Alexander Thynn (Viscount Weymouth), who had the original idea for this book, was born in 1932. He was educated at Eton and Christ Church, Oxford and served as a Lieutenant in the Life Guards and the Royal Wiltshire Yeomanry. He has written several novels and his murals are on permanent display at Longleat House. He is the founder of the Wessex Regionalist Party. His wife is the actress/journalist/author Anna Gael and they have two children.

Venetia Murray was educated at St Paul's Girls' School in London. She began her career as a journalist on the *Daily Express*; later she travelled extensively as a freelance writer in Europe, Africa and America, working mainly for the *Telegraph Sunday Magazine*. She has written three novels, published by Collins, and lives in Wiltshire.

WESSEX MEMORIES

'Where have all the cowslips gone?'

*Edited, compiled and
with an Introduction by*

Venetia Murray

Foreword by

The Viscount Weymouth
(ALEXANDER THYNN)

Futura

A Futura Book

Copyright © Longleat Enterprises

First published in Great Britain in 1986
by Bishopsgate Press Ltd

This Futura edition published in 1987

ISBN 0 7088 3393 4

Set in IBM Journal by
🅰 Tek Art Limited, Croydon, Surrey.
Printed in Great Britain by
The Guernsey Press Co. Ltd., Guernsey, Channel Islands.

Futura Publications
A Division of
Macdonald & Co (Publishers) Ltd
Greater London House
Hampstead Road
London NW1 7QX

A BPCC plc Company

Contents

Foreword by Viscount Weymouth   vii

Introduction by Venetia Murray   xiii

Acknowledgements   xx

'Mother would know if she were here'   1
ERNEST BARTIN

'Gossip was practically the only form of entertainment'   9
LILIAN DOUGLAS

'Tyning pit was more than a mine, it was a living
community'   37
RON PERRETT

'You name it we carried it'   61
AMELIA BALE

'Feed my lambs'   68
ARTHUR WHITLOCK

'I did not think much of her as a Queen,
just a very small old lady in black'   86
NINA HALLIDAY

'Sailors were always my great heroes'   94
ERIC H. WOOTTON

'Madam made court gowns'   105
ROSE BISHOP

'Sympathy was an unknown word in those days'   112
WILLIAM CHARLES KEATE

'Back to square one and the dole'   124
  MAY ALLEN

'Nanny was a wise old dear'   141
  LADY SUSAN SEYMOUR

'Don't play near the railway'   148
  NORMAN F. NORRIS M.B.E.

The 'lost' village of Imber on Salisbury Plain   157
  DOROTHY WEBB

'The warm sweet earth of Wiltshire'   159
  JOAN CHURCH

'From pony boy to stud groom to chauffeur'   165
  HENRY CHARLES LANSLEY

'Bluebells was a very gentle game'   172
  FLORENCE HANNAH WARN

'A milking pail full of hot gin and cider was provided'   176
  AUSTIN BROOKS

'My mother said "Do you realise you will have
to answer the door yourself?"'   188
  LADY LISTER KAYE

Glow-worms in the hedges and sand-castles
on the beach   192
  HAZEL AUSTIN

'Those evenings held a kind of magic for us'   197
  GERTRUDE McCRACKEN

'The hedgerows were a blaze of wild violets,
horse daisies, cowslips and daffodils'   209
  R.C. FORCEY

Foreword

Alexander Thynn
THE VISCOUNT WEYMOUTH

Time all too quickly obliterates the traces of what we once were: unless we were famous or infamous that is to say. The life of anybody may be recalled for a while by sons and daughters, or even by grandchildren. Yet we seldom seek to remember the lives of people who were unrelated to ourselves, especially if they lived before our time.

Memories which are set down in writing however, acquire a different status. They stand as a permanent record of how one particular individual assessed, and coped with his or her changing environment. They become unique statements because that environment will never be the same again. So unless our senior citizens can be encouraged to put pen to paper on such a theme there is much that will be omitted and finally lost from our sense of local heritage.

This was in part my motivation in starting a Wessex archive here at Longleat. The idea of reserving space in what is already a world-famous library for the personal testament of Wessexians who have reached the age of retirement: to garner the fruit of this experience in terms of whatever tales that they might wish to tell.

It is my belief that we have reached a point when the people of Britain (or indeed of Western Europe as a whole) are beginning to look inward upon themselves to perceive their own regional personality. It is all part of rediscovering their role in the world: perceiving what they represent and how they relate.

The people of Wessex as much as anywhere else in Europe are entering this phase of self-analysis. We are beginning to question how we are different or even similar to the people who come from neighbouring regions. Yet the character of Wessex will only be revealed when we know enough about the life and times of the people who have lived here.

My interest in the subject relates to the fact that I too am someone who has kept his life on record. I started my own journal at the beginning of 1954. Subsequently I chronicled the events in my life even prior to that date, right back to my birth in 1932.

Add to this that I am the future curator of Longleat and its library. Most of my ancestors have regarded it as a duty incumbent upon this role, to select for themselves some personal angle upon literature to feature as their own collection for the library. There was one who collected books about the French revolution. More recently my father collected the first editions of Victorian books for children. And the theme I have selected for myself is this idea of a Wessex archive.

It excites me to think that the journal which I shall continue to compile until I stand at death's door will one day rest on a shelf in this archive alongside the work of so many others who have contributed the story of their lives in a spirit of candour and self-revelation. To a lesser or greater extent we shall all have been writing with the same end in view: furnishing information for posterity concerning what we ourselves were like and how we reacted as individuals with the situations in our life and times. We display ourselves for what we were and our environment for what it was.

Some people might question what it is that I might find so specially significant about the environment of Wessex. Some people might even question its distinctiveness from the rest of Britain. The concept is indeed important to me.

I was raised to regard myself essentially as an Englishman. Yet there is something too vague about that description. One can even point out that the original kingdoms, from which the English union was compiled were inhabited by peoples of different genetic stock. The Danish ingredient may have been strong in the North of England. The Angles (in their purest form) had settled in the East. Yet the blend peculiar to the West Country was of Celt and Saxon. And the resultant culture to emerge within their territory was to be anticipated as uniquely their own.

The Wessex culture which developed may have been determined largely by the fact that our blended peoples were settled within the most open stretch of rural agricultural land to be found in Britain. There were centres where the traditions of Celtic art prevailed. Indeed the hedgrow patterns remained predominantly Celtic. Yet all was to be regulated within the West Saxon sense of Law and Order: then left to our own devices within what our rulers may have regarded to be a rural backwater, despite the prosperity of Bristol and Southampton.

The Wessex identity was never actually suppressed but it was gradually forgotten. Our problem is that ever since the Norman invasion our cultural distinctiveness has been played down in the interest of a national centralism. As Wessexians we all know (somewhere deep down) that we are quite different from Londoners from Welshmen from Midlanders and from Cornishmen. Yet the habit of discussing the nature of that difference has been discontinued.

My concern was therefore to arrest that trend and assist people to discern what the character of Wessex folk might truly be — in terms of their own written word. Not necessarily the well-to-do or famous but ordinary people within as many varied fields of life that I could find. It was for this reason in the spring of 1984 that I put out an appeal to the senior citizens of Wessex to send me their autobiographies. It was transmitted within the regional press, upon radio and television and the general response has been most gratifying: no doubt with more still to come.

Indeed, I may hope that in a Century from now the material will still be coming in until this archive emerges as the most notable repository of typescripts for research into the character of our Wessex identity. I have no preconceived ideas as to what this character might be. And future volumes may reveal how commonwealth immigrants may change it as much as any stream of immigrants from places far closer to our home such as London, the Midlands and the North Country.

But let me speak with greater clarity concerning where I regard the frontiers of Wessex to lie. The easiest definition can be made in terms of what Wessex is *not*. It stops short of Greater London, south of the Midlands and east of Cornwall. I might speculate that the boundaries of Wessex could be drawn so as to run north from Selsey Bill, along the fringe of Greater London, and then west so as to encompass the entire watershed of the River Thames (west of London). In terms of Counties, Wessex will include the following: Hampshire, Berkshire, Wiltshire, Avon, Somerset, Dorset and Devon. There is greater uncertainty regarding the identity of West Sussex, Buckinghamshire, Oxfordshire and Gloucestershire. It is for those who dwell there-in to decide upon their regional identity.

In this selection of excerpts from the first batch of biographies to be sent to me at Longleat we have aimed at variety as much as quality. And it could be that additional volumes will follow in sequence as the process of Wessex rediscovering its identity takes shape. It is a process which is as yet in its infancy. The centralizing influences have for too long been dominant. Yet it is time to make a start towards the essential rediscovery of who we really are. And it is my belief that as good a start as any can be made by savouring the character in the lives of other Wessexians.

In reading these excerpts (if you happen to be a Wessexian) you may well discover something about your own identity: indefinable perhaps until we have far more material to hand. Like many others I feel this urge obsessively to discover whatever common ground in culture and in character might exist. And I link it up with an idea that the future evolution of Western democracy involves this rediscovery of the individual's sense of identification with a particular region: thus enabling the political maxim of 'One Man One Vote' to obtain potential, even upon the international scale. Hints of some future world order perhaps, where the individual region will carry as much political clout as any other, no matter where it be situated.

So it can now be seen that my interest in the Wessex archive is far greater than any mere nostalgia. It comes closer to being a search for the manner in which I relate to this conception of an ideal world order. I am striving to discern the nature of my own regional identity, but at the same time to perceive it as part and parcel of this ideal world order to which I aspire to belong.

It was in pursuit of both these goals that I launched my appeal for autobiographies as contributions to this Wessex archive. My success or failure will be marked by the extent to which a Wessex identity re-emerges by the end of the twentieth century, and the extent to which regionalism begins to flourish in the world at large.

Introduction

Venetia Murray

'The past is a foreign country – they do things differently there . . .'

L. P. Hartley

What is it that seems to give remembering the past of our own lives such magic?

One of the writers in this book puts it like this:- 'I spoke to him of the old days . . . His face lit up as he talked excitedly about those by-gone years that were still his life, and all that remained to cling to in a strange and alien world . . . It was a door that old people wait for us to open, and seldom do they miss the opportunity to escape to the past'. The writer, now over seventy himself, is referring to a friend from the generation before, whom he was seeing for the last time before he died.

When Lord Weymouth had the idea of asking people to send him their autobiographies he offered two incentives. There would be a small cash payment for manuscripts accepted, and they would be housed in the Longleat Archives. It swiftly became obvious that it was not the money which mattered, so much as the prospect of someone listening to their stories. They sensed that they were among the last generation to remember a way of life in England which has since faded. They wanted to set the record straight, on both the plus's and the minus's of the 'Good Old Days'.

In compiling this book it was difficult indeed to decide not whom to quote, but whom to omit. So many worthwhile and interesting stories have had to be put aside for reasons of space. Among the contributions finally chosen are the reminiscences of a shepherd, a miner, a Duke's daughter, a fisherman, a cobbler, a parlour-maid, a nurseryman, a carter's wife and a groom who became a chauffeur when the first cars appeared. There is a description of a 'lost' village, of a once-wild valley, of the old London South Western railway and of Glastonbury Tor as it was at the end of the last century. Their life-styles swing from getting by on the dole with six children in a back street of Bristol, to a shooting party. One man remembers the horrific conditions of the Somerset coal mines; another the great Cunard liners in the Southampton docks. Some of the contributions have been unearthed from family papers and sent in by the original writer's descendants. One such is the description of life as a child in Windsor at the time of Queen Victoria's funeral. The oldest writer still living was born in 1893.

These people were taught at school that they lived in a land where 'The sun never sets on the Empire'. They were brought up in a moral climate where an illegitimate baby was, at best, a social stigma, and at worst a catastrophe. A working class girl of their time had little option but to go into domestic service, and an upper-class girl was considered a blue-stocking crank if she wanted a career at all.

Poverty was a very real thing. It meant actual hunger. 'We lived on less than most people throw away these days' one writer remarks. Another proves the ultimate point:- 'When a tiny child died, the cost of a funeral was beyond the pocket of a poor family, so an arrangement was made to bury the infant at the same time as an adult's funeral . . . In front of the glass hearse, there was a little glass compartment running the width of the hearse and the little coffin was placed there and so buried in the adult's grave. We had a little brother, Gilbert, who died of pneumonia and this was the form his burial took. None of us attended, but I remember we had black sashes to wear on our Sunday dresses'. They did not know the adult being buried. Unemployment had even more sinister consequences than it does today, and the end of the road was often the Workhouse.

Each generation is liable to fantasise about the past, even if it is unconscious. Memory is an excellent editor.

But these writers have no need to fabricate. Their stories are so valid because it is true that almost every department of daily existence has altered since they were young. The Welfare State has done much to soften the divide between the classes which Have and the classes which Have Not. But it is not just the obvious advances — in science, communications, applied technology and further education — which have made life so much easier. It is, quite simply, society's outlook.

Today's young have their doubts about their elders tales. If it is true that Grandma began contributing to the family exchequer at the age of seven — albeit scaring crows for a shilling a week — and came home to nothing but kettle broth for supper, how come she is so cheery about it? 'Do us a favour' and 'leave it out' are liable to be the skeptical and dismissive reactions.

The grandchildren are wrong. The past has two faces. The old achieve detachment when they look back. Life is never all bad, and especially not in childhood. These writers have one other common denominator — they are optimists and survivors. They would not otherwise have had the energy or the inclination to put their memories on paper. In every single autobiography there are shafts of pure happiness.

What you have never known you cannot covet. What you have never had you cannot miss. And the old have reason when they say that the young have lost out in a number of ways.

There used to be a much greater sense of neighbourliness in the towns as well as in the country. Neighbours were interdependent from necessity. The modern attitude to travel and holidays has only developed since the last war. Many people in the past spent their whole lives in the same community. That gave them a sense of security and a lovely warm feeling of belonging. One woman, remembering her youth in Bristol, says:- '. . . this, then was our street and I believe there were at least one hundred children of varying ages living in it. Life in my childhood was very, very hard, but at least it was never boring, and loneliness or lack of playmates was unheard of'.

Again, before the arrival of canned entertainment everyone had to invent their own amusements. Gossip seems to have made an excellent substitute for television. The corner shop was the accepted meeting place for the women, the pub for the men. Both stayed open all day and until eleven at night. 'You could get almost anything in Vokings (shop) . . . paraffin, firewood, pickles in huge jars, beer, lemonade, jams, again in huge twenty-eight pound stone jars, ice-cream in the summer, bread, vegetables, cakes, tobacco, shoe-laces, cotton . . .'

This writer's description of life reads as pure 'Coronation Street' circa 1910 . . . 'Or she went down the corner shop for her beer four or five times a day since the older people did not bother much with tea, and coffee was almost unheard of. She had beer with every meal and often for a meal. She went to the shop with a man's cloth cap on her head, a black blouse done up high in the front, black skirt and a capacious black apron which was considered the proper dress for local shopping'.

The sweet shop was Aladdin's cave. No-one wasted money on packaging in those days, which meant the children could agonise for hours, hypnotised by the gorgeous displays of goodies in the front window. The names of the sweets themselves have nostalgic charm — Acid Drops, Pear Drops, lemonade crystals, . . . 'for a farthing there were lots of things one could buy; there was a strip of toffee called Everlasting (which it was not); a braid of liquorice which broke into strips called Shoe-Strings; a slab of black toffee called Wiggle Waggle which blackened the tongue and lips; Bulls eyes were marbles of sweet which could be eaten, but when rubbed on a rough wall revealed a flat surface with rings of varying colour; sweet shrimps; white or pink fondant mice, and, also for a farthing, you could get six pretty little boiled sweets called 'Rosebuds'.

Once upon a time, too, the English countryside epitomised all that is charismatic about the past. 'The fields . . . seemed to abound in butterflies, the Red

Admiral, the Tortoiseshell, the Small Blue . . . skylarks used to rise from the grass and sing away in a sunny sky. I still live in the country but now I come to think of it, I haven't heard or seen the skylark since before the last war'. Someone else remembers the verge side flowers, 'campions, ragged robin, periwinkle, centaury, self-heal, ladies' bedstraw, mullein, and gentians . . . but there are no more now where I knew them to be'. The ultimate comment on industrial sprays which kill the wild flowers comes from the lady who reports that 'hedgerows of cowslips are seldom seen now, but we buy the seed by post and try to rehabilitate them'.

Children's games were seasonal. No calendar dictated their timing. Suddenly it was a spring day and everyone brought out their marbles. They played many variations of marbles freely in the streets. Cars were still rare, the privilege of a tiny minority, and it was easy to jump out of the way of a slow-moving, gentle cart horse.

In the summer they made their own toys; hoops, skipping ropes, and all kinds of tops. They constructed kites from brown paper and string, using a pebble to correct the balance; made pea-shooters from the stalks of cow-parsley with haws from the blackthorn bushes as ammunition. On moon-lit winter nights they ran 'chalk-chases' — a cross-country version of hide-and-seek. This game was called 'Jack, Jack, shine the light' because the leader carried a flashing lantern.

The Day the Pig Was Killed was always a memorable occasion. The pig plays a star role in many of these reminiscences. It provided the family capital in terms of food for weeks. Even the inedible bits of the animal were turned into tallow for candles. But then anything which could be utilised always was. The word 'disposable' had not become common currency. Nature provided much, and anything which could be eaten was gratefully acknowledged — however difficult to catch or wearying to harvest. The search for food became a treasure hunt; an element of one-upmanship came into the tricky business of spearing eels or inventing a new snare for rabbits. Poaching seems to have been regarded by society much in the way that minor smuggling is today — a fair cop if you got caught, but if you knew the ropes you didn't get caught.

Wessex used to be alive with travelling 'salesmen'. There were pedlars and gypsies and carters selling or carrying all kinds of wares — from watercress to fly swatters, mackerel to clothes pegs, toy windmills to hot rolls. The barrel organ and the hurdy gurdy man gave the streets music. Tramps had their own code — a chalk cross on the wall of a house showed the owners were good for a free meal. Barter was often the currency of trade, and the modern concept of extended credit unheard of.

The sinister side of village life sometimes echoes the England of Thomas Hardy's Wessex novels. One man has remembered all his life the shock of seeing what he refers to as a 'skimmington' enacted by his neighbours. His account differs only in small details from the 'skimmity ride' which led to Lucasta's death in the 'Mayor of Casterbridge'. That cruel custom of mocking a woman suspected of adultery was made illegal in 1882, but like many other rituals it continued underground for many more years. Diggory Venn, the reddleman in Hardy's 'Return of the Native' has a later counterpart in Dorset before the 1914-1918 war:- 'Another regular roadster was the redding woman, who travelled the roads selling redding to the farmers. She had a very savage dog that would not let anyone go near her tent'.

Certain themes appear regularly in the autobiographies. Religion had a much stronger influence on manners and morals than it does today. Much of the country was Methodist, but whether Church or Chapel, attendance was compulsory and taken for granted from the first steps to Sunday School. Many belonged to the Band of Hope, in a vain attempt to counteract the inevitable consequences of an enormous number of pubs which stayed open all day.

The people of Wessex seem to be particularly keen on music. The piano in the front room was as commonplace as the aspidistra. Again, like Hardy's characters, there is much emphasis on carols and dancing, and sing-song evenings at home.

Politics were a diversion. Women's suffrage was not complete until 1928 and one writer even recalls a rotten borough. Election night was liable to end up a riotous farce; the concept of feudalism was still in the air — but so also was the spirit of 'noblesse oblige'.

In editing this book I have had two firm intentions. I did not want to 'prove' any socio-political point. These stories show both the charm of the past and how difficult life could be. Nor did I want to impose my own style of writing in any way on the contributors. I have edited their copy only so far as it was necessary to make easy reading. The validity of these memories sings out from the way they are written. Senior citizens of Wessex are highly capable of speaking for themselves.

Venetia Murray. May 1985

Acknowledgements

I would like to thank the following people who have helped with this book; first and foremost, Viscount Weymouth, without whose original idea there would never have been a book; Robert Charles and the Longleat staff for their help and forbearance throughout the project; Therese Lang for taking so much trouble with the publicity; the Marquess of Bath for letting us operate from Longleat; Sheila Powell who had been so much more than a secretary, and who has consistently created order out of chaos. And finally Rupert, Christina and Sophy for their moral support.

'Mother would know if she were here'

Ernest Bartin
STREET

From the oil lamp to the electric light; from the horse-drawn carriage to the multifarious motor car; from the tradesman to the microchip . . .

I was born the 29th February 1916, at Fort Stream, West End, Street. At that time Street was almost completely controlled by the Quaker family of C. & J. Clarks, of the shoe factory, whose trade mark is the Tor of Glastonbury.

Father worked at Clark's factory, but he could also make a boot or shoe from beginning to end. I saw him take more than one boot for a cripple who had one foot shorter than the other. The difference in length was made up by building up cork between the upper and the sole. His father, too, was a shoe maker and I sat and watched my grandfather many times making sheepskin slippers in his living room. When a batch was finished he used to take them along to the factory, hand them in and be paid — this was called 'outwork'.

I recall quite clearly a Mr. Bobbett who lived close to Ashcott, three miles from the factory, passing by with the slippers he had made. He carried them on a long straight stick, the slippers resting a-straddle the stick, and swaying as he carried them on his shoulders. A three mile walk to the factory and a three mile walk home.

The fields in those days seemed to abound in butterflies, the Red Admiral, the tortoiseshell, the small blue, a small red and black one, maybe a moth. I can't recall its name. Nearly every blade of grass seemed to have a chrysalis attached to it in protective covering. I don't see them now.

Is it because of the use of these modern chemicals? Skylarks use to rise from the grass and sing away in the sunny sky. I still live in the country but now I come to think of it, I haven't heard or seen the skylark since before the last war.

Cowslips in season abounded everywhere; I had an Aunty living at Teignmouth in Devon, and they never grew there, so we used to pick cowslips for her and send by post.

My mother's father had land on the peat moors; in those days they cut the peat and stooked it in ricks to dry, and then travelled the area to sell the peat blocks for fuel. Bull-rushes grew everywhere in this environment, and when about three I tried to pick some and fell in the peat bog. Father had to take his belt off and pass it to me to pull me out. Those peat moors, between Glastonbury and Burnham on Sea are in the Vale of Avalon around which the stories of King Arthur and the Knights of the Round Table and the sword Excalibur were written. The Somerset and Dorset Railway used to pass across these moors, and I travelled by it many times during the winter, when the whole area was under water. The people moved about in special flat bottomed boats. This railway was affectionately known as 'The Slow and Dirty'.

The period of which I write now is about 1919 to 1924. Our house was lit by means of an oil lamp. We had an out-side toilet and baths were taken in a large, galvanised tin bath in front of the fire. The fire was an open black grate with a small oven alongside. For hot water bottles, Mother used to put bricks in the oven to warm, and then wrap them in clean cloths to warm the beds. I remember when she had her first glazed earthenware hot water bottle.

Halloween night we used to have mangolds and hollow them out, carve faces in them, put a candle in them and they looked quite attractive in the dark evenings. I can't ever remember any accident with the matches or through carrying lighted candles around. Writing of matches and fire reminds me when Mother had her first gas stove, what an occasion. I remember the first meal she cooked was sausage and chips. Funny how these little things come back to me, and yet things much later in life I can't recall at all.

We made nearly all our own games. Pea shooters we made from the wild cow parsley, using the hollow stems. Our ammunition was 'haws' from the blackthorn bushes. The problem was that the cow parsley made blemishes on the lips. Guns we made from a stem of the elder bush. We removed the pith for a barrel, cut a slot at the back end, inserted a piece of sprung metal from Mother's old 'stays' for the firing mechanism, and this would shoot matchsticks quite a distance. I always had a small pocket knife in my pocket and was always cutting something or whittling sticks, or removing sections of the bark to give an ornamental effect to a stick. I used to sharpen the knife on a piece of whetted 'blue lias stone', which was plentiful in the area. We used to cut and shape our own piece of wood for playing cat o'nine tails, and make our own spinning tops. They spun on a 'hob' we begged from Father.

Ah kites! We used to be good at making kites. Two laths joined in the shape of a cross, string attached to each end, tautly, which made a diamond shape; and then with a paste made from flour and water we attached a strong piece of brown paper. Then we made a long tail of a piece of string and rolled up pieces of paper cut into four inch lengths and bound it to the string. Then we attached the whole to the kite. If we went to the fields and the balance was not quite right, we would tie on a lump of grass to even things out.

Marbles were another summer pastime. We played in the gutters going to and from school. I wouldn't like to play marbles in the gutters these days. For a hoop we had an old pram wheel. Another very interesting thing we did was collecting cigarette cards. Some of these were very educational. For those who have never known, in our days cigarette packets used to have a card in them. You had to collect different ones to get the whole set. The subjects differed, might be British Battleships, British Regiments, Flags of all Countries, Footballers, Cricketers, Nature Studies and so on. This having to 'make-do' for ourselves made most of us into a Jack-of-all-trades.

Horse-drawn traffic was plentiful. People would got for a leisure ride in their pony and trap. A shire horse would come along pulling a farm 'putt', stepping out quite daintily for such a large horse. I can only remember seeing one horse being 'broken-in' (getting trained to pull a wagon). That was a shire horse and the farmer had it on the end of a rope, sending it round and round the farm yard.

The day of the 'penny-farthing' bike had gone, but push cycles were becoming popular — strong, sturdy, heavy models. All the cycles had chain guards or oil baths to keep the bottoms of the trousers out of the chain, and to keep the trouser leg bottoms clean from oil. If your cycle had no chain guard we used to put cycle clips round the trouser bottoms to keep them clean. The ladies' cycles had cords from the back mudguard to the wheel centre to stop their large billowing skirts from tangling in the spokes of the back wheel. The lights on the front of the cycle were oil lamps. They did not illuminate much but they showed other users of the road your position at night. Father had a 'King of the Road' acetylene gas lamp, and we were not allowed to touch it. These operated this way — there was a section underneath wherein you placed lumps of carbide, over the top was a section where you put water, and you turned on a small tap which permitted water to drip on to the lumps of carbide which gave off a gas which burned brightly.

Father changed employment and we moved to Burnham-on-Sea in 1924. People of Street, Glastonbury and the surrounding areas speak broad Somerset dialect. For example — 'Ahsnow' means, 'Yes I know'; and yet, for some reason, we used to start our sentences with 'Ah snow, he fell in the ditch' or similar. 'Be-ee' (are you, 'did-ee' (did you), 'cassn't' (you can't), 'dussn't' (you don't). If you met someone you would greet them with 'Ullow, ow be ee?' The reply more often than not would be, 'I be, ow be thee?' But in Burnham the Queen's English is more generally spoken. The number of times I had to visit the Burnham school-master to have the cane for talking improperly I can't recall. I soon learned to write correctly, but when I spoke I often reverted to dialect. And, as a matter of fact, I still do, and I like to hear it.

When I left school, I went into a House Agent's office to learn the trade. My wages were five shillings a week for the first year, ten shillings a week for the second year and fifteen shillings a week for the third. This was a good tradesman's wage in those days. I was successful at this. I more or less ran the office. My employer suffered from diabetes, and rested on his bed in the back of the office. So I used to do all the showing people round the different properties, and take and check inventories of furnished lettings. Believe me, there were a lot of items to check in the larger gentry houses in Burnham. Because my employer could not get out, to give me an incentive, he added ten shillings for every house I sold by myself. I was only aged fourteen to seventeen at the time.

At the end of the three years there was a disagreement about money. I was disgusted and threw the job in. I would have liked to go into auctioneering or a solicitor's office, but I would have had to pay them to learn the trade and receive no wages. My parents were in no position to finance that, so I had my taste of the dole queues.

In those days if they offered you two chances of employment, even if only for a week or two and you did not accept they stopped your dole. I did a fortnight delivering milk on a wheel bike, what a peculiar sensation it was trying to balance. Eventually I did about six months in a butcher's shop, delivering and learning to cut the joints. I did not fancy spending a life-time 'butchering', so got a job at the United Dairies factory, just labouring. After I had been there a fortnight, one of the Gentry from Burnham, who knew me from office days, was flabbergasted when he saw what job I was doing. Immediately after he left, the factory chemist sent for me, and I was put in charge of a tank room. Later I looked after the milk sterilisers. From early 1938 there was a large increase of the unsweetened sterilised milk being produced for the Government. Even at this date they were building up stocks, so someone must have had an inkling of the war that broke out in September 1939.

Cars and motor cycles were just beginning to become popular when I was a child. They were not the sleek designs we know today. The first ride I had in a car was in a Riley, with a 'dicky seat'. There was room for two inside the car and a hood could be pulled over in bad weather, but the dicky seat was at the rear of the hood, so it was always in the open. Steam wagons were still using the roads, and they used to stop and collect water for their tank close to where we lived. (There were no driving schools in those days, or driving tests, and when you took out a driving licence you could get an all vehicle licence which entitled you to drive even a steam roller).

We children attended the Primitive Methodist Sunday School. My brother played the flute in the flute and drum band and I played the triangle. When I was fifteen I started to learn to play the trumpet. My brother taught himself to play the mandolin and then advanced to the violin. We used to play in the local 'foursome', travelling to the different villages playing at dances. We had a baby Austin, soft top and cellulose side windows. Four grown-ups, and the pianist was a hefty fellow, one trumpet and case and music, one violin and case and music, and the music stands, and the set of drums tied on to the luggage rack at the back. It used to be a nightmare on foggy nights. Get home about 2.00 a.m., and start work again at 7.00 a.m., in the morning. But we enjoyed it.

I married in 1937 at the age of twenty-one, and thirteen months after our son Michael was born. When he was eighteen months' old I was called to active service. I enlisted in the Dorset Infantry. After twelve weeks basic training I was made a lance corporal, then soon corporal and thereafter sergeant. One of the hardships was that they raised the price of postage stamps from 1½d. to 2½d. My army pay was five shillings a week. I had seven aunties to write to, my parents, my wife, my brother and sister who were married and had their own home so about half my army pay went on postage stamps.

When I was eventually demobbed, I returned to my

pre-war employment in the United Dairies. They wanted to promote me and make me a manager of one of the departments. The elderly fellow who had done the job during the War started making disparaging remarks, so I said blow this after six years of war, and threw it in. After about a year I got a job as foreman in the cellar of Burnham Brewery. I left that job after two years and found employment first in a high tensile steel wire factory as despatch foreman, and later in a factory which produced ladies foundation garments. I was responsible for quality control. This meant checking the feel of the cloth. It is surprising how much this differed in firmness. Checking the shade was a difficult affair. When I started the whites were somewhat 'cream', but with the advent of these whiter than white washing powders, cloth producers vied with each other to produce a more brilliant white. Black could be anything between a greenish black, blueish black or brownish black. In brown we eventually had forty three different shades.

One item I have over-looked. Owing to the black-out at Christmas time, in 1939, it struck me forcibly that there were no lighted Christmas trees showing in the windows, and no lights to cheer me on my way to work, and I swore that if I got through the war I would never again draw a curtain to block out the light. Since my demob I never have drawn a curtain, and I also consider it my way of remembering those who 'fell' that I may live.

I am just thinking of the changes I have seen in my lifetime. There are so many. Mother used to do her washing in a boiler built into the scullery. Today nearly everyone has a washing machine and spin dryer. I recall helping to rake up the hay with the wooden rake, and tossing it up on to the waggon to carry away. These days everything is automatic, even the tying up of the bundles of hay. The cinema. We used to sit enraptured watching the silent films, where captions were put up on the screen and a lady sat playing the piano to accompany the film. I remember the first talking picture coming to Burnham in 1928, it was 'The Desert Song'. In those days Burnham youths used to roller skate to Weston-super-Mare and back to visit the 'talkies' at the Odeon. Al Jolson in 'The Singing Fool' was all the rave. We used to see on American films cars drive up to a gate or large door, and the gate or door would open without anyone touching it. We thought it was too far-fetched and must be faked.

We never see the barrel organ these days. We never see the man come round collecting rabbit skins or jam jars, who would give in return for these items a small windmill on a stick. Gypsies don't come knocking on the door now selling their own hand made clothes pegs made from stout stick and secured with a metal band. Gone are the days of the caravans, where there was usually a lurcher dog tied to the back axle and following on behind. Another character was the scissor grinder, and the china rivetter, who repaired china in the road outside your door.

I was recently looking at my uncle's Boer War Medals; my father's First World War medals, and my own from World War Two. The Boer War medal is quite thick and a thing of quality. The World War One medals not quite as good a standard, but the Second World War medals look like something purchased from a cheap multiple store.

We are getting into times now when you cannot generalise and say that because someone lives in an area he is representative of that area, people are becoming so integrated. I live in the hamlet of Downend, adjacent to the village of Puriton in Somerset. My next door neighbour is a Londoner, next door again, Mancunian, next again a real spinster of Somerset, and next door again the wife is from Finland. I myself am Somerset, although my grandmother on father's side was Cornish. My wife is Wiltshire. She often says, in dialect, 'Somewhen' for 'sometime'.

I am grateful to Lord Weymouth for instigating the recording of some of my memories. Many times during the past years since my mother passed away at the age of ninety three, I have thought of something and can't remember it clearly. And I have said to myself 'Mother would know if she were here.'

'Gossip was practically the only form of entertainment'

Lilian Douglas
BRISTOL

'Mum' said my son, Geoffrey, after I had again told him how different things were in my childhood. 'Why don't you write a book about your life, I'll bet it would be interesting'. 'Nobody would be interested in my life', I replied, but after listening to the staff at the office where I worked part-time saying 'Come on Lilian, give us a laugh. Tell us about your childhood and how you used to pray for just bread' I decided I would get on paper my memories of the past so that even if not published, my own grandchildren would appreciate the changes in living.

My father was 40 when I was born in 1910. By trade he was a carpenter, the son of a builder, whose liking for the bottle had caused his failure first as a builder, then as a grocer.

My mother was five years younger than my father. She was the eldest of my grandmother's second marriage and was a factory hand when she married my father. She had black, wavy hair, deep blue eyes and a lovely complexion although this was due partly to a heart condition she developed when carrying me. She told me that my father had ill-treated her to such an extent that she had developed a 'nervous heart' which beat twice as fast as normal. She often had very painful heart attacks which kept her in bed for several days. I adored my mother and used to worry over her as much as she seemed to worry over me.

At the top of our street was the local Register of Births but as there was a lane and side entrance to his house in our street, he and his wife were classed as residents. They were the elite, childless and employed one of the children to do their errands three times a day on a permanent weekly basis paying three pence a week, which was good money. The errands were almost always the same, beer and stout, with meals and for their nightcap.

In the next house lived Granny Hughes and her eight children plus her daughter-in-law with her six children, and, as both Granny Hughes and 'young Mrs. Hughes' were producing children regularly each year, we all got very confused over who belonged to whom and fascinated by the fact that the aunties and uncles were younger than many of their nieces and nephews. We always referred to the family as 'Them dirty Uses' because since they let all the babies roam around with nothing on their bottoms so that they wet and dirtied everywhere, the house stank to high heaven. We never played with them if we could help it but being such a big family they were sufficient unto themselves and didn't bother to come down the street much to play with us.

At No. 10 lived the Watts with ten children, six girls and four boys. Mrs. Watts was one of the biggest gossips in the street, and how she ever looked after her home and family I never knew, since practically all her time was spent standing at her front doorstep waiting for someone to pass to pounce on for a good old gossip. If no one passed, she would come across or down the street to where someone was cleaning their front step and nab them.

At No. 14 lived the Wookeys, Mr. and Mrs. Wookey, both of whom it was said were consumptive and their ten surviving children. Doris Wookey who was six months' older than I, was my best friend although I was always afraid to get too near her in case I caught consumption too, since this was a very common disease in my childhood days and accounted for one death at least in almost every family. All the Wookey family were very hard working, with Mrs. Wookey going out charring even though she suffered from an ulcerated leg. The children were always the most keen to do errands to earn money and they had the monopoly of most of the paying jobs. The rest of us children resented this and would jeer 'Where'ere there's a job, there's a Chook', but it didn't bother them at all.

Mr. Wookey's parents lived next door down, together with his unmarried brother and a married daughter and her husband. Old Mrs. Wookey used to be down the corner shop for her beer four or five times a day since the older people did not bother much with tea, and coffee was almost unheard of. She had beer with every meal, and often for a meal. She, as did most of the older women, always went to the shop with a man's cloth cap on her head, a black blouse done up high in the front, black skirt and a capacious black apron which was considered the proper dress for local shopping.

Below them were the Bartons with their three teenaged sons. They were a railway family and also took in double-homers, railwaymen on duty who had to spend the night in Bristol before driving their trains back to London or the North. They paid 1/6d a night and very often as one left the house, another arrived to sleep in the bed just vacated. To us, of course, the Bartons were well off and very much respected especially when one of them became a lieutenant in the Navy.

Next door up from us were the Deans, their two boys Billy and Syd and their daughter Cissie. My mother used to hate 'Ole Mother Dean', a fat, dirty woman, who loved her beer and practically wore a path to the corner shop. Her house was dirty and smelly and my mother was afraid the vermin and bugs, which she was certain were in the Dean's house, would get through to our house.

The Snells must have been a dirty family too because when they left, Mrs. Hazel had the neighbours in to show them the bugs crawling up the walls of their rooms.

After the place was cleaned up, Mrs. Hazel let the base-ment to the Frys who, to my mind, strongly resembled frogs. He was a lamplighter and when they moved in to No. 26 they had one son, Freddie, a fat, unattractive child, and a daughter, Gladys, also fat, pasty and the image of her mother. Within a few years, what with annual births interspersed with twins, their family increased so much that when they left, they had a baker's dozen, all of the same ilk.

Next to the Hazel's was the corner shop run by Mr. and Mrs. Voking. This shop was the hub of the whole street, even though there was another grocer's and off-licence on the opposite corner. In Voking's shop, you got up to date with all the gossip and local news. If there was no-one (standing) outside the houses to chat to, the street gossips would come down to Vokings to get some small article and would stand at the side of the counter saying 'I'm in no hurry, go on serving' and would chat to Mrs. Voking and any adult customers who came in.

Vokings opened about six or seven in the morning so that people could get something for their breakfast, and except Wednesday afternoons and Sunday afternoons, they stayed open all day until 10 o'clock at night.

They sold practically everything except clothes. The side of their shop facing our street displayed a mouth-watering selection of sweets and confectionery and what hours we children spent gazing at the display before parting with our farthings. There were long sticks of liquorice as well as ribbons of it. There were sherbet dabs with liquorice pipes one side to suck up the sherbet, and a stick with a dab of toffee the other side to lick the sherbet. There were fancy sweet animals, Frys 5-Boy Bars, Cream Bars, Jelly Babies, Dolly Mixtures, Gobstoppers, Toffee Bars especially Sharps, Coconut Bars, whilst on the shelf behind would be the big jars of Acid Drops, Pear Drops, Rosebuds, Fruit Drops, Mintoes, Lemonade Crystals, Sugar Mice and many more that I can't even remember. I only know that the Sherbet Dabs at ½d each and the Acid Drops were my favourites. Indeed my mouth was often sore through constantly sucking Acid Drops.

You could get almost anything in Vokings from paraffin, pickles in huge jars, beer, lemonade, jams again in huge 28-lb stone jars to ice-cream in the summer, vegetables, bread, cakes, tobacco, shoelaces, cotton. There must have been a wonderful turnover, but it must have been terribly hard work.

There were stables practically opposite our house, and then came the better-class houses in our street. None of them had basements and each had a tiny front garden and gate — which made the occupants feel far superior to their opposite neighbours.

The Blakes lived with their six children; May, their fourth daughter being about my sister Beatty's age, a neat tidy, insipid girl, who was always held up as a model to Beatty by my mother, and the youngest girl, Ivy, who was the talk of the children since she wore white socks until she was fourteen.

The Police Station was the next dwelling and had three or four cells for prisoners there.

The street's biggest gossip was ole Mother Church. She spent hours at her front door, which incidentally fronted on the pavement, watching for someone to pounce on for a gossip about her various complaints, the worst of which was her leg. On getting these details on paper it seems that quite a number of the women suffered from bad legs, which I think were the result of childbirth. Mrs. Church's husband was a seaman and despite her gossiping, her house was immaculate. She was the mother of six children, but only the two youngest boys came into our orbit, Harold being about nine years my senior and Reggie about three years' older than I.

It was said she was a terrible nagger and that's why her husband had become a sailor to get out of her way. I know she made the children take off their shoes before stepping over the threshold because all we children used to make fun of them doing it. I once went into her parlour which was a small room about 10ft by 8ft and there were thirteen chairs in it as well as a big table in the centre and the table with the aspidistra in front of the window.

This then was our street and I believed there were at least one hundred children of varying ages living in it. Life in my childhood was very, very hard, but at least it was never boring, and loneliness or lack of playmates was unheard of. The street, which was of cobbled stones, was

our playground. We played Jack across the Water with
the road as water. We played skipping, and Higher and
Higher, jumping over the rope, always in the road, only
moving back for the occasional horse and cart coming
down. We played rounders, cricket and football in the
street with the stable doors as goalposts and wickets. We
played tops, marbles in the gutter, fivestones, hopscotch
and Knock out Ginger. We tied ropes round the lamp-
posts and looped them, then played swings round the post
until chased by the police. We played dapball, conkers,
blind man's buff and hide and seek — and boredom or
frustration were never thought of. If you quarrelled with
your playmates and went in snivelling, you usually got a
clout alongside the ears and were told to get on out again
and either hit them back or find somebody else to play
with. Life was never easy — always we had to make our
own fun but it was the more enjoyable for so doing.

The front door of our house opened directly on to the
street as did the fourteen other houses that side. It had
two fairly deep steps, one of stone but the top one was of
wood and was covered with brass which had to be polished
each day. The front door was usually kept open all
through the day and was my favourite seat although it was
very, very draughty as the wind used to rustle up the stairs
from the basement and I would sit there shivering.
    When you opened the front door there was a long passage
covered with oil-cloth and two or three mats. Every day
the mats had to be beaten outside up against the wall, the
passage polished, the step brassoed and the bottom step
and the window sill scrubbed.
    Along this passage half-way, was the front room which
was sometimes used as a parlour, sometimes as my parents'
bedroom but usually was rented for one shilling a week
and at the end of the passage was the back room.
    Then came the stairs leading down to the lower regions.
These were uncovered and had to be scrubbed three times
a week. I remember you went down three steps, then there
was a sharp turn where, later on, there was a naked gas

jet hissing away, then down another eight stairs.

At the bottom of the stairs on one side was the cellar. This was not cemented and was very uneven with odd pieces of stone jutting out here and there. There was no window but an iron grating on the pavement outside, through which the coal was delivered, and this coal filled half the cellar. Wood and junk filled up the rest of the cellar. When the sun shone, the shafts of sunlight used to highlight thousands of particles of dust flying in the air and in my ignorance I used to stand at the side of the shaft of sunlight thinking I was getting out of the dust.

To the right of the stairs there was another long passage which was not covered with any oilcloth, and had two lines which were usually filled with damp sheets my mother was always trying to dry.

Halfway along the passage was our living room. This was furnished with an old brown horsehair sofa, a big kitchen table which had to be scrubbed and whitened after every meal, six hard wooden chairs and two wooden armchairs. There was, of course, the fireplace. At each side of the fireplace was an oven where all the cooking and baking was done, and a long trivet fronting the fire itself, where the saucepans stood to boil any food. Above the fireplace was the mantelpiece on which rested father's pipes and various other objects, and this was decorated with a piece of velvet or plush. All the fireplace was black and it took at least an hour every day to blacklead the grate and as there were no ashpans underneath the fire, you had to keep shovelling up the ash and taking it out so it wouldn't clog up the fire when you were baking. Then there were the fire irons which also had to be blackleaded daily. In front of the fireplace was a dilapidated rag mat which my mother had made.

At the far end of the passage was the kitchen which was a very dreary place. It had, I believe, flagstones, but they were very uneven and very hard to keep clean. Then there was a horrible grey/black greasy stone sink which we had to try to keep clean, but with seven and sometimes ten people using it this was nearly impossible. Next to the sink was the boiler, under which a fire had to be lit every time you washed clothes — which meant Mother being up before six on a Monday to get the fire going under the boiler, then all the whites had to be boiled and scrubbed and dollied. At the other side was the old high iron mangle through which the sheets had to go specially folded. Then there was a long bench down the other side of the kitchen, and a shelf for the iron saucepans and frying pans, and later on there was the gas stove which too was black. Outside, round the corner, was the WC with its double wide seats either side of the pieces of newspaper which one of us had to cut up every week, and which were common usage in those days. Then there would be the galvanised iron bucket which had to be filled with water and emptied down the WC after use — flushes were unknown, at least in our district at that time.

Then there was the garden itself with the fowl house all down one side and on the other side a few cabbages, a crown of rhubarb and a blackcurrant bush struggled feebly for existence. I can never remember there being more than four blackcurrants on that bush and can't think why my father didn't dig it up.

My parents' bedroom was the front one overlooking the street. My first memories of it was of the walls being covered in a light green distemper, although later on it was papered with cabbage roses climbing all over the walls. This was naturally the best bedroom in the house and there was a brass fender and brass firedogs covering the fireplace and a really fancy cloth tacked on to the mantelpiece with baubles hanging down. There was oil-cloth on the floor and two rush mats. My parents had a huge brass bedstead with very fancy brass knobs on it and a flock mattress over the springs. Then there was a big chest of drawers and a washstand with its washbasin and jug. There was a big blanket box which I believe my father made and there were several framed texts on the wall — 'Thou God Seest All' 'Trust in the Lord' 'Praise the Lord' and also a picture of a boy 'When did you last see your Father?'. There were lace curtains at the window and a blind so that to me the room looked very elegant, although the beam in the ceiling had dropped and my father used to say 'One of these days that bedroom ceiling will fall in'.

Then there was the back room which had oilcloth on it but no mats, so was usually icy to the feet. There were two iron bedsteads (not fancy) in here and my sister and I slept in one and my brothers Charlie and Mervyn in the other. The room badly needed decorating as the roof had a leak and there were stains running down the walls. We used to wet our fingers and make pictures on the wall. It faced north and most of the year was icy cold. We did have a fireplace in it, as all bedrooms in our street did in those days, but there was no central heating and you only had a fire in your bedroom if you were really very ill. We didn't have curtains but we had a blind on a roller which had to be pulled down at night, and we just had a candle or a little nightlight to go upstairs. We too had plenty of large texts framing the wall 'Thy will be done', 'Suffer little Children to come unto Me', and 'Jesus Loves Me'. We used to lie in bed in the winter shivering in our nightgowns watching the breath congeal every time we stuck our noses outside, and shiver again as we got up, putting our feet on the cold oilcloth and going downstairs to wash under the cold tap in the kitchen.

The showpiece of the house was the parlour — furnished as expensively as possible, curtains almost tightly drawn so the sun could not fade the furniture and used only on Sundays or when there were visitors outside the family circle.

In our parlour there was the inevitable black fireplace with its two side ovens but here the fender and firedogs were brass and looked far more elegant. The mantlepiece was decorated with a chenille pelmet with dangling baubles and on the mantelpiece itself were sepia photographs and ornaments whilst at the side of the fireplace was a pipe-rack with about six clay pipes in it of various designs with a tin of paper spills below it. We didn't have any framed texts in the parlour but we had several pictures, mostly of horses and traps or farm horses pulling the hay with the farmer seated in the cart or leading the horse. Then there was the Grandfather clock with its handing pendulum and loud tick chiming the hours away to which my father kept the huge key and wound it up each Sunday, I think, whereas the one in the living room was smaller (I believe it was known as a Grandmother Clock) and this had to be wound nightly.

There was patterned oilcloth on the floor plus a good rag rug and two large rush mats. There was a leather horse-hair sofa with fancy legs, far less bumpy than the one in the living room, and a round mahogany table on a central stand with a curving fancy base so that a dozen could sit round it without being hampered by table legs. The top could be switched to a vertical position when not in use to save space but it rarely was. On the table was a chenille cloth and in the centre was the big ornate paraffin lamp which had to be kept carefully trimmed and filled with oil.

At each side of the fireplace was a leather armchair and around the room were six dining chairs with leather upholstery. There was a large sideboard (which I believe my father had made) and there was a cane table covered with an embroidered cloth on which stood an aspidistra in its fancy pot. Nearly every house had its aspidistra which had pride of place in the front room window framed by the lace curtains and everyone tried to make sure theirs was the best aspidistra in the street.

There was a large cupboard in this room as indeed there was in all the main rooms and I believe the family Bible, insurance policies, letters and the like were stored in there.

On the inside of the door was a large hook to hang your clothes on. There were no wardrobes for people in our circumstances and every door had its big hook for clothes and, of course, in the bedrooms would be the cupboards with wooden racks with huge hooks.

That then was our house as I remembered it before my fourth birthday. I think our house was fairly typical of the homes of the working class before the First World War.

Religion played a very big part in my childhood days. We

went to sleep and woke up faced with large framed and unframed texts exhorting us to 'REPENT, THE DAY OF JUDGMENT IS AT HAND' and 'TRUST IN THE LORD AND YE SHALL BE SAVED' and 'EXCEPT YE BE BORN AGAIN THOU SHAL'T NOT ENTER THE KINGDOM OF HEAVEN' and so on. Schooldays started with Scripture lesson and Prayers. Then you had to kneel down on the cold oilcloth at the side of the bed to say your prayers and were only excused this if you were ill. Then you said them in bed.

You could almost call Saturdays Sin days because there was no day school with its morning service, no Sunday School Prayer Meeting or Evening Service, so you could relax. Usually in the morning there were all the errands to do, but in the afternoons, if you were lucky, there was the 'Picshers'. We all queued up at the Knowle Picture House on the Wells Road for the Saturday Matinee which was ½d (later raised to 1d), then surrendered our tickets to the commissionaire and rushed trying to grab the best seats. We took our oranges with us which stank the place out, the peel of which we threw at other children, and watched enraptured the serials where Pearl White, Mary Pickford and Ruth Roland went through hair-raising adventures with 'Continued Next Week' just as the villain had them in his power, or they were hurtling over some cliff to what seemed certain death. We would shriek at the heroine to look behind her at the villain who always came right up to her unseen, we would yell at the villain and cheer the handsome hero as he came to the rescue. The films, of course, were silent and for background there was a pianist but with the row we made, she needn't have been there and often was not. The commissionaire tried in vain to keep some semblance of order although we were not naughty children, only high spirited. It never occurred to us to damage the seats or to be rude to the commissionaire and although the place had to be cleaned up after us, it was only orange peel and paper on the floors.

Sunday, however, followed after Saturday and on Sunday you were not allowed out in the streets at all.

Neither were you allowed to knit, sew or read anything other than the Bible nor do any work except the bare essentials. It was God's Day and rarely did anyone step out of line. When we were very young, we were sent to the Gospel Hall in the morning, us girls dressed in our best clothes, with our hair taken out of its rags and combed in ringlets with a piece of hair ribbon, our poke bonnets and if cold, our muffs, our black stockings and our buttoned boots.

Although they preached of the love of God, the emphasis was on repentance, with God and the Devil fighting for possession of our souls. If we didn't repent of our sins and love God, we were threatened with the terrors of Hell fire and eternal damnation.

Heaven was pictured as a wonderful bright place in the shape of a massive hall with God in the middle, sitting on a golden throne surrounded by angels playing huge harps. I was never musically inclined and was terrified at the thought of dying and having to go up there playing the harp for ever and ever. I used to lie in bed and nearly go mad picturing eternity — time never ending.

The alternative was even more horrifying — the Devil in black with his helmet and pitchfork, surrounded by fallen angels similarly attired, with their pitchforks near a vast raging furnace.

You had to make your choice, either up playing the harp for ever with the angels or down burning in the roaring furnace with the devils pitchforking you into the flames and this too for ever and ever.

After tea, if my father and mother were on speaking terms, they would dress up in their best, father with his suit and best cloth cap and stout walking stick and off we would go for a long walk through the fields and byways. That was the recognised finish for a Sunday, with my parents stopping at the Talbot Hotel for a round of drinks, leaving us children outside for sometimes two hours with a packet of biscuits or a glass of lemonade.

My brothers used to deliver milk for the son-in-law of the Head of the Chapel and the dairy was at his house. My brothers used to tell me that beer was delivered to them in crates, for medicinal purposes only but they needed that medicine more than once every day, whilst they and their colleagues preached about the evils of drink.

There were no Roman Catholics in our street and we who attended Gospel Hall put Catholics in the same category as the Devil's workers.

I was four years old when the First World War started and I have no vivid recollection of the start. I only knew it just added to the misery that was part of my early childhood.

First of all I adored my mother and never stopped worrying in case she would die or wouldn't be there when I came home from play and later school. She had a bad heart, was told to live on the level and there we were living at the bottom of a hill in a basement house. My mother used to be ill and have to stay in bed for several days and I would hang around the bedroom till somebody sent me downstairs.

Because of his ill-treatment of my mother, I can't say I ever loved my father even though I was his favourite. I know I was afraid of him as were the rest of us children. My mother only had to say 'Here's your father coming' for us to scoot up the stairs to bed as though the devil himself was chasing us, yet except for my brother Arty, on whom his beatings had no visible effect, he never lifted his hand to any of us.

Still he was of a morose disposition and there was no friendly family atmosphere in our house. My father would come in in the evenings, wash himself and sit down to his meal with Charlie and I hanging around in case he found the steak too tough and we could have it. Then he would change his clothes and down the pub he'd go every night. On the weekends my mother would accompany him and we children had to go on to bed. When I went to bed on Friday nights I used to pray that when I woke up it would be Monday so I wouldn't need to face those terrible weekends.

Sometimes my parents wouldn't come in till after midnight as the pubs kept open till 11 o'clock. I'd lie with my eyes wide open until I heard them come in but usually this only prefaced the start of the trouble. After a while, we would hear voices raised and the four of us would jump out of bed, run down the two flights of stairs and cling on to mother and try to stop father from beating her. I remember one time he swung the poker round to hit her but he was so drunk he swung it right round and knocked himself out. Another time the rowing was so bad Arty climbed out of the back window on to the roof of the next two houses, down on to Vokings stable and up to the police station, but the police didn't interfere much then as wife beating was so common as to be the natural finish to a Saturday night out.

Next day they wouldn't be on speaking terms.

It says much for my father's affection for me in that he didn't beat me as I would be mournfully singing the whole of the morning 'The drunkard reached his cheerless home. His weeping wife he forced to roam, Alone and friendless with her child' and 'Yield not to temptation, for yielding is sin, Ask the Saviour to help you, Some victory to win. Fight manfully onwards, Dark passions, subdue, Look ever to Jesus, He will carry you through'.

About 12 o'clock my father would go to the pub and would not come back until nearly three o'clock. My mother would keep his dinner hot on a plate although sometimes, if they weren't on speaking terms, she didn't bother and I have seen my father throw his dinner in my mother's face. Then he would go to bed coming down after we had tea and going out again to the pub. Sometimes my father would not speak to my mother for three weeks and all communications to each other were made through us children.

Because of our poverty and my father's frequent spells of unemployment when he didn't get any money to keep us, our food was of the plainest. My father rarely had the same food as we did. He never had porridge for his breakfast. Actually, in the week, when he was working, I don't think he had any at all as often he would have to leave home about five o'clock in the morning to get to his job. On Sundays I know he had bacon and egg because the smell of it was mouth-watering to us children as we ate the boiled teafish which was our Sunday morning breakfast treat. My mother would go up the market and get this huge teafish costing only a copper or so, which would be soaked all night in the small tin bath and then boiled in one of the big saucepans or mostly I believe it was cooked in the copper boiler. Even after an all night soaking, it still tasted salty and I've never since really like boiled fish.

Tea, in our family in early childhood was four pieces of bread and marge and many, many times did I ask for more. Mind you, we did have some lovely teas. I can still recall the lovely boiled apple dumplings and puddings and the 'Spotted Dick', a boiled suet pudding with currants or other fruit in it, rolled up and put in a floured cloth and boiled for a few hours – the struggle to keep it on the boil and the fuss to get it out of the saucepan, then the joy of a slice with treacle round it or else the pudding in the basin with jam or treacle at the bottom so that it came all round the sides of the pudding when it was put on the table. Then sometimes for Sunday tea there was dripping from the meat, and bread and dripping was a major treat. Then on Sundays we might have toast done over the fire with a long toasting fork, covered with dripping, and rhubarb and custard.

In those days, all babies were dressed alike – first of all in the long swaddling clothes which they wore for a year, I think. Then they were 'shortened' and boys and girls alike wore dresses to below their knees. The boys would not be 'breeched' (put in trousers) sometimes until they started school at five, especially if they were pretty and it was common to see long, curly haired boys looking and dressed as pretty little girls.

However, with the war, we began to see some of the little boys dressed in long sailor suits with sailor hats with the ribbon showing their father's ship on it, the little girls would have the same straw sailor hat and dresses with

braid trimming of similar material to the boys' suits. They
looked quite smart to the rest of us and we envied them
their clothes. In those days you had to wear enough
clothes to weight you down almost. First of all for little
girls there was the long flannel or woollen vest, then combinations which came sometimes to your wrists and almost
down to your ankles. Then there was the liberty bodice,
followed by the flannel petticoat, the stays, the thick,
dark bloomers with elastic at the waist and below the
knees, then another lighter petticoat, the dark heavy frock
and the pinafore on top. You wore long black stockings
with elastic garters and finished off with boots which
buttoned up to your knee and which took ages to do up
with the button hook. In summer, not before June anyway
because 'Ne'er cast a clout till May is out', you changed
your flannel or woollen combinations for lighter ones and
had an embroidered underskirt instead of the flannel
petticoat.

The men wore long thick nightshirts at night and very
often a knitted nightcap to keep their heads warm. In
the day they wore cloth caps which they usually kept
on in the house. It was not usual for anyone — man,
woman or child, to go out of doors without wearing a hat
or cap.

I suppose because of the hard lives they lived, with the
constant childbearing and caring for their large families,
with all the attendant washing and cleaning without any
labour saving devices, the women aged quickly. At forty-
five, most of them were old. Almost as soon as they
became grandmothers, they changed their style of dress
and wore, usually, black high-necked long sleeved blouses
with a brooch at the throat, whilst outside their numerous
petticoats and whale-bone corselettes, they wore full black
skirts sweeping the ground with a black lace shawl and a
little black poke bonnet tied under the chin with a wide
black ribbon. No-one would dream of showing an ankle,
and their skirts used to trail in all the mud and dirt. Such
skirts would be washed very infrequently and, indeed,
the older folk didn't take kindly to the thought of washing

themselves too much, whilst as for a bath, that was an annual or semi-annual event.

When I started, school was a place for learning and discipline. There were no gimmicks, no sports afternoons, the only sport we knew was drill — with the old Arms Bend, Arms Stretch, Knees Bend, Knees Stretch etc. Lessons were learnt parrot fashion in the Infants with Ay is for ah, Bee is for bu etc., and twice one is two, twice two are four etc., but this way you really learned, and no-one went up into the next class if they couldn't read a little. Some children stayed three years in the same class but they eventually learned to read, unlike nowadays when there are different methods of teaching and you go up by age, not ability.

Incidentally, my brother Mervyn, who was very clever, had reached the highest standard by the time he was eleven, so that he had to remain in that top class for the next three years with the same lessons. Despite the handicap of having only one good eye, having to do a milk round every morning and a paper round every evening, together with a weak chest, he never missed school once during a period of five years.

I hated school at first and would do everything possible to avoid going, like sitting on the draughty top stairs in my vest after I had been sent to bed, hoping to get a cold so I could stay home. However, before I was six I had learned how to read and this opened up a whole new world for me. I became an avid reader, progressing from picture stories to Charles Dickens, Mrs. Henry Wood — in fact anything printed that I could get hold of, I would read. Of course, I never read the descriptions, all I was interested in was the actual story shorn of all frills.

By the time I was six, the War was making a much more definite impact on our lives. Supply ships were being sunk, food was really scarce and almost all the time we were not at school seemed to be spent queueing up for margarine, sugar and other day-to-day needs. Things became expensive — milk went up to a penny a pint, sugar to a penny a pound, whilst sweets and chocolates became very scarce as well as doubling in price.

More and more of the old folk whose sons were in the Forces couldn't manage and had to go to the Workhouse. It was pitiful to see such people clutching their few possessions making their way to the Poor Law Institution, as we knew it was the end of their life together. In the Workhouse, the sexes were segregated so that after fifty or even sixty years of being together, they had to say goodbye at the entrance to the Institution, — the wife having to join the other unhappy wives already there, whilst the poor man, heavy with the burden of having failed to provide under impossible conditions for their continued life together, joined the other poor lonely old men bereft of their partners, to wait for the death that released them from their misery and loneliness.

The Germans had inflicted heavy casualties on the Allies, and whilst I was too young to understand just what was happening, most conversations centred on the War. We children were filled very often with blind terror. The realities of war were being forced on us children by so many things, as parents and elder brothers were being called up or enlisting: there was the loss of the food ships and the serious shortage of so many basic foods. Again, the streets were filled with wounded servicemen and they were not a pretty sight. Some were wheeled about without limbs, just little stumps where their arms and legs had been amputated. Others walked on crutches having lost a leg whilst many others had one or even two arms of their jackets folded over their chest because they had had their arms amputated. Yet even more were led by their relatives blindly tapping their way through the streets. The worst were the shell-shocked soldiers who would walk up and down the main streets and suddenly start shouting and fighting. We children didn't realise these soldiers were ill and often we would follow them around taunting them until they turned on us when we would race screaming for home. Many Servicemen would have 'fits' and would be on the pavement foaming at the mouth and thrashing round surrounded by a host of small children enjoying the excitement, although I like to think there were the understanding adults to help them and shoo us children away.

There were aeroplanes about too — not many though, and on hearing the noise, we children would rush out into the street shouting 'Aeroplane, Aeroplane'. All the grown-ups would come and look and we would follow its progress through the sky until it was out of sight.

Christmas entailed an awful lot of preparation when I was young, especially the making of the puddings. The fruit would have been gradually bought and then down the butchers for a piece of suet. This would have to be grated, as would the carrots, apple, orange, lemon, and the candied peel, together with the bread. Then the raisins would all have to be stoned, all the fruit carefully washed and dried in front of the fire before using. The big wash-stand basin would be brought down to hold all the ingredients, which would be all mixed together and each one of the family would have a stir for luck. If people could afford it, silver threepenny bits were put in the pudding or tiny horseshoes. After the puddings were mixed in the washbasin and stirred, they were left overnight before being put in the basins as this was a major perfor-mance. The fire under the boiler would have been lit early in the morning and as soon as the water was boiling, the puddings would be gently lowered into the boiler, and as there were up to a dozen puddings being boiled, it was quite a job ensuring that the water was boiling when they were put in and then kept boiling for the nine/ten hours cooking time. Someone had to see that the boiler fire was kept well stoked so that the puddings did not come off the boil, and also to make sure that the water always covered all the puddings in the boiler.

After about four hours the lovely smell of the puddings cooking permeated the house and we children would sniff it with gleeful anticipation of the taster we hoped to get before Christmas. The whole of the downstairs kitchen, living room, passage and stairs would be running with water from the condensation of the steam coming from the puddings but this didn't bother us children as we were used to the damp walls anyway.

In the evening, after the puddings had boiled for nine to ten hours came the job of lifting them out of the boiling water and this was very tricky indeed. Out came the long wooden washing tongs and very carefully the first pudding was lifted out, put carefully down, and slowly the rest of the puddings were taken out. The pudding cloths were put in a bucket or bath of cold water ready to be boiled and then replaced on the puddings until they were eaten. The water in the copper which was very greasy had to be baled out and the copper cleaned ready for the next washday. The preparation and cooking of the Christmas puddings usually took three days and no housewife would really look forward to Christmas until they were ready.

About two weeks before Christmas, the butchers would start hanging the Christmas poultry on the hooks outside their shops. Turkeys were very rare in my early childhood. It was mostly geese and fowls (not so much chicken). Then there would be the legs of pork and the big smoked hams also hanging down whilst the window would have a boar's head in it, with an orange stuffed in his mouth. Many people bought huge legs of pork which they boiled in their coppers as they did the hams and forespurs.

As we kept fowls, we usually had a broody hen or an old cock and what a job it was plucking it or them (if we were lucky). We children had to sit in the cellar and pluck them. The feathers got everywhere, up your nose so you couldn't breathe, in your mouth, all over the cellar and they all had to be put in the big tin bath and were made into pillows or feather mattresses to replace the lumpy flock mattresses in our beds, but it took a very long time and a great many feathers to do this.

Then the shops would take on a festive air and would be hung with trimmings, tinsel and paper bells. Sugar ornaments like watches, animals and birds would be in the sweet shops, fancy confectionery and yule logs would be on sale but I don't remember Christmas Cakes being sold until well after the war. There would be fancy tins of biscuits, tins and bottles of sweets, and the toys would be on view. The toys were rarely mechanical but were mostly wooden, little wooden scooters, bricks, wheelbarrows, carts, metal soldiers and games like snakes and ladders and ludo, whilst there would be wooden dolls prams, wooden dolls beds, wooden dolls houses with furniture and the dolls themselves. These were made generally of wax but the more expensive ones had heads made of china in which the eyes moved and they had hair.

About a fortnight before Christmas was the recognised time for carol singing and we would go miles to earn a few coppers. There was no singing one little verse then knocking at the door — you had to go through the whole repertoire — 'Good King Wencelas', 'Come all Ye Faithful' 'While Shepherds Watched' 'Away in a Manger' 'Once in Royal David's City' and only after you had sung the lot, would you say 'Christmas is Coming, the Goose is getting fat, Please put a penny in the old man's hat. If you haven't got a penny, a ha'penny will do. If you haven't got a ha'penny, a farthing, God Bless You'. You would then knock at the door, wait hopefully for it to be answered and stick your tin in front of them and at the end of the evening, you and your companions would split up the takings.

Then, at last, it was Christmas Eve and bathed ready for Christmas, we would go excitedly to bed carefully hanging our socks over the bedpost before we tried to sleep. In our street, and all its poverty, we knew there was no Father Christmas but we still felt the excitement of anticipation as we waited for the Great Day. Then on Christmas morning, the sock would be filled with an orange, an apple, nuts, sweets, perhaps a sugar mouse, a game of ludo, a spinning top, a rope or sometimes a two shilling piece. The butchers and many other shops would have stayed open until midnight on Christmas Eve, and, as there was no deepfreeze, many a scrawny bird would go cheap at midnight if you cared to wait and take the chance.

The grocer would have given your parents a Christmas Box according to what they had spent. We usually got a ham. It would weigh over a pound and what lovely ham it was — none of your modern tinned variety but well smoked ham, cooked in the grocer's boiler (you could often smell the hams boiling when you went in the grocers.) Then we would have the pickled cabbage which my mother had done, there would be piccalilli and mustard pickle and Christmas was the one time when there was plenty to eat and indeed drink. There would be the wines — Bees, Parsnip, Dandelion and Elderberry; the beers, my father's favourite being Old and Bitter, whilst my mother liked her stout, Guinness usually, whilst we children would have fizzy lemonade, sweet cider and stone ginger. It was the one time in thc year you felt sated.

Next day was Boxing Day when again you ate and ate till you could eat no more although the dinner this time was cold. Cold meat and pickles. The shallot and pickled onions that had taken so much time and caused so many tears to prepare were eaten at an alarming rate — a seven pound jar would be gone in a day.

After Boxing Day we children went back to our normal play routine, except that we would become very friendly with the children on the other side of the road who had wooden scooters and tricycles, so that we could have a go on them since none on our side of the road ever received expensive toys like that. Naturally, with so many of us 'having a go' the scooter or trike would soon be broken and then there was no need to include 'them kids' in our games.

One day at school I was writing the date at the top of a page and it was 1917. I thought 'I'm seven, isn't that old!' I felt really grown up. I was in the Juniors, I could read, write, do sums and composition and had started work — doing a paper round.

Mervyn and Charlie did a milk round in the mornings

before they went to school and a Paper Round after school. They used to buy the Times & Echo from a wholesaler named Lethaby down by the Three Lamps. The papers were sold to them for 3 a penny and they in turn sold them for ½d each whilst any left over would be returned to the wholesaler. Mervyn and Charlie had their rounds and I had to take over New Walls Rd., Angers Rd., County Street, Highgrove Street, Firfield Street, Stanley Hill, Frederick Street, Summer Hill, Parliament Street and end up at 37 Park Street. This took up to two hours each day but it was just something that had to be done and it was no good snivelling about it.

The war was making life more and more harsh. It seemed almost everyone was in uniform. Now practically every family in our street had husbands or sons in the Forces and casulaties were very heavy. Wheelchairs and crutches seemed the order of the day and casualties were hitting our street. Billy Dean, the elder son of the family next door was killed in action and Mrs. Dean could not be comforted. Mrs. Moby's husband was missing, believed killed. Another son in the street had been torpedoed. My Uncle Alf had been gassed with mustard gas and so it went on.

There was talk of peace, of an armistice and then suddenly on the 11 November 1918 the Armistice was signed. We had WON the War.

The guns boomed, the hooters and sirens sounded, the bells rang and everyone ran shouting in the streets. Not everyone was rejoicing, however. There was Mrs. Dean crying bitterly that her Billy would never come back, and there were others who had lost loved ones, sobbing for their loss.

Officially there was much rejoicing but then came the aftermath. The men in the Forces came back home but not to the Heroes Welcome they had been promised. Their former employers refused to take them back and there were no jobs for them to come home to, only the meagre dole. Those who had stayed at home stuck tight to their jobs and bitterness and poverty was the Serviceman's reward for fighting for his country. Many were reduced to selling shoelaces from door to door and suddenly it was not the Italian with the hurdy gurdy and the monkey but British Servicemen with the barrel organs, going round the street, playing, singing and begging.

Uncle Jim came home from the Marines. He was married and had three children, the eldest being six months' younger than me. He got a job as a lorry driver but within three years he was dead. I grieved sadly over him as he was such a handsome jolly man, over six foot and well proportioned. He left a widow and five children under ten and my poor Aunty had a terrible job trying to feed and clothe them. I know the Church helped as much as they could, but my Aunty and my cousins were forced to a life of abject poverty until the eldest child could go to work.

Now that the War was over, everybody expected life to be much easier and gayer but too many were sadly disappointed. There were few jobs for the soldiers and after spending over four years' fighting for their country, they came home to fight for sheer existence. The amount of dole was minute and the men had to go on National Assistance, which meant someone coming to your home, going through the larder, making you sell anything of value before you got food vouchers or clothing vouchers and, if you lived with your parents, you got nothing because they were expected to keep you.

With the ending of the War, my father, who had been in more or less constant employment during the war became out of work for very long periods and so my mother had to rely more and more on her own brushmaking and on us children for money.

Life was settling into a pattern, a little brighter for us as despite father's unemployment, there was more money now coming into the house. Beatty was nearly 14, and working whilst Mervyn and Charlie were both doing a milkround every morning and as well as earning 1/6d each per week, they were getting a breakfast. Then Mervyn, Charlie and myself were doing paper rounds after school and we had quite large rounds so that with every third paper we sold being ½d profit, we were not doing so badly.

At school, Mervyn was doing his second year in the top standard. He had passed easily the preliminary exams for a scholarship, as had Charlie, but my mother would not let either of them take the final scholarship exam as she needed the money they earned too much to allow them to give it up, as they would have had to if they won a scholarship.

In January of 1920 our class took the preliminary scholarship examination and I was one of three who got through it. I was quite forward at school, having jumped from Standard 1 to 3 and then from 3 to 5 so that at nine I was in Standard 5 which was the scholarship class and comprised some fifty pupils.

My mother had not been able to let the others take the scholarship exam, she agreed to let me try.

We had to wait two or three months before knowing the results which were published in the Western Daily Press on the first or Second Saturday in June. Mervyn got the paper on his way home from his milk round and there was my name high amongst the Passes.

I was so excited I didn't know what to do. I told all my friends and aquaintances, all relations who lived near, but at the same time I was not sure if my parents would let me take up my scholarship. Beatty, however, was now earning good money working at Wills, and Mervyn would be leaving school that summer. Mother was still doing her brushmaking, so it was decided that I could take up my scholarship.

When the official confirmation came, I was so high on the list that I could choose any Grammar School in Bristol and after a good deal of chasing around, getting advice from all and sundry, it was decided to put Colston|Girls' School as my first choice.

I remember my first sight of Colston Girls' School in Cheltenham Road, the outside facade, the entrance to the main hall with the footman in resplendent uniform, the big Assembly Hall, the various classrooms and that long trek to the Annexe, the interview, accompanied by my mother, with the Headmistress. My mother, who worked so hard and lovingly for her family's well-being, could never forget that she had been a factory hand and felt embarrassed and out of place meeting the Headmistress.

When I started there were six hundred and forty girls and school fees were about £3.00 per term. There were many daughters of quite wealthy parents who preferred to send their children to good Day Schools rather than boarding schools and even in 1920 these children were brought to school in the family car either by their father or their chauffeur. As all pupils wore the same type of uniform, it was not possible to tell the scholarship girl by their clothes, but you could invariably recognise a first term scholarship girl by her speech which was much broader than the clipped speech of the daughters of the well-to-do.

My scholarship covered the school fees and thirty shillings a year for books. A fortnight or three weeks after the beginning of the Autumn Term, all the scholarship girls lined up in the Great Hall to receive their thirty shillings. People say how humiliating that must have been but I never found it so, nor to my knowledge did any of the other scholarship holders, — rather, I think, we felt a sense of pride at our achievement and pleasure in receiving the money towards our books.

About the time I started school, the 'bob' became all the fashion. Beatty who had lovely wavy hair asked if she could have her hair cut to a bob but my father refused to allow it. Beatty who had now been at work for eighteen months at W D & H O Wills, rebelled at this decision and had it cut. However, she was so scared of what my father might do, that she stayed out of his sight for over a week until he had got over his rage at her defiance. My mother, of course, had to break the news to him but beyond refusing to speak to Beatty for a fortnight, he took no action. The bobbed hair suited Beatty very well and she suggested to my mother that it would suit me too. Much to my amazement, my father raised no objection to my hair being cut so I had it bobbed. It was a real transformation. My hair, formerly strained back off my face in a tight plait now framed my face, the sides turning towards my face. I had been given a side parting whilst the other side was shaped to form an attractive wave with the ends curling forward to my face. Being freed from restraint it fell naturally into waves and made me look very different. My mouth, recently very gummy through the extraction of first teeth, now showed new teeth and I looked far more attractive.

Even at that time there was trouble with the Brown Shirts — but this was overshadowed by the unrest and economic depression in England. The lowest paid job advertised caused queues of several hundred applicants and fierce was the struggle to get the job.

Life was not all gloomy though. We had lots of fun and revolutionary changes in our way of life were beginning to be felt. We still played in our streets with their cobbled roads, but slowly these were being tarred over.

Before Guy Fawkes Night we enjoyed weeks of preparation and collection for the huge bonfire that our street lit on the Summer Hill Bank. All the rubbish and unwanted broken furniture was collected from miles around and a big guy was made and put on top. As soon as it got dark, the huge bonfire was lit and in and out of the smoke we'd go to light our sparklers and fireworks. We stayed there for hours stoking the bonfire, eating our oranges or apples and the hot half-cooked potatoes that we had begged or just taken from home. How wonderful those potatoes tasted, smoky, burnt skin and hard uncooked centre. I suppose it must often have rained on Bonfire Night but I can't remember those occasions.

There was always something to do, someone to play with, nobody was bored, neighbours were in and out of each other homes, their joys and troubles were yours too, and you knew almost as much of your neighbours business as you did your own and vice versa. Of course there were bad neighbours and since gossip was practically the only form of entertainment, some of it was malicious but not much.

If someone was ill, there was always a neighbour to visit them and bring a little something to try to whet their appetite. When a new baby arrived, neighbours acted as midwives and looked after mother and baby if there were no relatives handy to do it. When there was a death, again it was a neighbour who would 'lay the corpse out' and collections for wreaths would be made from every house in the neighbourhood. As a mark of respect between the time of death and the funeral, blinds would be kept drawn in the front windows of every house in the street and not raised until the funeral procession had left the house. Life was very hard, but we did not need the paid help for the above contingencies we now receive in today's impersonal society. In our poverty I think we tried as best we could to keep the Commandment 'Love thy neighbour as thyself'.

Despite the economic depression the standard of life was beginning to improve. Few people realised that progress and machinery could in fact mean prosperity and more jobs. Horses and carts were slowly being superseded by vans and motor cars, the wireless was on the market, gas lighting was replacing the old fashioned lamps and gas cookers were taking much of the hard work out of cooking, hitherto done in the side ovens of the coal firegrates. The Trades Unions were becoming better known and were fighting to get the working week reduced with a five and a half day week, and in fact, were successful. My father only had to work from 7 a.m. till 1 p.m. on Saturdays — but this did not better our existence much as he, in common with the average working man, went straight from work to the pub and didn't come home until 'turning out' time.

'Tyning pit was more than a mine, it was a living community

Ron Perrett
RADSTOCK

I wrote my first short composition at Radstock Board School. That was fifty five years ago and I remember the subject. We had been told a story of Robin Hood and we were asked to write about it in our own words. I can also remember the use of two words. They were 'so saying'. I had seen them somewhere and I had thought how clever their use in linking together words and action and was determined to use them. Here was the opportunity and I wrote 'so saying, he jumped on his horse and rode away'.

I have remembered that sentence all my life, which is really quite remarkable when oftimes I cannot remember what day of the week it is.

I remember a neighbour of ours called Bill Selway. He was a miner and a man of great passion for the miner's cause, a quality that found ample expression in the turbulent days of the General Strike. Though small of stature, he expounded his political beliefs with a strident, compulsive voice. To me he was an exciting man; a firebrand in an explosive world of injustice when the labour movement was a mighty crusade with a battle to win and a legitimate flag to fly.

I last saw him not long before he died. His mind and body had grown tired together but the old fire still smouldered. I spoke to him of the old days. It was a door that old people wait for us to open, and seldom do they miss the opportunity to escape to the past. His face lit up as he talked excitedly and quite rationally about those bygone years that were still his life and all that remained to cling to in a strange and alien world. Many times I have helped to free the elderly from their exile of dreams, just by listening and showing interest in their reminiscences, though I must admit, there have been times when I have had to be rescued.

I always feel depressed by the ageing of all such colourful and exciting characters. When I see the encroaching years taking over the agile mind and body, when I see faltering steps and stooping shoulders where there was once unimpaired mobility. When I see the bloom of skin and the sheen of hair become dulled, I feel the same melancholy that comes with the long shadows at the close of a warm autumn day. It is the sadness of a summer slipping away. How unlike my mother I am. She found growing old a gracious and beautiful experience, completely void of fear and despair. For her, the winter of life was only a transition to eternal spring. But then, she possessed unshakeable faith in God and His promised house of many mansions, which she never once doubted.

I was born in Radstock in 1914 alongside what was then the 'Somerset and Dorset Railway'. If I had any notion that a cacophony of whistles and the letting off of steam heralded my breathless arrival, I was soon to be disillusioned. Throughout my life at 35 Waterloo Road these noises never ceased, save on Sundays.

I can hear now the noise of the buffers colliding like the hammer on an anvil. This reverberation was transmitted from an engine at one end via some twenty trucks to one at the other. It always seemed to me to be all so unnecessary since the last wagon would be unceremoniously rejected and so the clamour would be once more repeated in the opposite direction.

My mother was the second child and first daughter of Thomas and Elizabeth Beard of Radstock. She was to be one of a family of eleven — seven girls including a twin, and four boys. In addition, there were two further twins that died at birth.

My grandfather was a miner, as were initially all the boys. Grandmother baked all her own bread in the huge kitchen stove. She made every garment and mended every garment. She planned every meal with economic precision. Shoes for the family were cleaned and laid in a row every evening, ready for the next day. She sent her children to school clean and well clothed, even if gracelessly so.

I can remember mother telling me that after washing and putting her eight children to bed, she retired to her own and gave birth to her ninth. No wonder then, in a moment of great stress, she confessed that if things did not improve she could no longer face life. Grandfather left the pit at Writhlington where he worked, walked to Braysdown Colliery and begged for a better paid position.

He was successful and life became a little more tolerable. But even so, she died on July 25th 1916 at the age of 60. The doctor diagnosed a worn out heart. 'Her body is very strong', he said. 'If I could have given her a new heart, she could have lived another decade'.

Within two years, grandfather married again. He chose another Elizabeth who was to prove the most perfect successor. She had worked all her life in gentleman's service from servant girl to cook general. The long period of graduation below stairs with all its graciousness had rubbed off on her. Her speech was precise and articulate. She carried herself with poise and dignity.

I loved to take afternoon tea at the little cottage, just the three of us. The china was most delicate, the bread and butter wafer thin and the cups never more than three quarters full. She served us all with no less propriety than she had given to nobility. It was a dear cottage filled with the warmth of welcome and a pervading peace that enfolded all who sought is sanctuary.

Whenever a rare opportunity presented itself, grandfather would embark upon some topicality of the day, mostly political, or he would produce the Daily Herald, pointing out an article of interest or the leader column which he considered quite the most important feature of any daily paper. Throughout all his political thinking shone his one inspired dream — the betterment of his class and its evolvement through the brotherhood of man and Christian principles. He always challenged injustice and oppression of the people. He always believed that in God's world what was morally wrong was never economically necessary and what was ethically right was economically possible. In a happy and calm eventide, his bitterest moment was the defeat of the Labour Government in the Autumn of 1931 and the forming of a coalition by Ramsey Macdonald whom he revered. His photograph took pride of place in his small cottage parlour and looking down seemed to dominate its very life.

I called on him the following day and the photograph was missing. I asked him what had happened to it and with with tears streaming down his face, he told me he could do no other but remove it.

My father was the son of a railway guard. He married my mother in 1905 and they went to live alongside the railway where they were to remain all their lives. My father was very deaf from birth. His eardrums were perforated and much money, so ill afforded, was subsequently spent in a vain effort to draw him a little nearer to a normal world of sound. He was to remain extremely deaf for the biggest part of his life, since there was insufficient money to purchase a hearing aid sensitive enough for such a serious ear condition.

He was never to hear our baby talk or our childish laughter. He never shared the sweet whispered language of lovers in love. Not for him the song of the birds or the sigh of the wind. He did not hear the hoof beats of the horses he loved and their comforting clip clop on the road. He missed the sound of harness put on and taken off, the ring of the brasses, the champing of the bit. And more than all these perhaps, the intimate equine language of horses expressing in their own way, their love and gratitude to him who so loved them. He lived in the world but only in its remotest and loneliest corner.

The welfare state later provided for him his first successful aid. I remember well with what childlike wonder and excitement he heard for the first time the commonplace sounds of the home.

Whilst everyone sympathises with the deaf, I think sometimes insufficient thought is given to those who live close to them. To a lesser degree within the family circle, my mother shared my father's isolation and loneliness. She was as shut off from him in those early days as he was from her. She could share no confidences and if there are such things as shouted intimacies, then the thin partition walls would have ensured their utter defeat.

I had seven aunts and if I skip lightly over their contribution to this saga, it is merely because they lived their lives where bright rays of glamour but seldom if ever penetrated, and in an age when strong personalities in women were deemed to be immodest. It was very much the age of male predominance and the woman-folk would sit, for the most part, quietly admiring the perception and the enlightenment that gave their men such an understanding of their social environment and that lifted them far above their deprived background.

My four uncles — with one exception — were all socialist, even though the 'reds' came in varying shades. Uncle Alf and Uncle George were vastly different personalities. Alf was the rough diamond, George the Kohinoor, although the polished and refined side of his nature was always subordinate to the gentleness and sensitiveness of him. George joined the Church whilst still young, as did all his kin, and showed exceptional ability as a Lay Preacher among the neighbouring Churches. He was instrumental in forming the Baptist Church at Peasedown, becoming its first Lay Pastor. The Baptist Ministry beckoned. It was a hard road he was to follow before he realised his ambition.

Up at five in the morning and a three mile tramp to the pit head. Then an eight hour stint in the black labyrinth of arteries that the fields of Somerset shamefully hid with their cloak of green.

The long slog homeward with his father and three brothers to a scene I can only inadequately describe. The shadows of the small dark kitchen are deepened by the imported blackness of the mine. The pungent combination of coal dust and sweat fills the room. The small stove that has cooked for five is fed and restoked to heat the large iron kettles and their steaming benevolence joins with the tin bath to wash the filth and the weariness down to the whiteness of self-respect once more. What a cauldron of heat and human emotion this kitchen must have been. Not the place for divine study you may think, but it was all that was available.

He passed his examinations and qualified to enter Spurgeons College, London.

His first ministerial appointment was at St. George, Bristol. His preaching was eloquent and compelling. It appealed to his congregation and spread beyond. His Church filled to overflowing and it became necessary to place chairs in the aisles to accommodate the new influx. He remained a Minister all his life.

If I admitted to having a favourite amongst my uncles, I think my uncle Walter would have a slight edge. From the same humble cradle as the rest of the family, he emerged with an early thirst for knowledge. He was an avid reader. He realised that any learning had, to a very great extent, to be self acquired. Like many of his day who saw human degradation and its effects, he was determined not to accept it as the inevitable. He must have read much reactionary doctrine that began to emerge at that time, but he tempered all this with his own religious experience. He believed that his Christ of the New Testament was also a social reformer. As a member of his Bible Class when a teenager, he had a very great influence upon me. He read to us not only from the Bible, but from the lives of great reformers such as William Morris, poet, artist, designer and an ardent Socialist. Much of his own religious thinking in those days of deprivation was based on the fundamental concept that Christ fed the five thousand before he preached to them.

He was also deeply involved in public life and was a member of the Radstock Council for many years, and all the time worked tirelessly and passionately for socialism and the election of the first ever Labour Member of Parliament for the Division.

His bookshelves were a revelation and an indication of the broad canvas on which the pattern of his life took shape. I still have a copy of Tolstoy's 'War and Peace' he gave me. To him that work was no problem. Yet he spent most of his working life as a miner, starting with his brothers in the Somerset coalfields when he left school. Amongst his many activities was his long term as miners' representative, at the Foxcote mine where my brother worked. He himself worked as a breaker at the coal face.

Mining was always remotely a part of my life as a boy. Coal was in the blood of my mother's family. My brother was a miner and my sister was later to marry a miner. In addition, there were ten pits within three to four miles of Radstock and three within a mile radius of my home.

Tning pit, closed now, was more than a mine, it was a living community. In a strange way, another link we had with the pit was the slag heaps surrounding it and one in particular that long before I was born had been deemed of sufficient height to close. To the credit of the pit owners, it had been mercifully planted with fir trees. These, together with ferns, grass and wild flowers that came uninvited to live, transformed its black unclad ugliness into a green hillock, pleasant to the eye and soft to the tread. It was commonly called 'the batch'.

Two pits had been involved in this man-made hill, — Tyning and Ludlows. The waste from Ludlows was carried up by miniature tubs on two narrow gauge tracks. They were operated on an endless rope system, full trucks of slag going up on the track and mined coal coming down on the other. The rope was made of thick steel and was carried over large metal drums like huge cotton reels placed at intervals between the rails. As children, we were fascinated by the perpetual motion of the trucks, ropes and drums. All three were well endowed with thick grease and mother would always know by our clothes where we had been playing. A particular stage of this busy little cableway was visible from our houses and from a distance the tubs looked like a slowly moving procession of black beetles.

My brother became a collier at the age of sixteen. He had previously worked for the Co-operative Society for two years. Why he decided to enter the industry I do not know. All his friends were miners and I rather think he felt locked out from their fraternity. I am sure he must often have regretted this step in the years that followed. Mother pleaded with him to stay out of the pits but he was quite adamant.

He started at the Foxcote Colliery one Sunday evening on the night shift which started at 9 p.m. and finished at 5 a.m. next morning. How well I recall the sad return from evening Service that Sunday and the shadow that fell over the household. My brother changed from Sunday best to sackcloth and mother prepared his sandwiches that were carried in what was called a 'tommy bag', and his bottle of tea that was always drunk cold. We watched with increasing dread, the minutes tick their way to 8 o'clock. Then came the moment of departure. He was not very big and in his rough, ill-fitting pit clothes, he looked even more diminutive. His features beneath his collier's cap were small and delicate. He was a quiet, pathetic figure but he strode bravely away, very much a man from that moment and with a wave and tears in our eyes, we watched him out of sight. My mother broke her heart that night. He had first of all to walk two miles alone to the pit head. The horror of that first descent in the cage can well be imagined. There must have been an awful finality in the crash of the closing gate, the downward lurch into blackness when the last thin wall of light holding back the unknown dark was at last broken. The icy splash of water from the dank shaft walls and every sound multiplied and echoed above and below. The inevitable feeling of being buried alive.

His first job was powder boy. He accompanied the shot firer and carried the materials necessary for blasting. Only four worked the night shift. They were the two shot firers and their boys and their task was to prepare the coal face for the arrival of the day shift in the morning.

The four, on reaching the pit bottom, would split up

and make their way to different workings by way of the main corridors, a further walk of two to three miles. This must again have been a traumatic experience, walking with head down along the long, narrow gallery dimly lit by the small arc of candlelight.

When the day shift had left the coal face on the previous day, the coal they had cut from the 3' high seam would have left a considerable overhang of rock above them. This had to be blasted away before they returned in the morning to resume further exavation. This could only be done by lying on the side and cutting the coal with a pick, the only posture possible in such a confined space.

These narrow seams were eventually to end prematurely the life of the Somerset coalfield and the closure of all the mines in the Radstock district. In the last twenty years, a great deal of mechanisation was introduced and mechanical cutters were installed but the nature of the seams limited their full potential and made coal production uneconomical.

The holes into which the explosives were placed would have been drilled by the face workers before they left on the previous day. The shot firer, on reaching the location, would insert cap and fuse followed by the powder rammed in with clay. The fuse was then lit and man and boy would retire to a safe distance.

When my brother later related to us the nature of his work that night, I found it hard to imagine and still do today, that first terrifying explosion that thundered from wall to wall in those narrow confines, echoing and re-echoing the ghostly labyrinth of tunnels like imprisoned demons howling for release. That first night must have been for him a succession of fearful nightmares.

After doing this job for two years, the next and only progression was to carting boy which was amongst the most crude and brutal occupations in the industry. A carting boy was responsible for the removal of coal from the face to the head of the main road, where it was tipped ready for reloading into larger wagons. From here it was transported by rail to the pit bottom. Because of the extremely low ceiling, it was only possible to haul coal from the face by crawling on all fours and pulling what was called a putt. This was a box about 3 ft long by 2 ft 6 ins high with runners on the bottom, somewhat like a toboggan.

Boy and putt were joined by a crude harness called a guss which consisted of a rope girdle to which an iron chain and hook was attached. The girdle encircled the naked waist, the chain went between the legs and the hook was linked to the putt.

For the first few weeks, my brother suffered the agony of all carting boys. With a full load, the soft body skin was chafed and cut by the ruthless friction of the rope that bit even deeper when the putt sunk into an area of soft strata or fouled an unsuspected pit prop.

Although the trouser knees were padded, it was insufficient protection against the unyielding floor. The knees were scratched, bruised and lacerated and the hands suffered a similar fate. These injustices of the flesh had to be endured daily until the skin because hard and calloused.

In the meantime, my mother each day washed the poor broken skin and rubbed in salt for hardening, crying bitter tears not only for the agony it induced, but also for the injustice and indignity that both suffered.

This work as a carting boy was punishing and exhausting and a walk of two miles homeward at the end of it all was a further drain on his strength. My mother would always have his dinner on the table when he came in, but many times we saw him push it aside and slumped forward with his head resting on his hands, would go to sleep instantly with sheer exhaustion in spite of the equally urgent need to eat. And the reward for all this was £1 or £2 per week.

With pit-head baths no more than a dream, both he and his family shared the affront of this imported dirt day after day. During the winter particularly my brother would often arrive home soaked to the skin. His clothes had to be dried by the following morning and the only heat available was from the small living room range. And so, all evening, and throughout the night, they would be draped around the hearth. The pungent, earthy smell mingling with the steam and rising like a thick vapour, added no comfort to our evenings by the fire.

From time to time, mother would have to repair the large protective patches on the trouser knees. When they were beyond repair, she would sew in new ones; an arduous and painful task. I can well remember the names of the two types of material used, but what their respective qualities were apart from their durability, I never knew. One was fustian and the other rush duck which had an unmistakably evil smell. Because of its toughness it was extremely difficult to penetrate and my mother dreaded this rustic needlework. She would sit all evening by the wholly inadequate light of an oil lamp, stitching until her fingers were raw.

There were jobs in the mine that although not having the same element of crudeness about them that 'carting' had, were none the less more undesirable in that they carried with them special health hazards. The 'branchers' as they were called, spent all their time blasting roads to new coal seams. They worked on the day shift. They were tough and strong and most of them well built men but they died at a relatively early age. The stone dust was even more deadly than coal dust and the advancement to chronic chest and lung infections was very much faster. Having said that, I would not minimise the health risks of the coal face workers or 'breakers' as they were called. Some spent most of their working lives hewing coal before the damping down processes of today were evolved and died prematurely from the dreaded disease 'silicosis'. This was the result of large deposits of coal dust settling on the lungs and, in time, solidifying.

The colliery owners seemed little concerned with these problems and in many cases were careless and indifferent to basic safety precautions. The industry was choked with discontent and unrest. Demands were made upon the owners for higher wages and shorter working hours but these were turned down.

In May 1926 the men decided to strike and found sympathetic support for their cause in other industries.

And so, for the first time in history, the country found itself in the grip of a general strike. I was only twelve then but much that happened at that time is still clear in my memory. Miners were all around me and the flames of bitterness that burned in them were kindled in me.

Meetings were held by the men on strike and my Uncle Walter often spoke with his accustomed fire and passion. He was to coin a phrase that is still repeated to this day in Radstock and district — 'We'll eat the grass of the fields men before we go back'.

He led a march of miners to the 'Sawclose' at Bath where a meeting was held. I doubt if their cause evoked any sympathy there, for traditionally miners were not popular with the people of Bath. The chasms of class yawned wider then than they do today but there was another reason. A small minority of colliers made a habit of visiting Bath on Saturday evenings returning on a special late train. It was a rare source of pleasure after a week of slavery in the mine but it was often much too generously celebrated. But like all minorities, they were used as a stick to wield against the majority and so the bad reputation was to become inveterate.

The General Strike lasted only nine days. The Government threatened the T.U.C. with legal action and it capitulated, leaving the miners to fight on alone. This most of them did until the December of that year when they were virtually starved into submission.

As the weeks and months dragged on, there were ever increasing fears of the winter, lest the conflict should not be resolved. Against regulations, many miners including my brother, mined surface coal on the Tyning batch. I well remember watching him one day burrowing deeply into the side of the hill. I still recall the horror and dread I felt that day, lest the unpropped roof should collapse. Too frightened to watch further, I raced home with the terrifying vision of my brother being buried alive.

This open-cast mining was hard and dangerous work and to some degree, unfruitful. It often meant moving five or six tons of slag to extract one bag of poor quality coal, which had then to be carried home. But with the prospect of a cold, miserable winter it was very precious indeed. At least it was for use in the home. Some miners did, in fact, make a practice of selling it.

It was a combination of poverty, boredom and a declining lack of loyalty to the cause that in the Autumn induced a small number of men to return to work. The very first of these in the Radstock area lived in our road and was well known to us. This first isolated break of solidarity led to scenes that, although considered justified, were at the same time distressing.

It was on a Monday morning I remember and I had gone with my brother and my sister's fiancée on a 'nutting' expedition which was a term used for the annual gathering of hazel nuts. News came to us that this man had offered his labour that morning at Middle pit and that a large crowd had gathered to await his emergence from the morning shift.

Excitement was hard to come by in those drab, depressing days and driven by the fear that we might be denied our share of it, we were soon on the scene. The road leading to the pithead was lined some two or three hundred yards on either side with a turbulent and hostile crowd and the clamour of angry voices grew in volume as more people came running.

And so, with the stark hideousness of the pithead as a perfect back-drop to this scene of ugliness, the stage was set for drama. Anyone in the crowd who expected the victim to walk into their midst cowering and afraid was doubtless surprised. He was a man of middle age, over 6 ft tall and broad of shoulder. He walked upright and arrogantly between a strong escort of police out of the pit yard and into the road with an air of stubborn defiance.

The excitement grew and angry shouts of 'traitor' and 'blackleg' were hurled. But for his protection, many would have physically attacked him. But he walked as though he did not hear and every malevolent look he took unflinchingly and threw back with equal ferociousness.

I think his arrogance and shamelessness evoked even

more indignation and so the situation became uglier. He ran the gauntlet up Coombend into the Market Place and beyond to the Railway Station. The crowd were unrelenting and men, women and children followed jostling and pushing and crowding in as near the escort as they dared.

Denied a physical attack upon his person, they made cudgels of curses and abuse to assail him. Past the Station, the eruptive cavalcade wound and into Waterloo Road. Our happy road, a thoroughfare that knew nothing of discord but only the laughter of children playing, and the cheerful salutations of people passing. How odd it all looked this day.

This first return to work was in some measure the opening of a flood gate and was to become a pattern all over the country. By the end of November work was resumed in all the important coalfields and after a strike lasting seven months, the men were forced to accept conditions even worse than those that induced the stoppage in May.

Wages were lower and hours longer. The bitter feelings of betrayal by the Conservative Government and by certain socialist members lived on in the hearts of every miner. They certainly did in my home.

We went to the Radstock Board School. I don't know why it was thus called. Then and at no other time in its long history had it ever boarded pupils and never in my wildest imagination can I see it proclaiming itself as 'The Radstock Boarding School', seminary for the further education of collier's sons and daughters'. Certainly not over the small wooden door in the wall through which we used to creep each morning.

I think my first childhood memory was of the schoolroom where my education started. I have thought very hard but there seems to be nothing before this. Initially, we were to be amused rather than educated. There were large frames of counting beads, bricks and modelling clay and the most fascinating of all, shallow trays filled with sand. We drew pictures with our forefinger and to erase and start again required no more than a slight shake of the tray.

The passport to the Grammar School or Secondary School as it was known then, was the School Certificate. All of us who were candidates for this examination were, for the next year, to be the Headmaster's special charge. If there had been factory farming in those days, we would have best been described as battery hens. We were placed in a special class and were fed twice daily. This was on a controlled diet of arithmetic in the morning and English in the afternoon. The only time it varied was when results in the morning were unsatisfactory. Arithmetic would then be fed again in the afternoon.

My teacher was a great lover of poetry and he helped me toward my own early love of verse. Reading poetry aloud for him in class was a wonderful experience. He taught us inflection of the voice, accentuation, pitch and tone, delivery and attack and above all, a passion for what we read.

The poem I loved best was 'Horatius at the Bridge' by Lord Macaulay. I had the impression that he liked it equally as much. It seemed admirably suited to voice reproduction and dramatic interpretation.

And so we cleared our throats and clearly and precisely in very audible voice began. Our teacher would stand in front of us like the conductor of an orchestra, ready to lead us through the poem of 28 stanzas, beckoning our voices with raised hands as the fortissimo passages approached, and muting them with a downward movement for pianissimo effect.

I remember verses from this poem now, after all these years. They are both good examples of our first introduction to drama in the form of power and pathos.

> 'Come back, come back Horatius
> Loud cried the fathers all
> Back Lartius, back Herminius,
> Back ere the ruins fall.

> Back darted Spurius Lartius,
> Herminius darted back,
> And as they passed, beneath their feet
> They felt the timbers crack'.

By the time we reached the word 'crack', the crescendo arising slowly from the first line, would have reached its powerful climax. Here a measure of competition crept in as we vied with each other as to who could produce the loudest crack. I sometimes thought our own roof timbers would beat us all.

Conversely our voices would recede to a mere whisper as we took up the tragic cry of Horatius.

> 'But he saw on Palatinus,
> The white porch of his home,
> and he spake to the noble river
> that rolls by the towers of Rome.
> O Tiber father Tiber
> to whom the Romans pray
> A Roman's life, a Roman's arms
> Take thou in charge this day'.

These lines would almost reduce me to tears.

There was a little sweet shop, that conveniently stood on the road to school, halfway up the hill directly opposite my grandparents' house. It wasn't really a shop at all but a very small cottage converted for this purpose. It was kept by an old lady by the name of Miss Rivers. She was small and softly spoken, and ever patient as we stood deliberating, sometimes at great length, as to the best way to spend the ½d tightly clenched in the hand.

She always wore black dresses that accentuated the whiteness of her hair. The sweets were laid out on two large tables facing the door. They were so big in relation to the tiny parlour that they had veritably taken it over and squeezed the old lady into a corner by the fire. There she sat in a high backed chair, always knitting when she was not serving us. To me it was more than a sweet shop — it was a fairy grotto.

We would often be given a ½d to take back to school in the afternoon and on the way we would gaze thoughtfully through the tiny window panes of the 'shop'. But choice was not easy and time was short and so we would wait until we were on our way home.

We could have liquorice in sticks or strips, a liquorice pipe or liquorice bootlaces. Or we might buy a packet of sherbet with a round dab on a stick for licking, or with a tube of liquorice sticking from its top for sucking through. We could buy four aniseed balls, a packet of sweet shredded pipe tobacco or a gobstopper that changed colour as we sucked it. Of course, we had to watch this magical process which meant its removal from the mouth every few minutes. But often we would chance all on a lucky dip. The bag had a magic about it and the mystery of the unknown. What a permutation of sweetness and with a ½d in the hand, who could make a decision?

I am quite sure that the Saturdays of my childhood were no less eventful than those of today and not the least bit over-shadowed by the contemporary scene of Dr. Who, Starsky and Hutch and Match of the Day. Radstock market was the weekly event. Inside, the personnel never changed in all the years I can remember. Outside, with a few exceptions, the stall holders came and went like door to door salesmen. The dubious nature of their wares often necessitated a very long absence.

In those days, the market lasted all day. It was often past ten when some stalls closed. It was a place for late night shopping, a weekly rendezvous for friends and a centre of entertainment.

Summer and winter the vendors vied with each other to attract the biggest crowds. They all followed the same method, leading their audience through the preliminaries by means of jokes, clowning and buffoonery to the ultimate points of sale.

Goods thrown up by the assistants were piled over the arm of the salesman, one upon the other until with a final slap of the thigh the bargain lot would be held aloft and the cost of the unique and never to be repeated offer, finally revealed. Those were wonderful days of deflation. Towels, sheets and pillow cases were reduced from a pound to five shillings within the space of minutes. Strongly competing, no more than a few yards away, were quack doctors dispensing palliatives, laxatives, tonics, corn cures, back and stomach pills, liniments, embrocation and ointments. Coloured gentlemen sold tooth powder with guarantees of teeth no less white than their own and lotions for the immediate restoration of hair. There were sales of china, hardware and haberdashery and a great deal of rubbish that today would have resulted in the prosecution of the seller. I can remember worthless German War Bonds being sold in bundles of fifty for a mere sixpence, with more than a veiled suggestion that they could well become a recognised currency once more.

The shop most familiar to me was the Co-operative grocery department, a part of the C.W.S. block of shops at the bottom of Wells Hill, empty now for many years. Since my mother was secretary of the Co-operative Womens Guild and closely involved in the labour movement, most of our purchases were made here.

From the age of ten I was entrusted with all but the main weekly shopping. It was a job I can never remember disliking. I was always fascinated by the network of overhead wires along which sped small containers, like miniature cable cars, carrying the money to a cash desk high up at the end of the shop and duly returning the change. They were launched by the assistant with a downward pull of a lever and they travelled at great speed.

Radstock had then, what might be described in the loosest sense, a debating society and community centre. It was in the main, very commonplace and unacademic and was entirely male. It assembled daily on a long wall. Here at all hours of the day, old and young came to sit, some occasionally like myself, some as regularly as the clock that spelled out the hour above the covered market. They were commonly known as the Bridge Committee.

In the late afternoon the miners drifted in to take their

seats after the grime of the morning shift had been washed away. They sat shoulder to shoulder like birds on a fence. In winter, even the cold, hard, comfortless stones were no deterrent. Here the first editions of the evening paper were read and the results of the afternoon race card eagerly scanned. Here the days events were discussed, the humorous highlights extracted and recounted, jokes retold and on a more academic plane the topical issues of the day argued and debated.

There were few vacant seats on Saturday mornings when the bridge wall became the monopoly of miners. Saturday was paying out day at the pits and it was here many brought their wages. The mining of coal was done by teams of two face workers and one carting boy. The wages for the team was paid out on one ticket and many face workers calculated and apportioned the share out on the wall. It was not uncommon to see wives also present on this occasion for the purpose of ensuring that the hard won wages were not irresponsibly squandered in the saloon bars of the Bell and Waldegrave inns.

We played football and cricket at the relevant times of the year. But they were not the only games we played. There were many others that were as seasonable as Bank Holidays, the flowers in the garden and the clothes we wore. We never consulted the calendar before we took our hoops out of the shed or our jar of marbles from the top shelf. But, somehow, we knew the time had arrived to do so.

We played marbles in the spring. Equally attractive to me as the game, were the marbles themselves, especially the large taws. These fascinated me with their brightly coloured veins of red, blue and yellow. I used to wonder how these colours could be so beautifully blended and fashioned within those magical spheres of glass and, in fact, I still do. Less glamorous were the small brown members of the marble family. It was quite possible to lose twenty or more of these in a series of games, so that we quite often made our own by rolling out balls of clay and baking them in the oven. Unfortunately, they tended to jump and wobble and to take a drunken course not intended by the thrower.

There were several variations of the game. In the standard version, we each put the number of marbles called for within a circle drawn on the ground. This was called the pound and basically the object of the game was to knock out as many as possible with the taws.

Summer saw the emergence of hoops and tops. Hoops were made of cast iron of about ¼ inch thickness and were propelled by a short rod of similar gauge with either a shepherds crook end or a ring that enclosed the hoop and became an integral part of it.

We used to drive these at great speed and on the uneven road surfaces of those days, they would rattle and bounce like flying dervishes. Not surprisingly, they often broke. We took them for repair to the blacksmith whose shop was in the big yard just off the Market Place. We were not normally allowed inside but since we had a hoop in need of repair we were to a lesser degree customers, albeit unprofitable ones.

We would stand a little timorously in the corner, half shrinking from the noise and heat as raw metal was tempered and hammered into shape. Here was a symphony of sight, sound and industry. The charcoal was stimulated and blown to white heat by the hand operated bellows, bright incandescent arcs of fire flashed between forge and anvil in the long iron forceps and under the rapid hammer blows, cascades of sparks were expelled, illuminating the suspended gloom of black walls and ceiling.

Tops were made of wood and were of two shapes. One was some three to four inches long with a flat circular head shaped something like a mushroom, the other short and dumpy. Both had a steel tip at the tapered end. Around the top we drew circles with chalks. Their many coloured permutations produced varied and fascinating effects when in motion.

Starting the top required a measure of skill and patience. It was coaxed into a somewhat drunken gyration either by wrapping the string of the whip around it and unwinding it with a sharp sideways movement, much as one would start a small petrol engine, or by giving it a twirl with the fingers. Whilst it was still revolving and before it lost its impulse, it had to be activated by the whip, swiftly and accurately applied. I can recall now the joy of that moment of success when it suddenly burst into life and sustained by its own speed and momentum, would spin with a proud and joyful independence.

High on the list of summer games was 'chalk chase', a glorified game of hide and seek. Two were chosen to hide by the age-old process of elimination reached by the joining of hands in a circle and the chanting of verses. These, although often meaningless, had a delightful folklore element about them. They were accompanied by the pointing finger of the leader in the middle, assimulating a roulette wheel. When it finally stopped and the words 'out go you' were pronounced, it was a moment of undisputable destiny. It was a method both simple and lyrical, fair and unchallengable. How much better than the dull, unimaginative tossing of a coin.

No game had a more beautiful setting, leading as it did both hunters and hunted deep into the countryside, down lanes, over fields and along the protective cover of hedgerows.

It is not difficult to understand why the majority of the games we played then are now extinct. Changing circumstances and habits have made many quite impracticable. How, for instance, could our game of 'ball in hat' be played today in the almost entire absence of headgear. The playing of the game necessitated a ball and required of each player a cap. These were laid out side by side, against the wall. A chosen player stood back the width of the road and, with eyes closed, rolled the ball into one of the hats. The respective owner then ran to remove it whilst the rest scattered in all directions. At the moment of picking up the ball he shouted 'stand', whereupon the runners would freeze. He then attempted to hit the nearest one with the ball. If he succeeded that player was out of the game. If the throw was unsuccessful, he could run again until the ball was reclaimed and the command to stand was shouted once more. To close the game it was necessary for the player with the ball to hit each one in turn.

Our winter pastimes were far more limited but only wet and extremely cold evenings confined us to the house. When the moon afforded us sufficient illumination, we often played what can best be described as a nocturnal chalk chase. It was called 'Jack, Jack, shine the light' but instead of carrying a piece of chalk, the two runners set off into the darkness with a lantern. Often on winter evenings sitting quietly in nostalgic mood, I have heard these words high and clear on the night air, shouted at intervals by voices blown about on the wind and my imagination having borne me this far, by peeping through the curtains I might have seen a distant light appearing and disappearing in the fields and hedges beyond. The words were a call for the two to hold up the lamp, a request they reluctantly conceded for the briefest of moments.

We provided our own heat with portable hand warmers, more commonly known as smoke tins. These were nothing more than empty cocoa tins perforated around the sides with the aid of a nail and a hammer. Inside we stuffed burning rags that had initially been ignited. By changing it from one hand to the other and swinging it backwards and forwards, we kept our hands warm, provided welcome circulation and at the same time, induced enough air through the holes to keep the rags smouldering.

Any comfort we obtained, however, was somewhat diminished by a sufferance that almost matched the intense cold in its unpleasantness. The tin became at times unbearably hot, searing the skin of our hands. The bellowing black smoke was inescapable. It choked us with its acrid fumes until we gasped for breath and filled our eyes until the tears streamed down our cheeks.

In retrospect, it seems to me that the winters of my youth were very much more severe than they are now. But then my father used to recall snow drifts eight or ten feet deep and thought that the winters of his childhood were even more extreme. Perhaps each generation feels the climate has changed in its life-time.

After fifty years it seems a good time to take stock. In drawing comparisons, I am never able to come to any firm conclusions. No sooner have I listed the merits of life when I was a boy than the relative advantages and virtues of our present society force me to cancel them out.

No generation has lived through more eventful years than that of my age group or seen more progress in the field of medicine and science.

The speed in the development of the latter has been a little frightening and continues to be an even greater source of concern both by its own dangerous progression and by its damaging spin-off effect on the environment. To me, equally disturbing has been the change in social attitudes and relationships. Television must take some of the blame. It has dictated our life's time-table to such an extent that on certain evenings it is desirous that we are at home at a given time. It has forced us to offer up silent prayers that our friends, please God, just for tonight shall not be friendly enough to call. It has proved to be the jealous and possessive master of many homes. It has shocked us and outraged us but the arguments against it must be qualified. To its credit it has stimulated our interests in subjects hitherto denied us. It has wetted our appetite for them and sent us searching through our libraries for a closer insight and involvement.

That it has destroyed the art of conversation and reshaped our leisure is indisputable but this proves little unless we assume that all conversation is, at best, as thought provoking as the programmes we view and that our leisure is used to equal advantage.

I cannot recall what we talked about as we huddled around the hearth on winter evenings but I doubt the profoundness of our discourse.

I believe a more serious threat to social relationships has been the migration from the terraced houses of towns and cities to the detached and semi-detached of outer environments. In the row of houses I grew to love, I can remember the involvement in each others troubles and misfortunes and the fun and laughter shared in the good times. Many families today live a bed, breakfast and evening meal existence. Our homes were lived in to the limits of each day.

Today there seems to be no place in the life schedule of many for the needs of others. Governments and organised charities have taken over the job of caring, a responsibility once willingly accepted by individuals. Without doubt our priorities have been disarranged by an increased prosperity and its consequent demands upon us. We do not have to be ambitious or aspiring to be caught up and enveloped in the commercial cyclone. The attempt to escape even for a few brief moments in the daily round to give ourselves to matters of a greater human priority becomes quite impossible, even amongst the most altruistic. We are not intentionally unresponsive but there is not sufficient time to become involved.

In writing this I have completed a journey into the past with a mere handful of memories. The more vivid of these have not been difficult to recapture, but some have been too detailed to enumerate, and so small that like gold dust they have slipped through my fingers. I have lived for the second time that period of my life very dear to me, amongst these very wonderful people. It has been with a closeness I would not have found possible by any other means.

'You name it we carried it'

Amelia Bale
DORCHESTER

I was born at Hurst Green, Moreton, in 1893, and my
parents, Mr. and Mrs. G. Hansford, moved to Pallington in
1897 to a larger cottage in the rental of Mr. T. Budden of
Waddock Farm, for whom my father worked. In this
cottage there was a large living room with a beamed ceiling
and a stone floor and two smaller rooms downstairs and
three large bedrooms upstairs.

There was no grate or range, just a large hearth fireplace,
where mostly wood and turf were burnt. There was also a
large brick built oven where my mother used to bake bread
and cakes once a week. The lardy cakes she made, I've
never tasted the like since, and sometimes during the week
she would make a griddle cake. This was a flat fruit cake,
cooked on a grid-iron stood up in front of the earth fire.

The bread oven was heated with faggots of wood and
furze, and it used to scare me to see that flaming oven.
Vegetables to be cooked were put in separate string nets
and boiled together in an iron boiler that was hung over
the fire from a back crook. We used to have to heat the
flat irons for ironing stood up in front of the fire.

I left school in 1906 and in 1907 I went in service to
Martello Towers, Canford Cliffs. It was a lovely house and
very nice people except for the cook, who was not at all
nice and very jealous. There was an elderly man working
there as 'off man' and I used to go out and talk to him
sometimes, he seemed so poor and lonely, but cook told
me off and said I was not to talk to him. At weekends
when Dr. Smith was away, Mrs. Smith used to take us two

younger girls with her to Church. We thought we were very grand, riding in an open carriage behind a liveried coachman and a pair of horses, all the way from Canford Cliffs to Richmond Hill Congregational Church at Bournemouth. Cook did not approve of that as it meant she had to get the lunch without our help.

I only stayed there just over a year, then I took a temporary job for a fortnight with a Miss Scott in Branksome Park. While there she asked me if I would like to go as housemaid to her sister, who was Matron of a fashionable Nursing Home on the West Cliff at Bournemouth.

In the summer months, with Matron's permission, several of us would get up early, put on a bathing costume and coat and run across the lawn and down to the beach for a bathe or perhaps run along the cliffs as far as Branksome Chine. Sometimes the Hall Porter would get a boat and we would go mackerel fishing. As long as we were back at 7 a.m. to start work, all was well.

I left Bournemouth in December, 1915 to get married, and early in 1916 my husband was sent abroad to Malta and the Middle East.

I was at a loose end, so I wrote to my youngest sister who was in service at Hatfield, to know if she would consider coming home to do some kind of war work with me. We eventually decided to join the Womens' Land Army and do horticultural work if possible. So we packed a picnic lunch and cycled off to Weymouth Labour Exchange to sign on. We did not have to wait long for orders and were sent to Affpuddle to Sir Ernest Debenham's estate.

Our working hours were 6.30 a.m. to 5 p.m., with half an hour break at 8 a.m., and an hour for dinner. We worked half a day on Saturday, making a five and a half day week, for which we were paid 15/-.

We were issued with a uniform which consisted of boots, canvas leggings, Bedford cord breeches, drill overall, felt hat, a waterproof and an armband. We did not like the leggings, they were not much good anyway, so we acquired some Army puttees which were much more comfortable.

We had to work at various gardens on the estate, at East

and West Farm, Affpuddle, Turnerspuddle, Bladen, Rogers Hill and Sitterton, and once we had to go to Southover to pick the apricots in a large glasshouse there. At Bladen, a large area of grassland was ploughed up and we made a market garden.

The apples on one tree at East Farm we used to call 'Apostles', they were a red eating apple, and if you cut it across in half there were twelve red spots round the outside of the core.

While we were there we had several different head gardeners, some male and some female. Some of the W.L.A. girls who came to work there did not stay long, having not been used to hard work.

We used to do a lot of walking and on our day off we would cycle to Lulworth, Ringstead or Osmington. One Saturday we saw a char-a-banc trip advertised from Puddletown to Weymouth, so we cycled to Puddletown to go on that trip. It was one of the old charas with an open top. We got to Weymouth all right but coming back the clutch started slipping at the bottom of Ridgeway Hill so most of us had to get out and walk to the top of the hill. My first ever trip in a motor chara.

The day the Armistice was signed at 11 a.m., we were given the rest of the day off. Peace celebrations were held at Bladen in July, 1919. My sister left the Land Army at the end of 1918 while I stayed on for another three months.

In 1919 my parents started a Carriers business with a horse and van travelling between Waddock and Dorchester via Tincleton, Woodsford and West Stafford, twice weekly.

They retired in 1925, and my husband and took over the business with a Ford 14-seater bus. We did three journeys to Dorchester on Saturdays and two on Wednesdays, and one journey to Wareham market on Thursdays. Most of the time in Dorchester was taken up with shopping for the villagers and delivering messages — besides taking produce and poultry to the market and collecting all kinds of goods for delivery on the outward journey.

You name it we carried it, timber, iron work, corn-meal, barrels of beer, coal, groceries and all kinds of provisions. One day I remember we had to take a Welsh harp to Dorchester and as there was no room inside, it had to be tied up at the back of the bus, which caused quite a few comments such as: 'What, are you taking your own harp with you?' when we met up with some of the other Carriers.

Shopping in Dorchester before the war of 1939 was easy and really a pleasure, and the shopkeeprs and their assistants were most helpful and obliging. Most of the shops would allow us to have goods on approval for our customers. One woman always used to ask me to buy her hats, she said I could always get one to suit her better than she could herself. Another person was heard to say that she always asked the Carrier to get what she did not like asking for herself. I was delivering a couple of rabbits to a cottage one day when I met the Vicar, who said; 'You seem to be the general provider, couldn't you provide me with a house-parlourmaid?'.

A few passengers travelled, but mostly, we carried goods for the market, vegetables, fruit, eggs and poultry as well as calves and pigs. For the animals we had some calf racks made to fit on to the tailboard. The pigs we carried caused many a laugh. One especially, evidently did not like the ride, so just lifted the racks and slid off. We did not miss it till we had gone several miles. We then turned back and found the pig quietly eating acorns by the side of the road. The runaway was quickly hoisted aboard again, the racks firmly secured with rope and all was well.

We often had to buy pigs and calves as well as vegetables to take back for our customers. On one occasion we had to take a hive of bees to the market, but the auctioneer did not want to know about them and told us to put them away in the farthest corner of the market. One day, the P.C. on duty noticed that we had two calves in the racks on the back. One was lying down and the other standing up, and he said they must both be standing up or both lying down, but he did not say how we were to tell them that.

Often the whole roof of the bus was covered with crates of chickens and ducks, these all had to be put in special pens and all had to be booked in. The eggs too had to be unpacked and put in boxes supplied by the auctioneers, to be sold. The largest number of eggs we carried on any one journey was 240 dozen, the average price then was ten pence a dozen in old money.

There was no rest on the other days of the week as during the summer we ran trips on Sundays to Weymouth, Sandbanks, Lulworth and other seaside resorts. We also went to all the local fairs and to Tidworth Tattoo, or there was furniture moving to be done.

When the war started in 1939, life began to change and being fairly near the coast and an R.A.F. camp, our timing was sometimes interrupted by air raids or warnings. Travelling at night too was a problem as we were not allowed much light, and often on moonlit nights drove home with no lights at all.

We retired from the business in 1946 after nearly twenty two years without a break. It was hard work in all winds and weathers but we got a lot of fun out of it, if not much money, and I hope we did a worthwhile service to the people in our area.

During my schooldays there were often gypsies camping for short periods in a large open space between two fields near my home. They were never any trouble, they used to make and sell clothes pegs and sell lace, bootlaces and other small things, but a local farmer was heard to say: 'These damned tinkers pinch wood from my hedges, then have the nerve to try and sell us the pegs they make'.

Another regular roadster was the *redding woman, who travelled the roads selling redding to the farmers. She had a very savage dog that would not let anyone go near her tent. Another yearly traveller was a man with a high sided cart carrying pots, pans, brushes, crockery etc. Occasionally, we would see a scissor grinder and a hurdy-gurdy man.

The cart-horses that worked on the farms had some

*Redding — a red ochre used to mark sheep.

lovely names: Blossom, Captain, Prince and others, and although they were slower than the tractors and other machinery that is used on the farms today, the hay-making, harvesting, threshing and other farm jobs were always finished on time.

The high banks of a narrow lane near my home were always a beautiful blaze of colour in the spring with primroses, bluebells, robin hoods and wild parsley. We had a favourite bank too, where blue and white violets grew in abundance. A small copse alongside a steep hill at Waddock was a beautiful colour picture in early spring, with a carpet of lent lilies. When I first remember it, during the time the flowers were out, one of the estate men would walk round to keep an eye on it; but people would come out at night and pick the flowers and pull up the bulbs. They gradually disappeared and the copse was left bare of flowers.

The field opposite that copse was always known as Daisy Field because of the large horse daisies growing there, but to the modern farmer, they were weeds, so out they had to go. We don't seem to see so many foxgloves now, or cowslips and wild orchids (or granfer griggles) as we used to call them. I used to know where some chicory grew and gentians; but there are no more where I knew them to be, the gentians were wiped out by the extraction of gravel, and the chicory by a road widening scheme. The biggest casualties seems to be the heal, ladies' bedstraw, mullein and lots of others. Every year my sisters and I had to pick a lot of agrimony for our Schoolmaster — he used to dry it to make Agrimony Tea.

There were acres of heathland on the ridge of hills to the north of the farmlands from the village of Tincleton, running eastward toward Wareham. A feature of that landscape was a clump of very tall pine trees on the highest point, called Clyffe Clump. In the olden days they were a landmark for the ships at sea. Originally there were between twenty and thirty trees there, but time and weather have taken their toll and they have never been kept up to the original number. I suppose they served the purpose they were planted for.

On that heathland we would find harebells, sundew and a different kind of orchid, as well as bell heather, Scotch heather and ling. We had to watch out for snakes and adders. We would occasionally see a fox but no deer there. At the edge of the heath at Tincleton there was a large sweet chestnut tree, so we kept that in mind for nuts in the autumn and we would search the small coppices for hazelnuts.

During the summer holidays my mother would take us to the seaside for the day, either Weymouth, Swanage or Bournemouth. I always remember the first time I went to Bournemouth, as that was where I first saw a whole hand of bananas at a stall by the pier approach, It always seemed to be lovely weather in those days . . .

'Feed my lambs'

Arthur Whitlock
PITTON

... In spite of the fact that there have never been more and better facilities for historical research most of the people of this country, especially its youth, have no conception, no vivid sense of the actual daily life which their own forbears of a generation or two ago lived, or of the very different life which they themselves would now be living, but for the phenomenal transformation, the magical change, which has come over this country during the last one hundred years or so. A change greater than that which took place between say, the thirteenth and nineteenth centuries. So that it would scarcely be untrue to say that the people of England of the early nineteenth century probably had far more in common with those of the thirteenth century than with the people of the present day . . .

This is the story of a shepherd, and the village he lived in over a hundred years ago. He died on February 4th 1942 and remains a legendary Wiltshire figure.

Arthur Whitlock was born in Pitton in 1850, the first of several children. He was my grandfather. There were many Whitlocks in the village. In fact, at one time they accounted for about a quarter of the population by name, apart from those whose name changed on their wedding day. The name Whitlock is found in the Church records as far back as 1687. The Whitlocks may credibly claim that Pitton has been their ancestral home for many generations. For instance, Sir Stephen Fox had a Whitlock grandmother and this probably takes one back to Elizabethan days.

Like his father before him he was a shepherd, and for well over half a century he journeyed about Wiltshire and Hampshire to noted flocks of sheep and was a well-known figure at the Sheep Fairs. He had an uncommonly intimate knowledge of all things that count and matter to a country-man, and was possessed of a seemingly inexhaustible fund of anecdotes. His pertinacious wit and good humour endeared him to all who knew him and won for him a very wide circle of friends in many walks of life. A life-long Methodist, he was proud of it. For him there was no place like Pitton. He was born there, and apart from some years spent at West Tytherley, Winterslow and Fawley, New Forest, lived there all his life, as did many generations of his family before him.

The village of Pitton is in the heart of Wessex about five or six miles east of Salisbury. It is a small village situated in Saxon style down in a valley, nestling on the side of the South Downs, while the Clarendon Woods, which reach almost to Salisbury, bound it on the West. In days gone by, the New Forest reached right to the hill above Pitton, known locally as 'Green Hill'. Pitton stands where the New Forest and Salisbury Plain once met.

Pitton was, until recently, a place of old timbered and thatched cottages, of farm buildings and wells, and at the end of the nineteenth century had a population of about 400 people. This decreased to just over 200, but in recent years has grown considerably.

A school was erected at Pitton in 1850, and it bears the motto 'Feed my lambs'. This was the year of Arthur Whitlock's birth. This 'lamb' was only 'fed' for two years before he went to work at the tender age of seven years, literally to feed actual lambs, for there were several large flocks of sheep at Pitton; money was scarce, flour and food very expensive, and even little Arthur's tiny wage was needed to make ends meet.

Despite only two years' schooling of sorts, not only could Arthur read and write and reckon, but he could, and always did, use his physical and mental powers so that he could turn his hand to almost any task, and achieved a skill at many things which few around could equal.

One of the important influences in his early years, and undoubtedly a decisive one, was Methodism, and indeed it exerted itself throughout the whole of his life. At first there was only a little chapel, with chalk walls, high box pews and doors like horses' boxes — A crude old place with a slate roof — to which Arthur at a very tender age was sent to Sunday services and School. There was no harmonium and few had hymn books for few could read them or afford to buy them. The local Preachers who came every Sunday, and usually stayed in the village for the day, gave out the hymns a verse at a time, and the tune was started by a 'precentor', an old fellow who, though he could neither read nor write, never made a mistake in 'marrying hymns to tunes', and never missed a service for years.

The conditions under which most country people lived were very hard and comfortless. People themselves were rough and crude, and Arthur Whitlock's career was to take him amongst the roughest and toughest at the markets, the fairs, the pubs and amongst the drovers. All the same, most Sundays, he was to be found at the Methodist Chapel, and he much preferred to listen to a local Preacher, who like himself, had to work hard for a living and rough it.

The Whitlock family was seated one Sunday dinner for some boiled ham, potatoes and some broad beans, when old John Noble (who was the preacher for the day and who was sharing the hospitality of that very humble home) asked 'Av'nt 'e any mustard Mrs. Whitlock?' 'No' she replied. 'Well, coodn'e borre (borrow) a bit seeing 'tis Zundee?' he persisted. Certainly just a very homely scene, but one can gauge the effect of coming right up against these Early Methodist preachers, not only in the pulpit, but in ones own home. Men who had perhaps read no other books save the Bible and Pilgrim's Progress; Men of deep piety, great fervour and inflexible convictions, who walked miles every Sunday after a hard week's work to preach to Methodist Societies, often in the open air; men of amazing sincerity and character whose faith and labours laid the foundations of Methodism. Many of them came all the way from Salisbury.

It is well to remember that the hungry forties had only just closed and left behind a vivid memory of hunger and starvation. People today simply have no conception what-ever of the daily lot of their own forbears of about one hundred years' ago. Poverty was a very real thing. Flour, the staple food, was then at a price which sometimes necessitated the whole of the family earnings being spent on that commodity alone.

The fear of unemployment haunted every home, for it meant starvation or the workhouse. My own paternal grandfather, born in 1830, was admitted, while still a boy, with his father and mother, brothers and sisters into a workhouse, simply because there was no alternative. Arthur Whitlock often said later 'We lived on less than people throw away nowadays'.

His first job at the age of seven was a yearly servant at a farthing an hour and a guinea 'come Michaelmas', every penny of which he handed over to his mother, so that he only had it while he carried it home. He worked for twelve hours a day, every day of the year, with no holidays, other than Saints' days and the work was very hard: but Arthur Whitlock possessed a supreme advantage over many, having an uncommonly strong physique and a splendid brain. Only so could he have stood up the conditions of his life so well.

One of his village contemporaries about the year 1860 used to go out to work as a washerwoman. She had to walk well over a mile to the farmhouse, arriving before eight o'clock in the morning. When she had to leave at mid-day to get her own family's dinner, her thirteen year old daughter had to take her place at the wash-tub. Later she returned and worked away until six p.m., and she received only one shilling for the day's work.

Arthur, at fourteen, was head-shepherd looking after a flock of six hundred sheep with an under-shepherd under him. No boy could do it today.

At this time, Jabez Horner of Winterslow arrived with horse and cart and a sack of flour to deliver and said 'Get one of Briant's men' (the Wheelwrights opposite). 'No' insisted Arthur 'tip it up'. Taking the sack of over 2¼ cwts., on his shoulders he carried it up the steps into the house. That summer he carried all the corn off the farm up the granary steps and into the granary, some 80 2¼ cwt., sacks.

One of the hardest jobs he had as a youngster was at the brick kiln at Knightwood, where he had to tread the clay with his bare feet all day long, and then walk home at night.

Showing both the tempo of work and the earning power of the labourer in the 1870's, he dug and planted with potatoes, ten rods* of ground in one day for half a crown. It is, therefore, not surprising that right up to his old age his physical powers were well maintained; when he was eighty five years he could walk six miles by road into Salisbury.

The food was plain and lacking in variety. People sing of the roast beef of Old England, but as Arthur Whitlock said 'One never had any unless um ole cow died'. There was a little mutton about, for sometimes a sheep died, or was killed by accident, but it was the pig which supplied the family with the bulk of meat from one year's end to another, and by the time the last of the bacon came from the rafters, the family knew what 'rafty' meant.

Certainly there were rabbits, hares and even game for those who could catch them without themselves being caught; but it was the family pig which kept the common country people going. Its death was certainly a family event, and delighted eyes watched its dismemberment into bacon, ham and pork, and mouths watered at the thought of faggots, chitterlings, trotters, chaps and great quantities of lard placed on one side.

Nearly every household baked its own bread once a week or once a fortnight. Usually the family bought a sack of wheat from a farmer, sent it to the miller for grinding

*old English unit of area equal to 30 sq. yards.

into flour, the shrewdest paying the miller for grinding it, and making sure to get the 'blues' or 'middlings' for the pig. Once the bread went 'rimey' (stringy), the place became tainted, and do what one might, for the whole season one coud get nothing else but 'rimey' bread. Tea was very expensive and therefore mostly beyond the common purse. Some aspired to it for special occasions, but often toasted bread-crumbs in hot water had to suffice.

Milk was not very plentiful and butter was greatly prized. At one time there was only one cow at Pitton for four hundred people! The sheep were the favourites of the old people, and numbered three to four to every villager. Fowls looked after themselves. They roosted in trees and outbuildings and picked up what they could, a few to each farmyard. They were, on the whole much smaller than fowls are today, and if one discovered where the hens laid their eggs, one had them. For a shilling one could buy two dozen eggs, albeit smaller than todays.

The potato established itself as the main vegetable, with the cabbage a close second, followed by the broad bean, the turnip, the marrow, and to some extent, the onion. Apples, pears, plums and gooseberries, currants and such like fruits were available, but even tomatoes were rare and only became plentiful, and then only in season, at the turn of the century.

Of the things which people feared most in those days, next to the fear of being workless, was fire. One needs little imagination to visualise what it was like to be in a thatched cottage in a village composed of thatched cottages, thatched farm buildings and even thatched, chalk walls, all sun-baked and ready to burst into flames with little to burn on the open hearths except sticks and logs and other spark-inducing fuel. This quite apart from the mischief of little boys, who naturally enough were fascinated by the advent of matches. Just imagine how you would feel if you had been burned out of house and home, or you had seen someone else burnt out, and that if a fire started and sparks began to fly about, every drop of water had to be drawn up the wells in buckets or taken from rain

water butts. Then perhaps you will realise something of
the latent fear which haunted the minds of the common
villagers all the time. What of dry summers when villagers
had to wait for the chalky water to drain into the wells
before they could get enough for personal needs and for
the cattle?

One great fire, over one hundred years ago, burned the
heart of the village right out, and this made an indelible
impression on Arthur Whitlock's mind as his own home
was lost in the fire. There was a high wind blowing at the
time and it was claimed that whirling pieces of burning
thatch fell in Salisbury Market Place, five miles away.

All household water had to be drawn every day from
deep wells, and sometimes for the cattle too, when the
pond dried up. Great labour was involved, almost daily, in
chopping up sticks, and sawing the wood needed for
cooking, baking and firing.

As to lighting, the departing sun imposed a natural
black-out on the villages, and the villagers went to bed
early. It was possible to walk into Pitton almost any evening
in the twilight or after dark and only see one or two lights
twinkling in the whole village. Matches were only just
replacing the tinder box, and few could really afford them.
Tallow candles were in common use, but as Arthur Whitlock
muttered 'They gave 'e mar stink than light', and they
guttered and spluttered all the time. It was hardly possible
to see to do much by their very indifferent, fitful light. To
buy an oil lamp and to keep it in use was really beyond the
worker's means. Therefore, if one stayed up after sunset,
one would sit either side of the capacious hearth, but there
was not much fun in this after a hard day's work in the
fields, and often there was no supper to be had anyway, so
Nature imposed a silent curfew and the villagers, or at least
the older ones, went to bed.

The clothes were simple though the smock was almost
gone. Most people had working clothes and Sunday clothes,
and they made them last. Black nearly always wore until
it was a fusty green. A tale is told of one old fellow who
accosting a well-attired galley-bagger (i.e. scarecrow) said,

as he exchanged some articles of clothing with it 'Why thee
bist better off than wot I be', and one need not be too
sceptical about the veracity of the tale. The sun bonnet
and the voluminous and ground-sweeping skirt had just
succeeded the crinoline. Most men had gaiters and used
substantial walking sticks or staffs. It was not an uncommon
sight to see men stuffing hay into their boots to ease their
feet when walking.

There was not a lot of travelling done, and as Arthur
Whitlock said, 'If thee's wanted to get anywhere thee's
walked, and if thee's wanted to get there any quicker,
thee's run'. People walked miles. Trains were coming into
use, but were a novelty. The well-to-do had coaches and
horses, and farmers had horses and carts, but the common
people walked.

Arthur Whitlock's work took him to a flock of sheep at
Andover, so he rose very early in the morning, walked the
fourteen miles from Pitton, arrived before eight o'clock
and called the shepherd. He worked hard until the late
afternoon, just stopping for his bread and cheese and beer,
and then walked the fourteen miles back to Pitton. The
next morning he was up early and off trudging to another
job somewhere else.

Roads, in today's sense, did not exist. Most of them
were old tracks. Country roads were a composition of flint
stones gathered from the fields and white chalk. It was
hard, on a white chalk road to walk a few miles with the
brilliant sun dazzling your eyes and the wind blowing the
white chalk dust all over you; or to walk that road again
after a week of rain. The main roads were called turnpikes,
and at certain intervals one came to toll-gates and paid the
toll for using the turnpike.

Pitton, in those days, boasted a wheelwright's shop and
a blacksmith's shop. In the village there were farm workers,
carters, thatchers, shepherds, woodmen, drovers, wheelwrights, blacksmiths, carpenters, a cobbler, baker,
gamekeeper and apprentices, not to mention the parson or
curate.

The event of the week was, of course, Market day. Early

morning the roads to Salisbury would be busy with droves of sheep and cattle being herded in by drover and dog to the stalls in the Market Place. Then would come the carriers' carts from all the surrounding villages, and later those who had trudged the whole way in, and who, when the Market was over, would trudge the whole way back home again. It was a merry convivial, jostling crowd, for Market day was not only a time for doing business, but for fraternising, news-exchanging, quipping and (in the inns and pubs) for revelry.

The Fairs were the great events of the year. Every market had its sheep or cattle fair. Weyhill Fair, near Andover, was at one time the largest sheep fair in Europe, and the monasteries of Europe sent their representatives to it.

Farming methods were altogether different from those current today. The farming at Pitton was mainly arable and therefore required many more workers to the acre. There were large flocks of sheep everywhere and comparatively few cows. Around 1830, farm machinery which had been introduced in adjoining districts had caused consternation among the farm workers, who, fearing that unemployment and starvation would result, promptly smashed it all up.

In those days, it was quite a common sight to see old men or women on hands and knees working their way across the fields stone-picking. Long lines of stone-heaps marked their work, and upon these heaps their paltry wages were assessed. The stones were later taken and shot up at the roadside for use in road repairs as required. Boys could be seen with strings of sparrow heads, for farmers paid so much per head in nesting season. Some active boys earned more catching sparrows than their fathers could earn at their work.

Sowing was done by hand broadcast, and Arthur Whitlock claimed to have sown so evenly that, even after the drill appeared, one could not tell whether the field had been drilled or broadcast by hand.

Reaping was also done by hand, and one must visualise men with scythes, one walking a short distance behind another, working their way round the field from morning till evening. Women and children followed to gather and bind the fallen corn with wisps of the same, and later to stack it in aisles till it was gathered on to wagons and made into ricks. Before the threshing machine came into common use, the corn was beaten out by flail.

Though all these workers were crude, yet there was 'finish' in their work. They had tools little heard of today. Who for instance has seen a rick-trimming hook? Yet with all their laborious days they could not only build a good rick which would stand against the weather, but smartly thatch it and trim the sides.

Perhaps one can best get the 'atmosphere' of the Pitton of those days by walking round the Churchyard and trying to discern the remarkable Christian names, by which they labelled their offspring. One might well imagine oneself back in Old Testament times, for Old Testament names preponderated. There were Josiah, Laban, Reuben, Job, Noah, Uriah, Isaac, Elijah, and Elisha, Lot, Abner, and among the giddy girls, Martha, Mary, Adwena, Zephaniah.

Few today would understand the dialect of these people, and many words would need translating or interpreting, for it must be remembered that they spoke 'Wiltshire' or 'Wessex', and quite possibly Alfred the Great would have understood some of their broad expressions better than young moderns would today. Certainly Chaucer and Shakespeare and Wesley and Cobbett would. Often an interpreter had to be called in to translate from 'Wiltshire' into English. Here are a few expressions in common use and their translations:

'Struth alive' — God's truth alive.

'Baint in no caddle' — I am not in a hurry.

'Thik cat be all in a furk' — That cat is agitated.

'Nar marsel' — Not a bit.

'Main pert' — Very well.

'Zort of tarblish' — Not up to the mark.

'Znork in' — Snoring.

'Zno' — Thee's know, or you know.
'Girt' — Great.
'Diddycoys' — Gypsies.

If you had listened to Arthur Whitlock for long you would have heard him say 'Cold enough to shram a cat' or 'Cross thik puddle' (the Atlantic); 'Kick, ah kick a gnat's eye out' — give tribute to the accuracy of a horse's kick; 'I baint or bis'n gwarn to 'av 'e' — I don't believe it; 'I lit wee' — I met with; 'Wot his tawk'n about?' — What are you talking about?' 'Jamie's sake alive' — (old Jacobean expression); 'Lar a massie all alive' — An expression of great surprise like Lord of Mercy. If he did not like anything, then he was not 'Ropt up in't' — not wrapped up in it.

'Arth' he was usually called, started in his father's calling as a shepherd, and then worked at various jobs on various farms all in and around Pitton. In 1873 he married Martha Noyce of Winterslow and brought her to Pitton. Before long, however, conditions forced him to leave for Fawley, in the New Forest, with his wife and two children. He was only there for a year or two before he returned in mid-winter with his family and furniture in a waggon to Winterslow. One old farmer there befriended him and gave him work keeping him on till harvest. In the middle of harvest a message came to Arth requesting him to shear a flock of sheep, and though his farmer friend now needed him badly, he was big hearted enough to let him go. Before too long, Arth had built up a considerable reputation.

For some fifty years or more he was one of the most noted of the Wiltshire sheep-shearers, and as such, he was in great demand for miles around. He was constantly travelling across country to flocks and markets, fairs and farms, towns and villages, and came to know and be known by a very wide circle, not only of shearers, farm-workers, farmers, but land-owners, auctioneers, Inn landlords and country folk generally. Often he had to be away from home for days on end, and if he could not stay at a farm or some cottage he would stay at the local Inn. His journeys familiarised him with the country for a radius of some thirty miles.

The extent of his reputation can be gained from a circular which he sent out in February 1896 which contained four pages of high recommendations for his work with lambs and calves since about 1880.

Arth had the capacity to feel things deeply and to express himself forcefully. When he learned that one of his daughters was keeping company with one villager, he exploded, 'I zoona chop 'er up and give 'er to the pigs!'

Of his pious wife, Arth used to say that 'She 'ood'n eat 'ar egg if she no'd 'twer laid ove a Zundee. Nor drink 'ar drop of milk if she no'd thik cow had had 'ar marsel of barley!'

Arth carried a catapult with him and sometimes made good use of it. On the way to work with two other shearers he took out his catapult and knocked over a rabbit. To his great annoyance, one of them named Ted, picked it up and put it into his bag. A little later in the day Arth persuaded the other shearer to take Ted out of sight for a while. Very speedily and very neatly he took the bulk of the rabbit apart, its head, shoulders and legs, out of the skin, which he packed up tightly with sawdust, sewed it up again and replaced it in Ted's bag. Ted, unsuspecting carried it home and that evening at dusk in the garden tried to paunch it! Finding it full of sawdust he flung it down in wild disgust. Next morning he passed the time of day with the other shearer, but did not speak to Arth. 'Wos up, Ted?' queried the innocent Arth! 'Thee's knows wos up!' snorted Ted, but unfortunately for him, he went round local pubs telling of 'thik' dirty trick'. The result was that for some months he could not enter one without someone asking whether he had seen any 'mar ov tha' zordust rabbits'.

Doubtless there are many very fine and very wonderful sheepdogs about the country still, but Arth's father had a quite remarkable one. His father was once minding a flock of about 600 sheep with his dog when he was urgently called to visit someone in Salisbury Infirmary. The only thing he could do was to leave the dog in charge of the

flock and go straight off in to Salisbury. Quite by coinci-
dence there he ran right into the farmer who naturally
enquired who was looking after the sheep, and on being
told said 'My eyes, I must be off after tha' '. On reaching
the flock he found the sheep quietly grazing by the side of
a field of corn, with the dog running up and down just
inside the corn and darting out now and then to nip
any sheep unwise enough to venture too near.

Arth observed Nature very closely indeed, and sometimes
by a certain whistle he could bring out an inquisitive stoat.

For the craftiness of foxes he had great respect, and
maintained that at night in woods it was impossible to tell
the whereabouts of a fox or vixen by its cry. Like a ventri-
loquist, first it would come from one direction and then
from another. Of all animals he found the fox the most
circumspect, suspicious, and cunning, and therefore the
most difficult to trap.

It may sound enigmatic to say that in those days foxes
were very powerful, especially if they were killed, but the
people of those times would have understood. Killing a
fox might make things so difficult that one might have to
leave the district and find a living elsewhere, since this
interfered with the gentry's pleasure. In fact, one of Arth's
uncles had to leave the district for killing foxes. When it
was discovered that he had killed some foxes there was
no future for him roundabout and so family and belong-
ings piled into a waggon and did not finish their flight
until his family crossed over into Wales, fugitives from
their native land. Their descendants are still there. The forbears of at least one family in Pitton originally arrived
there for the same reason.

When he was about 86 years of age he was quietly
resting on his couch in his living room when suddenly a
hare appeared in the doorway. With true instinct he made
no movement, but just watched it. In it came, hopping
here and hopping there, looking round, and then disappeared under his couch. Immediately Arth got up and
shut the door. He soon caught that hare and wrung its
neck. When his daughter returned he said 'I've had a

visitor'. 'Where is he then?' she asked. ' 'anging up in the larder!' he replied.

It would be going a bit too far to say that the old people had no amusements, for were there not General Elections! Certainly these bore not the slightest resemblance to the tame, insipid proceedings passing under that name today. People not only took a General Election more seriously, but it gave them the supreme opportunity for the emotional expression of long pent-up feelings. At Pitton, early in the 19th century, out of a population of over four hundred people, only two, being freeholders, had the right to vote. These both spoiled their voting papers by marking the names of both candidates. For one thing they did not rightly understand what they were doing, and for another they were actually afraid to give offence to either side. Meanwhile, a few years earlier the 'rotten borough' of Old Sarum a few miles away, which had few inhabitants, had two Members of Parliament appointed by its landowner.

Feeling ran so high that supporters of one side actually threw the contents of their own rustic conveniences over their opponents.

At one election in Salisbury, some forty colliers were brought into the constituency from Bristol by one of the candidates. This infuriated the Salisbury mob who chased them all over the City; and when the colliers sought safety in a loft, the mob broke open the trap-door. The colliers were dreadfully manhandled by the incensed mob. Some miners were thrown into the Canal, and others had their ears torn off.

Nevertheless, there was also a lighter side of General Elections. One old local worthy, with stout political convictions, found, on going to his stable on voting day, that his beautiful white horse was painted blue, the wrong colour.

Bob Porter, one of Arth's shearing companions, had a quite remarkable donkey. He often bought that donkey a pint of beer whenever he stopped at a pub, and sometimes he could get the donkey up on the table by holding a pint of beer up there for it. One of Bob's pals wanted to borrow the donkey for a week-end, and so Bob let him. When his pal returned he was rather worried, 'Bob' he said, 'Thy donkey bis'n well'. 'Wos, wrong widd'n?' asked Bob. 'Well', said his friend, ' 'E wood'n drink nar drop ov beer, zno'. 'Ar', said Bob ' 'E never 'ood ov a Zundee, you!' and believe it or not he never did. He was unaccustomed to it, never going out on Sundays.

To some gentlemen farmers Arth once said 'As gentle-men thee's 'av a very honoured name, but as farmers thee's be thundering bad'ns'.

It's perhaps only fair to add one of his bosses remarks, that when they wanted a gamekeeper they enquired who was the biggest poacher round those parts as they would employ him. They were advised to get Whitlock!

Getting to all the flocks of sheep was no small task. This often meant that he took short cuts across private pro-perty, but this did not matter as he was so well known. The present Lord Radnor's great grandfather, a steward, cantering with his Lordship, espied Arth crossing the Estate and galloping up in no uncertain terms told him to clear off. However, his Lordship then came up and turning to his steward said, 'You would not know this man yet, but he visits the flocks in these parts. If he could not cut across country his job would be impossible', Then turning to Arth he said 'All right Whitlock, you may cross my Estate at any time of the day or night. Good day to you'.

The then Duke of Hamilton was on the boundary of his estate at Winterslow with his gamekeeper when he saw Arth on the other side of the hedge, and said 'Good morning, Whitlock'. The next time that Arth saw the keeper he said ' 'Ow the deuce did 'is Grace know my name?' 'Oh' replied the keeper 'e once asked me 'ow twer we never got any rabbits this side of the estate, so I telld'n, Whitlock wer keeper t'other side the 'edge'.

Arth sometimes caught poachers, but he never had them hauled before the Bench, or as he termed it, 'the maggot-scrapers' (Magistrates). To invoke the law into English domestic affairs was an unforgiveable sin.

Winchester Gaol he always called 'The College', and he said that over the entrance to it were these words, 'The way of the transgressor is hard,' and over the exit, 'Go, and sin no more'. One old poacher who well knew the inside of 'The College' was pestered by his mates as to what it was like. 'Oh' he said, 'Tha'm very particaler! If thee's drop thee's eggshell on the vloor at breakfast, thee's get no beer ver dinner!'

Arth told of another inveterate poacher who had spent twenty Christmases in 'The College', and the very first Christmas he spent at large he sent a brace of pheasants to the governor, 'And telled'm 'e wer zorre 'e cood'n be there ter zeez'n'.

One of the choicest friendships of Arth's long life was with William Baugh, who later became Brigadier Baugh of the Salvation Army, one of William Booth's henchmen. Arth and William were ploughboys together, and both came of ancient Pitton families. They lived utterly dissimilar lives, but both had the greatest respect and affection for each other.

Once, when William Booth came to Salisbury Market to preach he met with the usual rowdy reception as was given to him by mobs elsewhere; but there was this difference and the General was quick to notice it. The crowd could not drown the singing. Two Methodist Preachers, by the name of Fry, were there with their cornets, and so the hymns rang out above the rowdy shouting of the unorganised mob. William Booth was immediately struck by the success of these cornet players and urged them to accompany him on his great campaign. They did so, and the 'Army' had its first band.

Arth was one of those villagers who, when a certain roadway and footpath were closed, so adding a mile on the journey into Salisbury, and another on the way back, decided to contest the case. They went out with axes and cut down the barricades as many times as they were erected across the footpath. Some villagers of Pitton and Winterslow fought out the legal battle one cold winter before the Court at Devizes. Judgment went against them for the roadway, but was given in their favour for the footpath from Pitton to Salisbury via King Manor.

It was this very case which attracted so much attention at the time, and the Western Gazette in publishing reports gave the caption 'Arthur Whitlock makes the Court laugh again!'. As for Counsel, Arth said 'They curly-headed old . . . be crafty old . . . They bide poking about for a bit, about summut, and then they jab at 'e!' Arth had stated in evidence that he had never worked for the owner of the estate, and then in cross-examination admitted that he had sheared his (the estate owner's) sheep. Quick as a flash Counsel was upon him. 'Now my man' said the barrister, 'It's no use your telling lies here. You have just told the Court that you have never done a day's work for the estate owner in your life, and now you say you have sheared his sheep on this very estate. So you did work for the owner after all, didn't you?' 'No I didn't', came the meek reply. 'Well, how do you make that out?' asked the puzzled, nettled lawyer. 'I only worked for the contractor', answered Arth much to the amusement of the full Court and to the discomfiture of Counsel. Nevertheless, the legal costs for the villages were crippling, so that they would have been burdened for many years, 'If' as Arth said 'Ole Lardie had'n stumped up!' (A reference to Lorch Ilchester, then Lord of the Manor).

Arthur Whitlock was not unprogressive, but he was almost entirely sceptical and very critical of modernity and of the young 'moderns'. 'I agree wee edikashun', he would say, 'but alluz they be teach'n nowadays 'ow to get their livin' wee'out working ver it. They get it wee their wits zno! 'Ard work won't 'ert 'e but there baint nar one round yer, but 'ood drop down dead at the thots of working like the old'ns 'ad to! There baint one round 'ere knows wot 'ard work be like! Look at old . . . Why, 'e likes work well enuf to lie down bezide it'. And when someone remonstrated saying 'You don't know. Perhaps he is not strong'. He sharply retorted, 'Ar and 'e don't know either. 'Es never tried to vind out!'

'Buildin 'ouses' he would mutter with withering scorn. 'Why they must 'av a bairth room! Why I 'av'nt 'ad a bairth zince me mairther bairthed me in vront of the vire!' As to hard work, when he was over eighty he always lifted three hurdles at a time with the prong.

It may be recalled that Lloyd George promised to make this a country 'fit for heroes to live in'. Surely he should have known that in the England of his parents' day the country folk had to be heroes. If one word describes them better than another it is the word 'heroic'. They simply had to be. It was a hard school indeed and it tested them to the very roots. They needed no toughening courses. They had one which lasted from the cradle to the grave, with no holidays and few or no relaxations. Nevertheless, it produced not only robust physique, but sound character and a sterling sense of values. There was a hard and relentless nexus between work and recompense. The word 'earnings' had a very hard, solid sound for the old people, although strangely enough not metallic, in spite of being on the Gold Standard.

Just a few hours before his death Arthur Whitlock sat on the edge of his bed feeling his pulse, and remarked, as though speaking of someone else, ' 'ar well, it won't be long now!', and in a short time he was gone.

He had run from the middle of the Nineteenth century into the middle of the Twentieth, and what a race it had been . . .

'I did not think much of her as a Queen, just a very small old lady in black'

*Mrs Nina Halliday
WINDSOR

My memories go back a long way. I was born in Windsor in 1892 when Victoria was still Queen. I remember my elder sister, who was seventeen when I was born, lifting me over a fence, streaked green with age, which divided a hay field from the path in the Long Walk that leads to Windsor Great Park, and of finding myself surrounded by tall red poppies, dog daisies and buttercups with tall grasses well above my head. I was quite lost in it, and it was very quiet and strange. I was very glad when she lifted me back. I must have been about two at the time.

I had many toys and books as I grew older. One which gave me much pleasure was what was called the 'go-cart', which I think my mother must have had when my sisters were small. Possibly it was built for a goat to pull, for it had long shafts to push it by, a centre back board with seats both sides so two children could be safely strapped in back to back, certainly a host of dolls could be tied in and I used it much more than the ordinary dolls' pram, into which I once pushed a very fat small boy cousin — he did not like it.

The first swing I had was one made from wooden slats which slid down around making a safe cage, and it was hung in the door-way leading from the green-house to the garden and my ambition was to swing high enough to

*Mrs. Nina Rosalind Halliday 1892-1982 written when she was eighty-seven years old, and submitted by her daughter Mrs. Joanne Land of Warminster.

touch the grapes which grew in the green-house, but I never succeeded.

There were two books which I loved. The first because its cover and leaves were cut in thick cardboard to the shape of a sailor in a straw hat which were worn at that time. It was my first meeting with the Navy and I liked it. The other book I had when I was older. This was a big book of Fairy Tales, but it was not so much the stories as the pictures that made it so precious. When one turned a page, the opposite one stood out in layers away from the background. The picture I remember now was of a Snow Queen sitting on a huge snow-ball, that was the flat part, then in front of that there were small figures and animals playing in the snow, and lastly a frame of leafy trees. The Snow Queen's wand had a glittering star at the end, and she, the snowball and the animals and trees were all scattered with glistening frost. There must have been five of six more pictures made in the same way. The Snow Queen had rosy cheeks and golden hair. This was a Sunday book which my father and I looked at together.

In the winter sometimes my father would take me to the five o'clock Evensong at St. George's Chapel in the Castle and we would sit in the choir where one could see all the silken, brightly coloured banners of the Knights of the Garter. There is a wonderful procession of Knights down through the Lower Ward, round through an archway, and up the wide steps through the great West Door on a special day in summer. They wear the Garter ribbon across their chest, beautiful dark blue velvet cloaks and hats with ostrich feathers, all led by the Sovereign. When I was young the choir was lit by candles. That, and the beautiful voices of the choir, men and boys, rising up and up, was lovely.

I always remember a strange dream which came more than once from when I was about four. I was above a long, curved, sandy beach, no people anywhere. The sea and sky were grey, the sea lapping at the edge of the sand with tiny waves. Standing at the edge in the water was an old grey horse, its head drooping with weariness. Everything was grey, it was just all weariness and loneliness. I did not tell anyone about the dream, but the peculiar feeling left with me I have never lost.

My father had a building business and kept one horse and van. The horse was called Tommy, and I was very fond of him. In winter I used to listen to the van coming back at the end of their day and run down to the stable yard to see if I could help. I was allowed to fill the pannikins with oats and chaff. It was lovely to plunge ones arms into the oat bin and feel the oats all slippery and sliding against ones arms. Usually it was getting dark and then two oil-lamps were lit and hung up, one just outside the stable and one by the harness room. Tommy had a nice clean bed made for him every night and in the summer bundles of red clover as a change from hay, and I used to take some to put in my bedroom.

There were twelve or fourteen girls and two boys in the Kindergarten school I went to. One boy was called Jack and one Bob. They wore sand coloured smocked overalls. I liked Jack, he wore navy blue shorts, jersey and stockings and when out of doors he always wore a scarlet knitted cap with a scarlet string and bobble, just like those the men wore who drove the big vans pulled by big Shire horses belonging to the Brewery his father managed.

In the summer holidays we went to Bournemouth for a month. A terrible amount of bustle in packing tin trunks, my mother's bonnet box with a wire contraption in each side. When the bonnets were put over the wire, a long hat pin was pushed through to secure it. There was also a flat canvas holder with straps which wrapped umbrellas, sunshades, two of my father's walking sticks, one sturdy for real walking, and one elegant with a golden end like a thimble, just for show, all wrapped into the canvas, rolled round and strapped securely. I had my own tin trunk, painted green.

I enjoyed being at Bournemouth, because the beach was sandy and there was the excitement of so-called bathing from what seemed like a small house on wheels, with two benches inside, always sandy, pulled down to the sea by an old horse. One went down some three steps into the sea. The 'Bathing Lady', as she was called, tied a rope firmly round one's middle and proceeded to push one under the water three or four times, then back into the machine to get rid of the sand and dry as well as one could. The 'Bathing Lady' was dressed in rusty black with her skirt pulled up and tied at the back, and a black hat, all rather forbidding until one got used to her.

On the beach I wore a macintosh garment with a bib and legs designed to keep one dry when paddling, which it never did. The light elastic at the knees got sandy and rubbed ones legs, and if one carried a bucket of water up from the sea it always seemed to slop over and behind the bib.

My father took me for trips on the steamer which called at the pier and we both loved it. It was no good trying to keep my floppy hat on in the wind so my father took charge of it, and I could get beautifully blown, and when we got back to the pier, he did his best to tidy my hair before putting my hat on again so as to make me look as tidy as possible before we got home. All too soon the tin boxes appeared and somehow got packed. It did not seem to matter how things were shaken and brushed, we always took home some sand, and I was allowed to take one piece of the broad-leaf seaweed which foretells wet or dry weather.

When I was young the roads were covered with gravel and so very dusty especially in windy weather when the sand blew up in clouds. It was very noisy with the horse drawn traffic. The butcher boys always had very smart horses, and the milk man too, with his rattling cans — one big one which stood on the floor of the van with a tap to draw off the amount the customer wanted in her jug, and cans of pints and quarts hanging around the rail at the sides of the van which was rather like the shape of a Roman chariot. It had two steps for the driver to get in by, and the big churn stood in front of him. People who were very ill found the noise of carts trying, and peat was laid down on the road to deaden the sound. We had it down twice, once when my mother was very ill and again when my father was the same. I liked to walk on it and I liked the strange smell and having it down made me feel very important.

When I was young there were musical plays in London called Musical Comedies with lots of gay tunes. My sisters used to go to see them and buy the music and play and sing them for their own pleasure. There was one very special one called 'The Geisha' and for a while Japanese things were very popular. One shop sold them in Windsor; flying storks with wide spread wings to hang from the ceiling, and other half storks to fasten to the wall. Paper fans brightly coloured, and dolls of all sizes in coloured crinkly paper, the small ones with arms and legs just stuck between the paper and a soft paper body. Coloured parasols of many sizes, and they all had a lovely strange scent which seemed to come both from the wrappings and the cloths. All the little dolls had rings of black hair and bald tips to their heads. I was given one lovely doll dressed in a green satin kimono, with a wide *obi or sash, and a bisque china face hands and feet, but she must have been made in this country, she had not the right scent. But the very best thing I had was the programme of the play, it was made of crinkly rice paper with a fully coloured picture of a Geisha on the cover and a red silk cord and tassel and it too had the same unusual attractive scent. I used always to play in my bedroom and my chief game was 'Plays' with different scenes and the small Japenese things were just right.

I must have been a horrid child. My sisters were dressing to go to a Ball. I had watched them choosing the materials from the patterns which had come from the dressmaker and wanted to see the complete result but was told that I could not watch them dress, so I lay on my back on the landing outside their room and drummed with my heels. However, I was finally told I could see them before they left. So I ate my supper and was got ready for bed and

*obi — a Japanese sash, with a bow at the back.

waited for what seemed ages. At last they came and I thought they looked lovely, one in striped blue silk and the other in corded green satin, very low necked and with short trains and small little puffed sleeves. They both had fans and long white kid gloves which buttoned right up to the elbow, there was lace all round the necks and one had a posy of white flowers and the other of violets on the shoulder. It was certainly worth waiting for and best of all they gave me a little white book with gold patterns on it with two leaves of scented powder called, I think 'Papier Poudre' — which I took to bed with me and sniffed at under the sheets.

When I was about seven a war was started in South Africa against the Boers and lots of the soldiers were sent from the Barracks in Windsor. They marched to the train with the band leading them and people standing all along the pavements cheering and clapping. During the war it became a craze to wear a little badge on ones coat with the pictures of the different generals on it — Lord Roberts, Baden Powell and General White are some I remember.

When I was quite young my father's friend, who was Mayor of Windsor, asked me to present a bouquet of flowers to Queen Victoria when she came to open the Royal Agricultural Show in Windsor Great Park. She came in the State Carriage drawn by four grey horses, known as the Windsor Greys, with outriders and postillions, all in their scarlet uniforms, and a Royal Guard from the Life Guards. After a speech of welcome had been read to her, I presented the flowers with a curtsy. She did not smile, but just took them and I did not think very much of her as a Queen, just a very small old lady in black. The soldiers and all the carriage attendants were very bright in their uniforms, the saluting guns boomed as the carriage moved off and it was soon over. The next morning a messenger came to our house with a package addressed to me and when I opened it there was inside a lovely red cloisonné heart locket with a pearl in the centre and an engraved message on the inside.

One evening after tea my father took me out to where

we could see the flag on the Round Tower, and it was at half mast because Queen Victoria was dead and 'nothing would ever be the same again'.

Windsor was a good place for pageantry — the Foot Guards were on Sentry Duty in various gates of the Castle and every morning about eleven o'clock the new guard marched up with their band playing and they continued to play whilst the new guard marched round the castle and relieved the old. On Sundays the North Terrace was open to the public in the summer, and two bands played on the Terrace under the Royal Apartments. It was very pleasant on a nice sunny day but my 'Sunday best' shoes always had to be patent leather and when they got hot it was terribly uncomfortable.

I liked better to walk across the Park with father to see an enclosed part where there was a herd of big wild boar which had been sent to the Queen by an Indian Prince. There were also red and fallow deer grazing and a small flock of goats.

Queen Victoria was buried at Windsor and we saw the Procession from a stand which had been erected under the Guildhall. The seats were covered in black material and everyone wore black clothes, but I had a dress, coat and hat of a lovely mauve colour — I loved it. The streets were lined by Foot Guards and the pavements were packed tight with people all dressed in black. It was a long wait as the train bringing the coffin and all the important people travelled very slowly from Paddington to Windsor — so that people at the stations which it passed could see it.

It was a wonderful procession, with the Life and Foot Guards playing the Dead March. The Guard of Honour led, then came the gun carriage covered by the Royal Standard. The new King, who would be Edward VII, followed with many of the Queen's relations and Kings and Princes all in uniform. The finest was the Emperor of Germany in a beautiful white uniform and white helmet with lots of gold on it and many Orders and decorations. Then came the Chiefs of the Navy the Army and members of the Queen's Court including her daughters and other relations in royal carriages, all, of course in black with long veils.

I seem to remember that a purple cushion was on the coffin with a small crown on it. The bands had muffled drums and as the procession came along one could hear the slow booming of the guns. All very solemn, so much black and such a small coffin, but so much colour as well with so many uniforms.

'Sailors were always my great heroes'

Eric H. Wootton
WEYMOUTH

I was born on the 27th March 1914 in a flat at 16, St. Mary's Street, Weymouth. The flat was over 'Lovell's Creamery' where ladies used to come in and sit on stools to have their glass of milk with either a splash of soda water or a spoonful of cream.

One of my first memories in this flat was an enormous gas chandelier suspended from the centre of the ceiling and I loved to watch my father extract the gas mantle from its cardboard box by means of a bent pin and after placing it in position set fire to it before lighting the gas.

On Sundays when I was dressed in my white sailor suit and white linen hat with H.M.S. Victory on the band, I was taken by my mother and father for a treat on a trip to Upwey Wishing Well on a coach drawn by two horses. The fare for the trip was one shilling return. The highlight of this journey was when the horses would draw the coach through part of the River Wey at Upwey. The driver of this coach was Sugerum Shorey who lived with his sister in the Toll house along Preston Beach Road and made a living chopping and selling logs at one shilling a bushel basket, which he used to sell from his horse and cart travelling around the town.

There were several hawkers who were notable characters in the town. One being a bearded man who travelled round selling fresh watercress. He would fill your cap for a penny. He was a very ragged looking man, his trousers were very torn and only reached his calves. He lived in an old shed in a field at Preston and lived to a great age before eventually being found dead in his shed.

Another was the mackerel-man, a Mr. Bateman, who would sell you a dozen fresh mackerel for a shilling. Mackie Bowles was another who would have a barrow at the front of Pulteney Buildings near the pier, loaded with cherries and when the sailors returned to the drifters they would buy bags of cherries. This used to take place at seven o'clock in the morning and many of the sailors were still drunk from the night before.

At this time the whole Fleet used to visit Portland Harbour to be inspected by King George V. This meant that frequently the town was really crowded with sailors. The sailors would sometimes take me aboard a drifter and I would then spend the day on a battle ship in Portland Harbour which in those days could house the whole Fleet. At night the ships used to give tremendous search-light displays. There would be several ships anchored in Weymouth Bay who would sweep along the front with their search-lights dazzling the late evening promenaders. Sailors were always my great heroes because my grandfather sailed on windjammers for most of his life.

At the age of four years I befriended a Bob Ozzard who had five sisters, always dressed in clean white starched pinafores. His father was also Bob and would row us boys out across the harbour to his boat, where he had a large basket attached to two ropes to the harbour bottom and when the lid was removed it revealed dozens of live green lobsters. These he would take home to cook at his fish shop.

At this period I also learned to row. The oars being too heavy for me at four, young Bob and I worked one oar while his father worked the other.

I spent much time on the sands. On one occasion when with my brother, he pointed out an elderly gentleman in knickerbockers standing at the corner of Bond Street and told me that it was Thomas Hardy.

I well remember in 1919 watching the soldiers returning from France, marching along the front having landed from boats at the old wooden pier. Children older than myself would help to carry their rifles for which their payment was sometimes a tin of 'Bully Beef' and sometimes a clip of live cartridges and even French coins. The sailors used to sometimes give us a piece of ship's cocoa. This was a mixture of cocoa and sugar and it was very hard but as children, we thought it was lovely.

Another sight along the front was old men pulling and pushing ladies in Bath chairs and children riding in carts pulled by goats.

Sunday afternoons were sometimes spent at the Kursel — Alexandra Gardens where the band used to play and weather permitting one sat on the grass or on a deck chair. If the weather was bad one could always sit under cover either in the Gardens or in the thatched shelters around the grass. Then of course, there were the paddle steamers, which were always a great attraction, like the 'Empress of India' and the 'Monarch'. Trips to Cowes, Lulworth, Torquay, Portland and Bournemouth were always very popular.

Living near the great Naval base of Portland, it was inevitable that we should be connected intimately with the Navy. At that time I was five years of age and had two uncles in the Marines and later a brother in the Navy and another uncle a Lieutenant Commander. One uncle, Billy Perrett, was a bandsman in the Marines and stationed at Portland. I remember the Christmas when the Marines gave a party for the local children at the Palm Court which was the dance hall attached to the Pavilion Theatre. We had a huge Christmas tree and all the children had a riotous time to the music of the Marina Band which was conducted by my uncle. The old wooden Pavilion Theatre had a most wonderful atmosphere which gave one the creeps even before the play started. The exits were lit by a single gas jet which gave the theatre a very gloomy appearance. There seemed to be many thrillers acted at that time and as children were allowed in they often afterwards had nightmares. I remember at the old 'Jubilee Hall' in St. Thomas Street, seeing 'The Murder in the Red Barn' which had a long lasting effect on me. But the

Pantomimes at Christmas were very jolly affairs.

Although the War had ended there were still come sad events taking place; I remember seeing, on a dark winter's night the band of the Salvation Army, preceded by someone carrying a lamp proceeding along St. Mary's Street playing the 'Dead March'. It was an unforgettable gloomy sight and sound. There had been no survivors from the latest submarine lost just off Portland Bill.

St. Mary's Street and St. Thomas's Street, the main streets in the town, had some quaint shops and buildings which have now unfortunately disappeared. There was Wheelers coffee grinding and tea blending business, which emitted the most delicious aromas that were most enticing to passers by; there was Wellman's fruit shop which always had a Dorset Blue cheese in the window, these are no longer made; Curtis's always had a window full of ripe bananas and inside were two large glass containers, one contained lemonade the other raspberryade, behind which was a clockwork apparatus which made a boy's head bob over a fence and when he disappeared a dog's head would appear. The lemonade was sold for a half penny per small glass, a penny per large glass. There was the Market House next to St. Mary's Church where one could buy second hand books for a few coppers, and potatoes were seven pounds for six pence. And there were sweets made by Mr. Roberts, the local confectioner where we had tremendous fun with the electric shock machine. Five or six of us boys would join hands and have a penny worth of electricity which would bend our elbows and knees and screw up our fingers. Lumley's the bakers sold delicious fresh hot brown doughnuts with a large quantity of jam inside for the princely sum of seven for six pence.

During bad weather a French fishing trawler would sometimes shelter in the harbour until conditions improved. The sailors would cook their dinner in a large iron pot over a fire on the deck, in which they boiled large pieces of fish and whole potatoes. They would all sit round the pot with their knives in their hands stabbing the fish and potatoes and eating them with great relish off their knives. They were always willing to sell to anyone who wanted a cod at a reasonable price. One evening my brother Harold and my father were strolling along the harbour when Harold decided to go on board a trawler and buy some fish. After conducting their business mostly by signs, as neither could speak the other's language, my brother with a large cod in his hand stepping from the trawler to the quay, slipped and and fell into the sea. As he was a non-swimmer, the men managed to hook him under the collar with a boathook and drag him to an iron ladder attached to the quay wall. He still had hold of the cod. The weather was cold so he took to his heels and ran home as fast as he could. When my father arrived home a few minutes later my brother was drying himself in front of the fire but decided he should reward the fisherman who had dragged him out of the water by treating him to some of the local beer. He asked my father to go back to the harbour and treat him in a nearby pub. His father had no difficulty in making the fisherman understand his signs that he would be welcome to a free drink. The rest of the crew also understood, and also the crew of the trawler moored alongside. In the end my Father found himself treating about two dozen thirsty fishermen and it cost him quite a lot of money.

I arrived at Melcombe Regis Boys School and my fishing career began. A favourite spot for fishing was the old dam in the harbour where the water was comparatively clean and I caught dabs and whiting. When I could borrow a boat I would fish for eels and prawns in the harbour. The eels were caught in a small net on a pole. The harbour then had only a few boats in it, and one old boat that had been there for many years had grass weed growing on the bottom and sides and dozens of small eels used to feed on it which I would catch with my little net and take home, skin them and fry them. They were delicious.

At around this time, 1924, a favourite past-time for children was to gather round the 'Vauderville', a wooden structure on the sands and watch Val Vaux and his Vaudessques which included his wife Ruby Lee, a soubrette.

These shows caused much merriment amongst us children. Of course there was always Punch and Judy, donkeys to be ridden and paddling to catch shrimps and spider crabs. Also there was always plenty of room on the sands for cricket in the summer and football in the winter.

To the east of Sandsfoot in the Underbarn, there was a wild cliff covered with brambles gorse and shrubs and a few windswept trees. Below this is a narrow sandy beach which was not much used especially in the winter. We found this an ideal place to collect driftwood, light a fire and bake potatoes in their jackets in the embers.

In those days Radipole Lake was a great attraction. In the summer we played cricket on the dried out bed called Chaffeys Lake and caught tadpoles and sticklebacks. One particularly hard winter I was able to skate on the ice from the iron railway bridge nearly to Radipole village with my dog which I had at this time. My dog, Nip, rushed across the ice after a stone thrown by a passerby and disappeared into the water. I managed to haul him out by his collar and rush him home to dry him out.

I remember with a friend walking to Upwey, where at different times of the year, we could gather bluebells, primroses, and horse chestnuts or conkers as they were then called. There were some magnificent chestnut trees over-hanging the river and in the autumn it was very easy to collect half a satchelful of fallen nuts, there was no need to climb the trees.

In 1925 I won a scholarship to Weymouth Secondary School, later to become the Grammar School. At the age of sixteen we sat for the London School Certificate, roughly the equivalent of present day 'O' Levels and to help us recover from the strain, the senior boys were given the opportunity of a week's camping at Lulworth during the summer holidays in August. We assembled on the pier at the appointed hour and about fifty of us embarked on the paddle steamer 'Monarch'. We were under canvas for a week during which time it rained almost continuously. After a few days we were so wet that there was nothing left dry to put on, not even our pyjamas.

One very unusual occurrence took place on the only fine night during that week. We were supposed to be in our tents but three or four of us decided when it was getting dark to creep out under the back of the tent and walk down to the village. We continued our journey across the fields and came to a field that was completely covered with millions of glow worms. I had an empty matchbox with me and capturing one or two put them in the box and to my surprise found them to be still alive and glowing in the morning.

About half way down the cliff there was a level area covered in short turf which was just large enough to hold two small tents and allow for a camp fire to be built at a safe distance. There on warm summer evenings we could descend to the beach by a convenient path and swim in the cool clear sea, sometimes by moonlight. In those days we could camp for a whole week-end and not see another person.

In 1930 I left school and joined the two million looking for work. As I had done pretty well at school I was expected to take an office job which, after the open air life I'd been living did not appeal to me very much. I would have liked to have joined the Navy but being somewhat short sighted that was not possible, as sailors with glasses were unheard of in those days. After a few weeks being bored with nothing to do I obtained a temporary job at a nearby small holding, where I learned the basic elements of fruit, flower and vegetable growing. I found this very interesting and the outdoor work pleased me but I never thought that, apart from the war years, I should spend my life in horticulture. The pay was very poor for very long hours, so after about nine months I moved to a nursery, this time mostly greenhouses, where the pay was slightly better but the hours were longer. When I reached eighteen my pay was one pound and six pence.

I moved on to the Weymouth Corporation Nurseries. I found this work most interesting and spent much of my spare time studying at home, there being no such thing as day release courses.

Part of our duties were to decorate the Guildhall and hotels for important events. I decorated the Weymouth railway station for the arrival of the Duke and Duchess of York and the then Princesses Elizabeth and Margaret as children. Later on for Princess Anne, and for many other functions such as conferences and choosing the Mayor's. Even the town Church St. Mary's was decorated for the Mayor's Sunday; I also decorated for many weddings and funerals in the town.

In spite of working long hours we still had plenty of energy to enjoy ourselves when not working. Some Sundays, four of us would hire a rowing boat from an old fisherman for five shillings for the day, which was from ten a.m. until ten p.m. on condition that we returned the boat clean and tidy and safely tied up to the moorings. At this time I was friendly with an old fisherman and life-boatman who gave me detailed directions of how to find the remains of an old ship wreck named the 'Abergavenny' which was situated about two miles out into Weymouth Bay.

One Sunday in November, the four of us set out on a fishing expedition, the sea was calm and after some hard pulling we arrived at the appointed spot early in the afternoon. There were several boats anchored near the spot where I reckoned the remains would be, so we anchored a short distance away from them. The anglers in the motor boats did not seem to be getting much luck but we must have anchored directly above the fishes feeding ground. We started hauling up fish as fast as we could bait our hooks and pull the lines in. This was so continuous that we forgot about the time and we suddenly realised that it was now not only dark but a thick fog was coming in.

By the time we had hauled up anchor we could barely see the length of the boat and with no compass we had no idea which way we were rowing, towards land or out to sea. Fog horns were sounding all round us and there was nothing for it but to carry on rowing, steering as straight a line as possible and hoping for the best. We started rowing at about five p.m. and by ten p.m. we were lucky enough to find ourselves close enough to the shore to see the lights at Bowleaze Cove which meant that by the time we had rowed another three miles back to our moorings in the harbour it was about midnight. When I arrived home my father said that I had arrived just in time to save him alerting the lifeboat. After that I always carried a compass with me but I never got caught in a fog again.

A very old ex sea Captain was quite a local character. He was a small thin man with a close cropped white beard and could often be seen dressed as usual in a reefer jacket and a seaman's peaked cap selling from a tray of paper flags in aid of the local lifeboat. One day Jim, a friend of mine, told me that Captain Gulliver, the old seaman, had given him permission to use his boat whenever he wished, and he assured me that if I wanted to use it he would put it right with the Captain. A few weeks' later, one sunny Saturday afternoon I persuaded my father that he would enjoy spending an afternoon on the sea with a fishing line. He was not at all fond of the sea and had never been fishing before. Eventually we arrived at the rowing boat which was moored to an iron ring set in the quay wall directly opposite the Cove Inn. It was a fairly large boat resembling an old ship's lifeboat, pointed at both ends and painted white.

At about one p.m. we set off down the harbour and rowed across the Bay to the Portland breakwater close to which we anchored and started fishing. The water here was as clear as crystal and about thirty feet deep. I was idly staring down through the water at the rocks at the bottom when from a gap between two boulders I saw the head of a huge conger eel emerge and take in a piece of spare mackerel which I was using for bait, and take it back into the hole to eat. I immediately unwound a thick hand line with a large fish hook attached, baited it with a whole mackerel and lowered it slowly until it dangled in front of the hole. Within seconds the mackerel was snapped up. Bracing my feet on the side of the boat I gave a mighty heave on the line in order to get the eel away from his hole before he could wrap his tail round a rock in which case it would have been impossible to move him. It was obvious from the pull on the line that this was a very large eel. After a tremendous tussle I got his enormous head out of the water at the side of the boat but his body extended under the boat with his tail thrashing the water at the other side which made it at least six feet long. My father took one look at its huge mouth and moved hastily to the far end of the boat and did his utmost to persuade me to leave the monster to the deep. I did not agree with his point of view. But after an unsuccessful battle the eel broke loose and disappeared below the surface. I could have wept with frustration but my father who was a non-swimmer told me that if the eel had come aboard the boat he would have jumped overboard deciding it would have been much safer.

By the end of the Twenties the town was getting quite lively during the summer, being crowded with visitors especially when the carnival was held. Dancing took place along the esplanade, music being relayed from the bandstand by loud speakers. As none of us could dance we decided to take some lessons with a local dance teacher called Madam Fay. Our lessons were held in a bare room in a house in Rodwell Road which was reputed to be haunted. Although we never saw any ghosts while we were there we heard plenty of moans and groans from Madam Fay as we trampled on her toes.

At about this time I achieved one of my great ambitions when I formed a partnership with two friends and bought a motor boat 'Louise'. She was fourteen feet in length, had a sort of middle age spread, was driven by an ancient converted Ford car engine. She cost us eleven pounds, but provided us with many times that amount of pleasure. She turned out to be a very contrary old lady, something unexpected happened during practically every voyage.

The first time I took her out alone before I had reached the harbour mouth she blew a gasket which meant a hard pull against the tide to reach her moorings near the old 'Dam'. During the three years we had her everything possible that could happen to a boat happened to 'Louise', including losing her propeller, and having to constantly clean the rust from her carburettor which drained from the ancient petrol tank.

The 'Louise' survived many calamities but ended her active life in September 1939 when on returning to harbour after a Sunday morning trip we were told that war had been declared. However, before being called up we were able to sell the engine which the buyer removed but 'Louise' sank into the harbour mud and disappeared for ever.

After volunteering for the R.A.F., I was sent to Padgate for an intelligence test and on my return to Weymouth learned that I had been placed on the deferred service list due to the fact that the Parks Department was now growing food instead of flowers.

On June 15th 1945 I was married at Henlow Church to a W.A.A.F, who was sent to work with me as a punishment for cheeking the Commanding Officer. This turned out to be the best thing that had ever happened to me and I have never regretted it.

I began to have trouble with my sight when I was forty three and had an operation on my right eye. I was one of the first patients to experience the Laser beam. However, in spite of the efforts of the hospital staff it was not successful and from then onward I could see only from one eye.

Having had forty four years of unbroken employment except for the war years I retired from work when I was sixty. But soon after my sixty fifth birthday I found myself back in the Eye Hospital. Five operations on my left eye for another detached retina proved unsuccessful, and I have now been blind five years. My grateful thanks goes to my wife for having so patiently typed this autobiography.

'Madam made court gowns'

Rose Bishop
SOUTHAMPTON

I was very young when, looking out of the front room window, I saw a dark carriage drawn by two very black horses with tall black feathers fixed on their heads. It was not till I was much older that I knew that it was my father's funeral.

I don't think it was very long afterwards that my mother and I went to her sister's at Southampton. It was a Sunday morning and we arrived in time for lunch. As it was a lovely day we went on to the shore, and I was very happy playing on the beach while the elders did a lot of talking. I was told years afterwards that when my mother caught the train back to London I did not cry or make any fuss.

I knew I hade two brothers, one Edwin — in the navy, in submarines. I also had a sister, Beatrix, eighteen months' younger than I was, whom I don't remember at all. I had been born in 1907.

I settled down to live with my auntie in Southampton. My uncle was a deck-steward or head-barman on big liners, away seven weeks and then home for a few days. They had a very nice house which they had had built. My aunt, although she had no children, was a very lovely and understanding person. I met all my other aunts and cousins, had good holidays, and settled down to a very happy life.

The day before a boat was due to sail my aunt and I would go aboard and go all over the boat. The tables were set, the dance-floor with the band was all ready for the passengers, with singers trying it out, and we were waited on in my uncle's cabin. It was wonderful. Then when a boat was due in the lady next door would knock on the wall for my aunt, who would go out to the garden. The ship would then be looking awfully empty and untidy.

My uncle would bring home bananas from Madeira, on a stem about 3 ft long. My aunt used to heat a long steel poker in the fire until it was red-hot and put it right down the hollow stem to ripen them. All my uncle's nine brothers were on the boats, and his two sisters' husbands as well. I came to love the boats and the sea. Whichever brother was home would collect all the others with their children, hire open cabs, and take us out to the New Forest for the day. We would have a big swing put up. In spring-time the forest children would pick primroses, tie them in bunches and throw them into the cab, and my uncles would give us ha'pennies and farthings to throw out to the children.

I went to a school called Foundry Lane School. On 24 May, Empire Day, we were marched up on to the common dressed in white embroidered dresses with ribbon at the waist, and very much starched.

I never thought of my mother, although sometimes she would send me a sixpenny game from Woolworth's and once, on my birthday, a white pinafore with blue ribbon. To me my aunt was my mother.

The years went by and I was thirteen and a half. One day my aunt had a letter by the morning post. The first I knew about it was my aunt was all upset, walking all over the house and saying, 'If your mother wants you when you leave school she can have you now'. She sent a wire to my mother telling her to meet the train at Waterloo.

I was suddenly put on a train in the guard's van with a packet of sandwiches. I remember the guard was very nice, found me a box to sit on and sat on another himself. We were surrounded by packets and boxes.

Waterloo Station was very busy. My stepfather met me and took me by tube to Chalk Farm. We did not like each other from the start.

The home I went to was very poor. My sister and brother were there. My sister was a very pretty child with thick corn-coloured hair, lovely eyes and skin, and very spoilt. My mother only had a small kitchen, one bedroom and a sitting-room. For the first time I had to share with all the others, and it did not go down well. My stepfather called me 'the lady', and said I was too big for my boots and would come to no good. I was always blamed if anything went wrong, and began to keep quiet and after a time gave up fighting. I think it made me 'take everything and not answer back'.

I left school at fourteen. My mother put me in service in a very big house in Regent's Park. I had to wash up, scrub and clean, sleep in and take tea to the bedrooms in the morning. There was Madam and her husband, a son who worked and a daughter. On Sundays I had to go to Church with the cook, whom I didn't like. She frightened me.

I didn't like the job at all and my mother did not gain much out of it, so a friend of hers took me down the West End to answer an advertisement for girls to learn embroidery. The workrooms were in Hedder Street, Piccadilly — one floor for machine embroidery and one for handwork. Madam was small and dark and her husband tall and quite young; they were, I found out, Serbs. I was taken on to work at seven shillings a week, 8.30-1, and 2-5, to start the following Monday. My mother thought it was worth a try, and I was given sandwiches and four pence for the fare.

A very sedate lady called Miss Gill took charge of me and said I was the new match-girl. I was soon to find out what that meant. I was given some silks to match beads and sequins in Oxford Street and Marble Arch. The West End is always crowded, and as I didn't really know where I was going I took a long time. The shops were very good as they knew Madam.

We could stay in the workroom for lunch but must not have anything that smelt as the materials would carry the smells.

Madam made court gowns for balls and parties. Once a year when rich people gave very big parties to present their daughters at court we would have these beautiful gowns to do. The work we did was done before the dresses were made up. Very lovely material — velvet or crepe or silk — was tacked on to a frame two or three yards long which had wide webbing, then white canvas was tacked on, then the dress sections were tacked on the canvas and the frame was stretched tight by two girls at each end. It had to be pulled evenly or else the material would be pulled out of shape. You then sat down and worked on the printed design, one hand on top and one underneath. Some times there would be about twelve girls on one frame.

After some months I was put to this embroidery work and some new girl took on the job of match-girl. I was very interested in it and liked the other girls, and time passed quickly.

We had one young girl called Grace who was a designer, and she would get very upset when Madam would come in and say 'Grace, just slip out to Regent Street with your book and pencil — I've seen a lovely model in a window there. Just copy it as quickly as you can'. Grace would say 'I can't do that, I'll get caught. You know we are not allowed to copy, and if I have to stand to do it I'll have the police on me'. But she had to go, and very often she would get away with it.

We always got laid off for a few weeks when the London season was over. I was earning 10 shillings a week when I left.

I still remember Madam very well, and her husband, who when he was happy would sing a song from one of the shows called 'Just a little love and a little kiss'.

Fox furs were worn then, and I made up my mind to buy a real fur with some of my money. My stepfather went mad when he saw me wearing it, and said a bit of a girl was earning more than he did for doing nothing. His money on the Midland Railway was not two pounds a week with stamp money taken out. He said I'd come to a bad end. He turned me out for the seventh time.

I stayed with my friend's family, but all I wanted was to go and see my aunt. One Sunday I found there was a cheap fare to Southampton — 5s 9d. return. I got to my aunt's in time for one o'clock lunch. I began to do this very often. It was going home for me. Once I found my uncle there, back from a long cruise, and he said to me 'I know you have never been happy away — would you like to come back to live?' I said at once that I would.

And I did just that.

I had my old bedroom back, a room with my own things in and lovely and clean.

One Sunday after dinner my uncle told me they had bought a shop — sweets and tobacco — to give me something to do. It was at the top of our road, in an arcade leading off a busy street. On the Monday morning my uncle and I went to the shop and I met the people who were leaving. They were very kind and told me about ordering etc., and the wholesaler who would call for orders. There was a big sale of cigarettes, as young men bought them while their motor-bikes were being seen to a few doors away.

A girl about my own age and her brother came in to see me — Midge and Reg. We were great friends from the start. They had a big furnishing shop. We went out together, but I did not have much time off. In those days shops were allowed to keep open as long as they liked, so we opened all day Sundays and very late in the evening — till 9.30 or 10.

There was a school nearby, and I found that an early start was essential as the children came in on their way to school. We started a small part of the shop for children only, with sherbet fountains, liquorice strips, and ha'penny chocolate bars. We took a lot of money this way, and got to know the children.

My aunt and I always spent a lot of time going to the Isle of Wight. There was a very good daily service. We caught the paddle-steamer that left at 2 from the pier at the bottom of the town. On the other side we travelled in a very big, open bus called a char-a-banc. On board most of the young people would sing, but there was no bad behaviour.

When a liner docked, the men always had plenty of money. Some of them used their motor-bikes to get home. One of them, called Joe, bought several boxes of chocolates (we kept all the best makes) and handed one of them to me. He asked me if I would go to the pictures with him the next night. We saw each other each evening till he went away again. He asked me if I would go on his bike, and I said yes. There was another customer there who had just come out of his apprenticeship at Bridport. He lived with his invalid mother. He asked me why I was off so early, and my aunt told him. It was a November evening, damp and very cold. He said 'If you go, you'll come off — the roads are awful'. He had a long black and white scarf round his neck. I pulled it off and said, 'I'll take this to keep me warm'. Joe came in for me and we set out. Near the football ground we skidded, and both of us were flung off. I wasn't hurt, but Joe had a broken leg and was in hospital some weeks. We wrote to each other every day.

But my aunt was always talking of Con, the young man who lived with his mother. She had bought him a shop further up called The Chocolate Box — a big shop, very high-class.

One morning Con came in early and asked me what was wrong. I said nothing was wrong, but I thought of going up to London for a few days to see my friend. I needed a change. To my surprise he at once said, 'Don't go. Let's get married'. I said, 'Don't be silly, I don't know you, and you have been engaged to a girl at Bridport and it's been broken off about three times'. He said it was true. Then he was gone, and I forgot him. It was Monday, and I was busy tidying up and the regular travellers were coming in.

About 12, when it was quiet, Con came back, and said, 'We'll get married at the Registry Office in the Avenue at 12 o'clock on Wednesday'. He took a paper out of his pocket and said it was a special licence. Saying he would see me later, he was gone.

But on Tuesday night he came again, and said, 'Hurry up, we have to buy a ring'. We went down town to Samuel's.

They were shutting up, but they did serve us. All the rings seem too wide. I hadn't thought about marriage and what it meant. I finally chose a very narrow ring (I think I thought no one would see it), and we went home. His last words to me were 'Be ready at a quarter to eleven.'

When Con called for me I was not ready. I was still in a state of shock, I think. We just made it. I thought Registry Offices were very shabby affairs, but it was a very nice room, green carpet etc., flowers and two men. I did not know the form of words at all, and when I had to repeat it I just could not get the words out. Everyone was waiting. I felt awful, wondering if I was married and why.

We went home and had a drink, and shortly afterwards we had to go back to Con's mother and his shop. I was shy and dreading meeting her, and Con I knew thought so much of her. I saw a very elegant lady sitting by the window, where she sat all day. She was dressed in black, with white hair pulled up and pinned on top of her head, slim, and pale. I noticed she had some lovely rings, and the sun was making them sparkle. She looked very autocratic and very French. She gave me a lovely welcome, and then we went downstairs.

Con had told my aunt that his mother was one of three sisters and her name was Mercy. They were French.

Con had been apprenticed in carpentry. I have his indentures — beautifully written on parchment and stamped where he started at Bridport. When I really got to know him he would touch wood and know at once what it was because he loved it so. He finished his apprenticeship at 21. In those days they always made their very big tool-box themselves — most beautifully done with lots of little drawers and big compartments for saws etc. That was the last job they did before they were qualified.

Con loved his mother and looked after her. But she must have been a very understanding person, for he had his freedom and was fond of sport. He had men friends and girl friends, but his mother came first. I think they had a lovely understanding. I saw it working when I married him.

'Sympathy was an unknown word in those days'

William Charles Keate
BANWELL

This is my life story as I remember it from the year 1902 until 1940. I was born on January 4th, 1902 in the village of Banwell, Somerset. Banwell, at the time of my school days, was the third largest village in Somerset. There was the Church, two Chapels, Methodist and Baptist and, unlike today, they all had large congregations. The five Pubs also had a large following, open from six in the morning until eleven at night. Beer cost three pence a pint and cider a penny. And it was very deadly stuff, so you can imagine that quite often there were a number of the community who took the day off, to visit the Magistrates at Axbridge on Petty Sessions day.

The drunks usually got away with a fine of half-a-crown if there was no violence, otherwise they would get seven days hard labour at Shepton Mallet Prison. There was a Brewery, two blacksmiths, one of whom also ran a shop where you could get anything from tin-tacks to an air-rifle, kitchen utensils or a new cycle. We could hire a cycle from Saturday dinner time until 10 o'clock Sunday night for half-a-crown.

In the year 1910 there were several things that happened that would certainly not be tolerated today.

I remember seeing a 'skimmity ride' — as such an exhibition was called at that time. I was coming home to dinner when I heard an almighty din and I wondered what was happening, but it seemed that a woman, whose husband was in the Army, had found some consolation in another woman's husband. When this was discovered, all Hell broke loose. The family of the wronged wife, and they were pretty numerous, collected all the buckets, tin cans, saucepans, in fact anything that made a noise, paraded in front of the sinful woman's house, banged their instruments and shouted filthy abuse at her.

She daren't go out, or they followed her; it was really vicious and she quickly moved to another village. She eventually became reconciled to her husband. The man, however, went from lodgings to anywhere he could find shelter and died some years' later in an Institution. I fancy that family would be kept very busy with the present day moral outlook.

We had an old man by the name of Hookey who lived in a hovel in total seclusion. The windows were covered in filthy rags, and bushes and brambles covered it from view. The old man had come to live in the village some years before. He had been a prospector in the Australian out-back and had met with an accident to his head. He was a tall, gaunt man with a long beard, always dressed in black, but looking back at it now, that could have been dirt.

He always wore an Australian bush hat with a very wide brim, and once a week he walked to Weston-Super-Mare and back, a distance of twelve miles, to buy his provisions. For some reason, he never spoke to the village people, a fact I find today not very surprising. As for us children, we created a fantasy world around him, and we swore he had a long knife down the inside of his trouser leg right into his boot.

The powers that were decided that the old man be put away; the big question being how to make him. He certainly wouldn't be persuaded by words, so the village policeman would have to take him by force.

The Constable, not being too sure about this, and neither too brave, decided to enlist the help of a few of the more brawny type of villager. It was then decided that old Tom Hurley, because he possessed a flat bottomed cart, should be pressed into service.

How they took him I only heard afterwards, but it

seemed that the Constable hid in the bushes while someone knocked on the door and under some pretext or other got him to walk down the path to the road, whereupon the Constable crept up behind, and tripped him up.

Soon the cry went up that they had him and were bringing him down on his way to Axbridge Police Station and from there to the Asylum at Wells. I had my face glued to the window as they passed. The poor old man was stretched out on the bottom of the cart, his hands and legs tied to each side. He had never hurt a soul in his life all the years he had lived there. There couldn't have been any need of it but such was the cruelty of 1910.

I always remember the cottagers who were standing at their doors as he went past saying 'Poor old man — what a shame', but it was sheer humbug as they were the people who had agitated for it. The funny thing about it was the County never did a thing to reward those six brave men and the Constable, who you would have thought, if you had seen them, had risked their lives and saved the village from destruction. I never heard anything afterwards about poor old Hookey, but many years later, his son came from Australia to see his father, and was not impressed by what he heard and made a lot of noise about it.

Living in those days was very different to what it is now and people supplemented their wages in different ways. One such couple were a man and wife who lived in a cottage near the bottom of our street. Their names were Bill and Emily Steel and they sold fish on days when they could get it. It was laid out on a table near the open window and many a time I have been sent there for a couple of bloaters for tea if we could afford them.

It wasn't all that often as my father's wages in those days were eleven shillings a week, of which he kept a shilling for pocket money. I was always told to ask for hard roes and the man or woman would pick them up in their hands and squeeze them around the middle. Apparently they could tell which were hard or soft roes. Perhaps they would pick up a dozen before they found the right ones, and throw the others back again. They never concerned themselves if their hands were clean or not, and you accepted that as a way of life.

On Friday and Saturday nights they sold faggots and peas and always did a roaring trade. You took your basin and they would put however many you wanted into it with a few spoonfuls of peas and a fair amount of gravy. You then ran home, as fast as you could, before they got cold and they were a very special treat.

There were three butchers shops but there were a few others who sold pork with a variety of other goods. My uncle, for instance, had a green grocers shop, but he also killed pigs on the premises and many a one have I seen killed and burnt in straw in the backyard, hoping to get the bladder for use as a football, but they did not last long.

Looking back at it now, I often wonder why they never burnt the house down as bits of burning straw would fly all over the place. Anyway, the pig was cut up and hung in the window for sale with a dish of what they called scallops — bits of fat fried very crisp — in the middle of the shelf underneath, probably surrounded by cabbages, peas, parsnips, onions or anything that was in season, with wasps, flies, and all creatures that on earth do dwell having a whale of a time.

Once a year my sister and I spent Saturday with my uncle as my father and mother went on their outing given by the mill owner to his employees, usually to London. We would be got up early, given a basket of food, taken up to Banwell Hill on which the village allotments were at that time. My uncle had four of five, planted with potatoes. We had to 'pull the vilt' as they called it, — which consisted of potato haulms — potato stalks or raims as some people called them, thistles, milk thistles etc., so my uncle could commence gardening.

I think the word 'vilt' must have been a local word for filth as I have never heard it anywhere else. After a back breaking day and fingers full of thistles and stained with milk thistle juice, we were given a good supper, a penny and put to bed, as our parents did not get home until the early hours of Sunday morning. It was all very exciting but I think we realized that 'Home, Sweet Home' was the best place.

Another thing I remember at that time was an Italian organ-grinder coming to the village with this monkey who used to pick up the coins people threw on the ground around him. On one visit, one of the louts, you had them in every village, put a penny in the fire, got it hot and threw it to the monkey who, of course, burnt his paws badly. The organ-grinder went mad, drew his knife, got the lout down and would have killed him if the others hadn't rescued him in time.

There was quite a lot of unnecessary cruelty in the Mendip villages in those days, as I suppose there was elsewhere. I think the fact that the Pubs being open all day had a lot to do with it and many a wife and children went hungry and suffered beatings through it.

Along with others, I joined the Scouts a year or two before the 1914-1918 War. We were formed by an American lady and her millionaire husband who came to live at Banwell Abbey. They bought all our uniforms, axes, poles, the lot. We had four patrols, eight in each one. Their chauffeur became Scoutmaster, and every Friday evening we were taken to the Abbey to sing hymns and songs. They had a huge American organ and the lady herself played it. After we had finished we were given cakes and lemonade.

Our job was to carry plates of cakes, bread and butter to the wounded soldiers invited to Garden Parties by all the local gentry. We picked up their crutches if they wanted to walk about or pushed the wheel chairs for those that couldn't. After they had gone, later in the evening, we cleared up the forms and chairs, picked up the waste paper and rubbish. Then we had our reward; we were given all the food that was left over and told to eat it all up, and this we did, as food, never plentiful in our young lives, was getting a lot more difficult to get. There was many a Scout's pocket wanted washing after one of these feasts, where he had tried to put away something he couldn't eat, for the next day, and there was never a lack of volunteers for those jobs.

Our Sunday joint was mostly a breast of mutton costing six pence, or perhaps a larger one at nine pence according to what money you had to spend. Sometimes, if he felt like it, the butcher's roundsman who called on a Saturday night would cut me off a sausage for my supper which I would get my mother to fry for me. It did not happen very often, but it was heaven when it did. Hungry, but happy days.

An event I remember vividly was a bailiff evicting a family from their cottage. Every article they possessed was thrown out into the road. The father was a navvy called Tiverton Pring, owing to the fact that he originally came from Tiverton in Devon, and his wife and seven children. It was really pitiful to see, as we went to school with these children and played with them very often. They were left in the road for hours, but, as night came, they were given shelter in a stable just outside the village; perhaps the Lord remembered.

It was not unusual to find stables in the streets in those days, as horses were the main means of transport. In our street alone there were four stables next to, or underneath cottages where people lived. On the opposite side of the road was a huge iron pump, put there to celebrate the Diamond Jubilee. It would take two children to lift the handle to pump it. Often you would have to pump a dozen times before you got any water, it was so deep. When it broke down, as it often did, you would have to put on a pair of yokes with two buckets and get your water from the pond — a distance of half a mile and do your best.

I remember a lot of village characters from those years. One such was called Boxer Baker. He lived with his old mother a few doors away. Boxer got a living with a horse and cart, somewhat precarious, I must admit, carrying things from one village to another. It was surprising the number of people who got a living with a horse and cart. He was a big powerful fellow, but at times suffered from head trouble, but there was no cure for things like that in those days.

But one day, on coming home from school, we were quickly pulled inside and the door locked. Yes, Boxer had gone over the top and the usual routine was followed. The Constable and six brave men overpowered him, took him to the Doctor who certified him insane and sent him to Wells Asylum where I suppose he died, as he was never seen in the village again.

Of course, it killed his poor old mother, but that was a small detail then. I remember his parading past our cottage several times with a cardboard box on the end of a garden fork which he would stab occasionally, and I know we were very frightened.

There was a man by the name of Billy Pople. I remember that he was a little fellow, not a bit more than 4ft 8ins., but his wife was a huge woman with a voice like a fog horn. One day, Billy decided to end it all as he couldn't stand any more of her ways. The method he favoured was pretty popular at the time for the tired of life community. He was going to cut his throat, at that time second in the ratings to hanging. Anyway, he proceeded to a little hill at the back of the cottage where there were a number of fir trees and a lot of scrub. We called it 'The Hanging' as, according to village gossip, through the years several people had used it for that purpose.

Billy wished the world good-bye and started to perform, but when the blood started to flow, Billy lost all his enthusiasm for another world, threw down his razor and ran home. His wife who, after being married for so many years, did not have a lot of love left for him, promptly sent for the Constable, who took him to the Doctor, who bandaged him up. The Constable took him into custody and gave him a new home in the cells at Axbridge Police Station.

Billy eventually came before the Magistrates at what was called Petty Sessions. They gave him three months' hard labour at Shepton Mallet to think over the error of his ways or to make a better job of it next time. Sympathy was an unknown word in those long ago years.

*

In my childhood days, many happy hours were spent gathering wild flowers of all descriptions. The first, in early spring, would be primroses and white and blue violets. There were banks of violets followed, as the seasons developed, by honeysuckle, scabious, ragged robin, moon daisies, cornflowers and some we called soldiers' buttons, and the wild orchid, bee and butterfly.

You knew exactly where to find the wild strawberry, the crab apple and the wild plum, the best nut bushes or the fresh watercress.

I suppose a time that would be remembered most would be late August and September when the blackberries were ripe and you picked them for sale. In the school holidays you were up early, and with your mothers — two families would always go together — set off at nine o'clock with baskets and buckets.

Often the dew was so heavy that your boots and stockings — no Wellingtons then — were soon saturated, but as the day wore on and the sun came out, they dried on your feet. About half-past twelve, as near as you could judge, you ate your bit of bread and cheese and had a drink of water from a river — if you were near one.

You would go on picking to what you thought would be round about four in the afternoon and if you were lucky in your choice of fields, your baskets would be full. Then you would walk home carrying the blackberries with great care. Sometimes, when getting over a stile, you might be a little careless and upset the bucket or basket and it was a heart breaking job trying to pick the berries out of the long grass, but it did happen.

You took them to a collecting point which, in our case, was a mile and a half away. Eighty pounds of berries for which you would get a penny a pound. Six shillings and eight pence for two days' hard work and wet feet; (of course that was old currency.)

How my hands have ached carrying one side of a bath full of berries and my mother the other. You had to watch the dealer very carefully, or he would bring the scales down with a bang and as he always used a four-pound weight, you were on the losing side anyway, but you daren't shout too loud or he would refuse to have them and you wanted the money too bad to risk that.

He had another way of trying to do you. As the berries became more plentiful he would say, in a casual way, 'Sorry, but they will be down to a half-penny a pound next week'. But you never fell for that one, and told him so. No-one picked for two days, so he would put the price up again.

At the last collection for the year, he would bring a cheap bottle of Port wine and hand around a glass each — not us children of course — and that was your lot, no more, no less, say he hoped to see you again next year, which he knew very well he would if you were still alive. Although there was a lot of rushing about to get to the best picking fields first, you always respected the one who did get there first, and wouldn't dream of going into that particular field. Everyone was poor and that was an accepted fact.

As you grew older and stronger you borrowed what was called an eel spear. This was five strips of metal, two inches wide and eighteen inches long, banded together with a three inch wide band about half-way round them and at the top was a socket into which you fitted a long handle. You then drove it into the mud on the bottom of the ditch and hoped you would get an eel between the prongs, which you often did. River eels were better than ditch eels as living in running water they did not taste of mud.

Eels were very rich in food value and you had no trouble in selling them. You got from six pence to nine pence a pound according to their size. After you had skinned and gutted them — a ticklish job as you had to know how to hold them, or you would be struggling with them until Kingdom come — they were boiled in a saucepan in milk, if you had it, or water if you didn't.

Another animal that now seems to have gone is the red squirrel. In my boyhood days, we could go on Banwell Hill and see half a dozen of them at any time in the fir trees. We would get a forked stick, trim it out and make a

catapult with a rubber you could buy in the ironmongers
for a penny, then go on the hill and try to hit one. But you
would't get one in a month of Sundays, they were far too
clever for us. They were pretty creatures and the countryside is the poorer for their passing. The last I ever saw was
in a farmyard in a small box going round on a wheel on a
spindle, so very sad.

Another loss is the number of butterflies that have gone
since my day. On a summer's day then you could count
twenty or thirty different species and we would spend
hours trying to catch them and when we got tired, we
would sit on the grass, dig out a square hole, put some
twigs across the top, and catch the grasshoppers of which
there were hundreds. What did not get out of the hole,
you lifted out and set free while you went on to something
else. You respected wild life and flowers.

Moorhens were another source of food. Today, no
doubt, you are disgusted at that, but if you had been
hungry as we were, I fancy it would be a different tale.
Everything that could be used as food was used. You did
not send to the village shop for a tin of stewed steak,
hamburgers or oven-ready chips, those things were in the
future, many years away.

The highlight of our village life in the winter must surely
have been Banwell Fair. It was held on January 18th and
from 8 o'clock in the morning, cattle of all descriptions
entered the village from its four different ways. Bulls,
cows, sheep, horses, even geese, turkeys and chicken left
over from Christmas were bought and sold. It was impossible for traffic to enter or leave the village as the animals
were penned in all the roads.

The Pubs always recruited a couple of strong, rough
men to assist in keeping order, as the Fair attracted the
gypsies who, after a few pints, would fight with the
drovers or amongst themselves. But as the Great War
became closer, it gave them all the fighting they wanted,
and Banwell Fair, as we knew it, died a natural death. The
Square was filled with stalls selling gingerbread, sugar

almonds and a speciality of their own making called toffee apples. They were laid out on the stalls with dust from the roads, plus the fumes of the naptha lamps and many a lonely little germ that wanted a home for the night would alight on them. Not to worry, we ate them, for germs were an unknown quantity in our young minds.

Banwell people felt very important when they learned of the arrest of Dr. Crippen and Ethel le Neve, the Hilldrop Crescent murderers. They were the first people to be arrested by radio and the captain of their ship, the s.s. 'Melrose' was married to a girl with village connections.

The Great War broke out on August 4th, 1914. My father being called up in 1915, I quit my job as grocer's boy and got a job breaking stones in a small quarry on Banwell Hill. You were given a double headed hammer and a bag of straw to kneel on. For every yard you broke -- a yard being a ton — you were paid one shilling and two pence and you had to break them down to three inches. You were called a snapper, a very apt name because if you hung about you didn't earn much.

The most I ever broke was seven tons in a week, and I had to work all the day light hours there were, and I got paid eight shillings, but as my father was coming home on leave it was very useful.

I left the little quarry and got a job as cabin boy at Sandford Quarry. This was a big concern employing a hundred and fifty men and several boys. They were working under contract for the Government Road Board. The hours were from six in the morning until six in the evening, as long as daylight allowed. I had to leave home at fivefifteen and walk a mile and a half to the Quarry. My first job was to keep a cabin clean for a dozen or so men to eat in. I made a good fire to fry their bacon and boil water for their tea. Their cups were, more often than not, jam jars made of stone. They were called gallipots.

I progressed to be a water boy for one of the drillers. The drills were driven by steam and your job was to keep the drill running smoothly by putting in little drops of water 'twas a good job in summer but God help you in winter, especially the winter of 1917, but my wages had gone up to eighteen shillings a week.

About 1923 I, with others, joined the St. John's Ambulance Brigade, passing my exams at Weston-Super-Mare. This was extremely useful at the Quarry and we dealt with many accidents — five fatal.

The War ended in 1918 on November 11th, and the Quarry went on its way merrily until 1928, but then the recession, as they call it now, began to bite. The days of Quarry Outings were over and the work force went down to forty men. One Monday a notice was posted in the office window saying the Quarry would close down at five p.m., on the Friday and so ended sixteen happy years of my life.

Now the visits to Axbridge Labour Exchange became the order of the day. You were given a form to fill out and in the post by Wednesday, signed by two householders to say you had not done any work that week, and then you had to go and get your money on the Friday. There was a manager and his wife in charge and on pay day there would be a line of men nearly half a mile long as it covered a lot of the Cheddar Valley.

The Manager, who had been a Sergeant Major in the Army and enjoyed his power over us, was a big, bloated pig of a fellow. I have known men standing in the rain for an hour and perhaps on getting under cover would remark that it was good to be in the dry. He would immediately get up from his desk, come to the doorway and order them all to go to the back of the queue and shut the door for half an hour. And you went, because if you didn't, he would and could stop your dole money for six weeks for so called insolence.

All this time the depression was getting worse. There were demonstrations, marches, and in some parts, violence. I had a variety of temporary jobs as they came along, but right to the start of the Second World War, times were pretty difficult.

'Back to square one and the dole'

May Allen
BATH and PORTSMOUTH

When my husband Henry, nicknamed Nobby, left the Royal Marines, he was unemployed and on the dole and our money was two pounds & one shilling a week. This was in 1926 and 27. Having six children and the rent of our house being eighteen shillings a week it was a very big struggle, but we managed after a fashion.

The hardest time was Thursday, last day before Nobby could draw the dole money. 'What have we to eat?' Nobby asked on Thursday morning. 'Nothing' I replied. 'Good Lord missus we had next to nothing yesterday and I'm hungry and you must be for I didn't see you eat much either, and what about the kids, what did they have?' 'Oh! they did well', I said, 'I managed to save some potatoes from yesterday's dinner and with the little bit of dripping from the Sunday joint of brisket, I fried a slice of bread each and spread the potatoes on and they enjoyed it'. 'Do you mean to say that satisfied them missus?' asked Nobby. 'Well no, not really' I said, 'but when they asked for more I hurried them out the house telling them to hurry or they would be late for school'. With that Nobby jumped up saying, 'That's it, missus, I'm off, I've got to get some money from somewhere'. 'Where are you going?' I asked. 'Havn't got the foggiest, but I mean to get something for the kiddies dinners, so don't send them back to school on empty tummies' he said, and off he went.

I was so worried I could not do any work. I had visions of him robbing a bank or something. I kept telling myself not to be silly, but time went on and on and the children came home asking where the dinner was. I kept giving them little jobs to do to pass the time and when I was just about at the end of my tether, Nobby came in. 'Here you are missus, get these cooked' and on the table he put some sausages and a loaf of bread. In no time at all I had the sausages under the grill, because I had no fat to fry them, when lo and behold the gas gave out. I had an awful job to stop from breaking down when Nobby said 'Quick you boys, get your hands down inside the chairs and see if you can find any money'. Arthur was the first to find a half-penny then Willie did, 'now then quick, one of you go next door and ask for one penny for the two half pennies,' which they did and we all had sausage sandwiches and my gosh did they go down good.

I could hardly contain myself wanting to know how Nobby managed to get the sausages and bread. As soon as the children had gone back to school, Nobby said, 'What about a cuppa? Don't tell me we haven't a drink'. 'It's O.K., we have just enough tea and milk for now but I don't know about teatime and the morning' I said, 'Don't worry, missus, I'll think of something, let's have that tea'. 'Please tell me what happened this morning?' I asked. Well, it's like this', Nobby started, 'I left here not knowing what I was going to do, I walked and walked when I saw a car outside one of those posh houses down town. I went up to the door and rang the bell. I don't mind telling you missus, I had a job to stand there and wait for someone to answer the door. Just as my nerve was going a lady came. She eyed me up and down and said 'Well, what can I do for you?' My God, missus, my voice came out like a croak. 'Please mum, can I wash and polish your car for you, I'll do it for a shilling, I'll make a good job of it'. Just then the lady's husband came to the door to see who was keeping her. I managed to tell him about the kiddies and not getting the dole until the next day. He listened for a while saying he always washed his own car, then said all right you can do it, and that is how I was able to buy the dinner missus. But there is still tonight and the morning . . .'

It being the end of September, the evenings were very

cold and dark so Nobby said to one of our boys 'Come on
Arthur, come with me' and took a sack from the shed.
After a while they came in struggling with a full sack.
Nobby tipped the contents all out on the floor, 'Come on
kids, pick out the bits of coke for the fire', he said. The
next minute I heard the pots and pans being moved so
went to the kitchen and was just in time to see a big shelf
being torn off the wall. 'Oh Nobby', I said 'don't do that'.
'Shut up missus, you want a fire, don't you?' In next to
no time he had a fire going, but it would keep going down.
We had a large tin tray that Nobby kept putting up to the
fire, but as soon as the tray came away, the fire went dead.
'I'm fed up with this missus', Nobby said, 'I suppose it is
to be expected for it's only the coke that has already been
burnt in the kiln to make bricks along the end of the road
for the new houses they are building. So up to bed all of
you, it will be warmer there', he said, 'You too missus'.
The children didn't like the idea of going to bed so early,
it being just after seven, but Nobby promised that I should
tell them a story, and that is how we kept warm, and I
racked my brains to make up a story and then talk loud
enough for all to hear until they fell asleep.

Hurray, at last Nobby has got a job. It is with a large
Furniture Shop where everything is sold on the instalment
plan. Nobby is to drive the van and he has a mate with him
named Jack. Now if a customer cannot or does not keep
up the instalments, it's Nobby and Jack's job to take
the furniture back to the shop. Not long after starting, the
boss sent for Nobby and said, 'Allen, I want you to go to
this address and pick up this furniture. It's a three piece
suite and bedroom suite. They are behind with their pay-
ments and look as if they don't intend paying any more, so
don't come back without it'. 'Yes Sir', said Nobby, and off
they went. It was a very poor street they went to and as
the van entered it a shout went up. 'Shut your windows
and bolt your doors the b .... are here'. Nobby said he
heard lots of doors slammed and the house they wanted
was at the other end of the street. 'Go on Jack, knock
on the door' Nobby said, which he did but instead of the

door opening, an upstairs window did and a sailor put his head out saying, 'What do you want?' When Nobby said the money or the furniture, the sailor said, 'We have no money mate, but you can have the furniture'. Both Nobby and Jack were ever so pleased to know they were getting it without any bother and waited for the door to open. Instead, out of the window popped the sailor's head and shouted for them to stand back. 'Here it comes', and it did piece by piece, a cheer went up, each time a piece smashed on the pavement from all the neighbours who had come to watch. 'But what about the furniture?' I asked. 'What do you mean? What about the furniture? We stacked it in the van of course, we couldn't leave it in the road. I don't mind telling you missus, we were glad to get away from there, we thought we were going to be torn limb from limb. I hope we don't have many jobs like that' Nobby said. 'What did the boss say when you got back' I asked. 'What could he say except that he would take the people to court, and that is what happened'. The day of going to court came and Jack and Nobby went. When the case came up, Nobby told about what happened and the Judge said, 'So you went to collect the furniture, did you?' 'Yes, your Honour' Nobby said. 'And did you get the furniture?' the judge asked. 'It was all broken on the pavement' Nobby said. 'Did you or did you not get the furniture?' the Judge asked 'please answer yes, or no', he said sternly. 'Yes, your Honour, but,' Nobby got no further. The Judge banged his desk and said, 'Case dismissed'.

*Oh, what excitement! Nobby has bought a second hand Motor Bike, a very old belt-driven Zenith. What fun we had! He made the side car much bigger, so that we could all get in except June, the eldest; she rode on the back of

*Mrs. Allen writes on two time levels — her own childhood and the period when her own children were small. She also switches from the past tense to the present. As it is a conscious, personal style, I have left it alone. Ed.

the bike behind Nobby. People used to stare as we went along, for it looked like Noah's Ark.

Oh dear! Nobby's job is getting him down, he has dreadful nightmares and it is always after some unpleasant job Jack and he has to do, like the one out in the country. 'We won't get very far here', said Jack, 'I've been before, and she's a right old battle axe. 'Well', said Nobby, 'she may be, but we have to try. You know what the old man said, 'Don't come back without the furniture'. What we have to do, is plan what we intend to do. So I suggest that I go to the front door and you go round the back, then I keep her talking while you get in, then once in, it should be easy to get the stuff out'. 'All right' said Jack, and off he went. 'Don't forget to give a little whistle when you are there', said Nobby. When Jack gave the whistle, Nobby rang the bell, the woman came to the door, but as soon as she saw the van she tried to shut the door, but Nobby had his foot inside it. It was just then that Jack called 'I'm in'. As quick as a flash the woman snatched a twelve bore shot gun off the wall and pointed it at Jack, who stood open mouthed. 'Get out, or I shoot' she shouted. Nobby saw the look in the woman's eyes and was really frightened for she looked mad. He tried to grab the gun from her shouting to Jack to run, but Nobby knocked it up just as she fired and the bullet went somewhere over Jack's head, and Jack fled through the hedge straight into a cess pool.

That night Nobby had a very bad nightmare. I was startled awake by Nobby shouting, 'Come on lads, this way, come on, come on'. My heart seemed to leap up into my mouth, for there was Nobby with the window wide open and one leg over the sill. I managed to grab hold of his shirt tail and hang on for dear life, for down below was a green house and if he had got out, I don't know what would have happened. Thank goodness he came to, and looked so surprised and said, 'What am I doing here missus?' In next to no time he was back in bed and fast asleep. But for me that was the end of my night's sleep.

One Saturday, Arthur asked his dad if we were going anywhere. 'Yes, might as well' said Nobby. 'Must make

the most of the lovely weather!' Where are we going to
dad, they all wanted to know. 'Just there and back to see
how far it is'. We started off, it was a grand day. We went
to Bognor Regis and we had been along the sea front and
were going through the town, when all of a sudden a
policeman stepped out in front of us waving us down. It
all happened so suddenly which was fatal for Nobby could
not start the motor bike again, and the policeman kept
saying 'Get off the road' and looking back over his
shoulder, Nobby said 'I can't start it'. 'Then push it' said
the policeman, his face as red as a beetroot, he helped push
us into the side. When we looked up we saw a beautiful
Rolls Royce coming very slowly around the corner of the
road and there was Nobby and the policeman standing to
attention and I looked right into the face of Queen Mary,
who smiled and said something to the King who leaned
forward and looked out and also smiled at us. I just
managed to say to the children it's the King and Queen.

Nobby's nightmares are getting worse. Last night we
couldn't have been asleep long, when I woke up to find
Nobby kneeling over me with his hands around my throat
telling me not to move, or he would throttle me. I was
so frozen with fright that I think that saved me. We
seemed to stay like that for hours, but it must have been
only a short time. He just lay down still asleep, but not
me. I could not put up with anything like it any more.
And once again I vowed and declared to get a divorce
from him. Then, next day, I would wonder how I could
manage to bring us six children on my own and he would
be forgiven again. 'Ah, my missus, you couldn't get on
without your old Nobby' he said. But, I made him understand he was to go to the Doctor the next day, which he
promised to do. But next day came and I had to send
for the Doctor, for Nobby was in no state to go to him.
After he gave Nobby a good examination, he took me on
one side and told me that my husband was on the verge
of a very big breakdown, and after hearing what his work
was and all it entailed, he told me that my husband would
have to leave and get another job, if possible in the country.

Nobby was off work for two weeks and was looking much better. 'I'll be going back to work on Monday' he said, but on Saturday a letter came with his cards and a week's money in lieu of notice and saying that another driver had been taken on in his place. 'Well! That's it, missus' said Nobby 'back to square one and the dole'.

*'When I was your age we used to play a game called Statues and another game, Sunlight Soap is the best in the World'. 'Please Mummy, what kind of a game was Statues', the children wanted to know. 'Well,' I said, 'the children would stand in a line with one in front, then the one in front would start at the end of the line and catch hold of that child's hand and pull him or her out, swinging them around then letting go quickly and whatever position that child was in, they had to stay like that until the end of the row'. 'Then what happened?' asked Arthur. 'All I know is that it was funny to see a crowd of children all making funny faces and some very weird stances'. 'What about the Sunlight Soap thing?' June asked. 'Well, I'll try to explain. We all stood in a row one side of the street with someone on the other side facing the wall saying Sunlight Soap is the best in the world and the row of children would run across and try to touch the wall without being seen. If you were spotted moving then you would have to go back and start all over again, and the one that touched the other wall first was in, and had to say again Sunlight Soap etc'.

'I don't think much of those games' said June. 'Neither do I' Arthur and Will chorused. 'Anyway, Mummy, how were you able to run backwards and forwards across the street? You told us you lived in the High Street', asked Arthur. 'How is it you didn't get run over?' 'There wasn't any traffic in those days' I said 'only horses and carts and we didn't see them very often, for they worked on the farms. There was a farm at each end of the street and every once in a while a man would bring a cow up through the street and all us children would run after him shouting

*Mrs. Allen reverts to her own childhood, talking to her children. Ed.

'Farmer one cow, Farmer one cow'.

What did you do when it was raining?' I was asked.
'I rather liked it', I said 'because we had a house called
Penny's House and it was three stories high. You see, my
father was, at the time, in great pain, because a horse
kicked him in the leg when on duty at Buckingham Palace,
for as you all know he was a Grenadier Guardsman in
Queen Victoria's time. Anyway, the kick turned to three
big ulcers which got worse as the years went by. So when
he was due home from work we children, Eva, Ruth,
Charles and myself were banished upstairs to the top floor
to play, but we were not to make a row. We had brass
knobs on each corner of our beds and we used to unscrew
them and make holes in the corners of the blankets to
make tents, we had some grand times pretending to be
camping out'.

I used to love Sundays because my mother would play
the melodian and we would all sing hymns, we were a very
musical family and all had good voices. She played the
melodian on Sundays because it had a plaintive sound,
just right for singing hymns to, but she played the concertina as well. Mother had three concertinas, the big
deep toned one was English and big in size with only
thumb straps to pull it in and out and mother's thumbs
were not strong enough for her to be able to play it for
very long at a time. Another one was very small, no
bigger than your Dad's hand and my mother could only
put three fingers in the straps. She used to play some tunes
on it, but it was really more of a show piece. The third
one was made in Germany and it was lovely, much lighter
to hold and play and had straps that went over both hands
making it much easier to pull in and out.

It was wonderful, she would play all evening for singing,
then to finish she would play 'The Campbells are Coming',
then drift into 'Men of Harlech', and end with the bells.
And she would swing the concertina up and around
making the bells sound as if coming over the hills. Mind
you, when she finished she was all in.

Sometimes friends of theirs called in on their way home.

They would be asked to stay for a while, how we loved that. It was such fun watching two men with brooms between their legs prancing around one another trying to knock one another over, and mother would play faster and faster till everyone was out of breath laughing. Before the evening was over, crowds of people gathered outside sitting along the pavement and joining in the songs. My sister Eva, being the eldest, would be sent to the Crown and Cushion pub to get the beer. They bought their own beer and food, and although beer was only two pence a pint, it only ran to about one quart, and in some cases only half a pint each; you see, money was very short in those days.

There would be new bread cut into chunks, cheese also cut into chunks, pigs trotters, bath chaps and chitterlings, and everyone would help themselves. I must tell you though that my mother supplied the pickled onions or I should say, shallots. I can remember all the family doing the shallots months before, jars and jars of them. I'm sure I never tasted anything like them since those days. Well, when the party was over, it would be somewhere around midnight, then all who cared to join in would go arm in arm, with a row of us children in front, part of the way to see our friends home. We would go as far as the bottom of Penny Quick where goodnights were said, and we would go back home while the others went on their way to Newton-St-Low. When we got to the top of the hill again we would all shout out goodnight and they would answer until we couldn't hear them any more. I was fascinated to hear the echo of the voices singing as we went along.

'It's no good, Missus', Nobby says one day, 'we cannot afford to pay the rent of this place, we will have to get something cheaper, so give our notice in tomorrow'. So now once again we are house hunting. Nobby would come home with a handful of keys, 'Come on Missus' he would say. Up one road down the next, from one empty house to another. No sooner Nobby went up into the bedrooms than he would come down and say 'Out'. I fell in love with one house and when Nobby said 'out', I refused to go. 'Alright Missus, you want proof, I'll show you'. He tore a little of the paper from the wall in the corner of the bedroom and there was a nest of bugs. 'Well' said Nobby, 'Am I right? Do you want to live here, because if you do, you live alone, for I won't', and off we would go again. At last, we found a place with just a small backyard. It was twelve shillings a week, six shillings cheaper, my gosh, how wonderful.

I have been earning ten shillings a week turning the Royal Marines trousers, four pairs a week at two shillings and six pence a pair. Nobby helps me to unpick them and I make them up again, when they are finished they look like new. They are in great demand, but four pairs a week is about my limit. Sometimes the stripes down the side are worn rather badly, so then I have to buy more stripes, which the Marine pays for, and I get an extra shilling. I go to jumble sales and buy coats and trousers for three, four to six pence and make clothes for the children, turned, cleaned and pressed. The children always look well dressed. Every Saturday Nobby looks at the childrens' boots and shoes and mends them with the leather I buy from Woolworths. Two shillings and six pence worth each week and woe betide any of the kids if they have done skidding or scuffing during the week. They were always well shod.

It is raining, pouring, and I have been washing all day. Nobby has bought me a Dolly Tub. I have never seen one before but Nobby says they use them in the north of England. What fun it is trying to find out what one has to do. 'What do you think of it, Missus?' Nobby asked, 'Have you got the hang of it yet?' 'Not yet, but I will before long', I answered. 'I hope so Missus, 'cause I feel bad when I see you with the skin coming off your hands after doing the washing on that rubbing board, you must be rubbing your fingers more than your clothes'. 'I can't think how the clothes will get clean swishing that Dolly thing backwards and forwards, it puts me in mind of a milking stool with a handle up the middle'. 'Never mind what it looks like, you just get practising how to use it and save your hands'. 'Yes dear, I will, you don't like the look of them all blooded and I don't like the pain of them'.

On a Friday night my sister Ruth or I would go to the butchers and get the 'Kecker', and it would have the lights and liver, in fact all sorts of things on it, and mother would make the most wonderful faggots from it. Once a week in the winter, Charles and I would have to carry the Bullocks Cheek from the butchers. It was a standing order. My friends used to watch us struggle across the street with it. I'm thankful to say the butchers was just across the street from where we lived so we didn't have far to carry it, for it was ever so heavy. There was the jaw bone with all the teeth in it and lots of meat on the cheek part. 'Oh, how nasty', said Willie, 'Did your mother cook the teeth as well?' Must have done, I suppose. Anyway, we never had any teeth on our plates. But the meals we had from it were wonderful.

We had a huge black pot and it stood on the back of the range all the time. Every kind of vegetable was put in it which we had for dinners, then at night before going to bed we all had a cup of soup and a piece of bread. During the day, the rest of the vegetables had settled to the bottom of the pot, so we just had the thin soup at night.

My mother would make lovely brawn from pigs' heads and we had some beautiful meals made of bullock's heart stuffed, breasts of mutton boned, skinned, stuffed and rolled then roasted. But I must tell you that our Ruth and I were sent up to Bath to Spears shop to get some pork bones for Sunday dinner, they were gorgeous. The butcher used to leave ever such a lot of meat on them and also put in our bag a lot of fat pork on the rind and mother would render it down and make scrumpy for us children, and sometimes we would give our friends some who never seemed to have the kind of meals we had.

Friday night was pay night and we always had bloaters for tea when I was young, but they were cooked differently. A lovely big fire was made up, a piece of string was tied across the mantelpiece and the bloaters were tied by the tails and hung dangling down in front of the fire. It was always my job to twirl the string so that the fish was turned round and round and it had to be done very gently or the fish would fall off the string down into the pan that was underneath to catch the oil from the fish. 'Why was it always your job, Mummy?' the children wanted to know. 'Well', I said, cocking a chest. 'I was the most careful. The other girls would twirl the fish round to see how fast they could make it go, and then the fish would fall off'.

I used to get all the glasses my mother had and would put water in them to make different sounds when I hit them with a knitting needle. I could play quite a few tunes on them, I said. 'Let us do it now', Arthur said. 'I'm afraid we can't, we haven't the glasses, they have to be very thin, and ours are thick'.

We were never allowed to sit idle, mother would be making a rug and we kids would help her, one would cut up the old coats or trousers, another would cut strips about two inches long, then the other would place them in criss-crosses and hand them to mother to stitch them up into a sugar sack that had been soaked and washed.

We all had certain chores to do each day and especially Saturday mornings. Each week one would have to clean the silver and, as we didn't have much, that person had to clean the knives as well. Now we use stainless steel ones but in my day they were steel and would go rusty, so they had to be rubbed backwards and forwards on a board with some stuff called bath brick, and it was hard work I can tell you. Then one day my dad brought home a knife cleaner. It was like two round discs and the knives were put between them and the discs would rub them. So it was much easier than the board.

Another child would clean all the boots and that was no easy task for we had to use blackening and one had to really use elbow grease to get a shine, I can tell you. Another one made all the beds. We slept on straw palliasses and each week mother would spray Keatings powder on the beds to keep the fleas away or they would get in the straw and as mother would say 'prevention is better than cure'.

Mother was at the window one day when she saw a tramp coming up the street. There had already been one for some boiling water and a spoonful of tea, and then another for a spoonful of sugar, when this one came he asked for a drop of milk. Mother guessed they were together but could not understand why they seemed to come straight to our door, not bothering to knock on anyone else's. After they had gone mother went to the front door and up high on the side was a cross in chalk, so she called our Eva and showed her the cross. 'Go along the street and see if any of the other houses has a cross on it like this one'. When Eva came back she said that no-one else had a cross, so mother washed it out and no other tramps bothered her.

Our father was on the Committee of the Conservatives and our front room was turned into a committee room. My friend's house, which was down the street opposite, was for the Liberals. Now we were all the greatest of friends and went to school together, except when it was voting time, then we were at daggers drawn with one another.

Their colours were red and yellow and ours was blue, and mother would tie our hair up with blue ribbon and the Liberals would have red and yellow. The fights we used to have trying to pull each others ribbon off. Do you know, it's a wonder I have any hair left. We should have been in bed, but mother let us stay up to see all the police on horseback going up and down the street. We only had gas lamps in the street and a man would come along each evening and light them up. But on voting night it was lit up like fairy land for nearly everyone had flares, mind you the smell was terrible from the smoke. I think that is what made it more mysterious.

Thirteen was the school leaving age, but when I was eleven I had a bad illness and so, as I could not seem to pick up my strength, I was sent to my grandmothers who lived in the heart of the country and I was with her for nearly a year, so when I came back home and went to school again I was only there a few weeks when I had to leave.

I went to work in a clothing factory and I was an apprentice for two years at three shillings and six pence a week. I thought it was wonderful and I worked from eight in the morning until one o'clock, then from two o'clock until six and no breaks like everyone gets now-a-days. I learnt to make men's trousers, cycling knickers, football shorts, and many other things. After two years we would be put on piece work and then you could earn as much as ten shillings a week. Out of that we had to buy our own cottons, pipe clay, soap, pencil and scissors. The soap was for the back straps on the trousers, they don't use them today. You would soap a piece of lining, put the straps on, then take it to a pressing machine, and the warm iton would stick the straps on the lining. Then you would cut them into shape and take them to another girl on a binding machine, who then bound them with tape. The pipe clay was for making the button holes, the pencil was for putting your number on the pocket when you finished your article, then if any fault was found they would know who was to blame.

I went to work when I was staying with my grandmother too, for one shilling a week. I was a crow scarer. 'A what?' the children shouted. 'That's right, a crow scarer'. I used to have to go across two fields of corn at daybreak and again as it was getting dark and I don't mind telling you it was frightening. I was supposed to frighten the crows but they frightened me more, for the noise of their wings was terrific, for there were hundreds of them. My grandma came with me a couple of times then left me on my own. I had a clapper, you know, like the men take to football matches. The first time I used it I gave it an almighty swing and knocked myself out, but I was shown how to use it and that was out at arm's length, but the noise of it used to scare me, but after a while I got used to it.

I must tell you that I caused my Gran a lot of trouble. She didn't have any water laid on, and had to get all her water from the pond in the garden which would have to be strained and boiled before use, to make my tea or cocoa. It was not fit for drinking by itself. One day, when I was getting some water from the pond, a large toad jumped into the pond. Well! I just dropped the bucket and ran into the house to tell Gran, and all she should say was 'Good, he's still with us then'. She went to great lengths to tell me what a great swimmer it was, and that he kept it clean. But never mind what she said, it made no difference, I would not drink anything after that except skimmed milk.

Then one day Gran could see that I was craving for water, so she said 'Come on, May, bring those bottles, we are going to Nupend to get some groceries'. I don't know how far it was to Nupend, but it took me and Gran all day to get there and back, so she only went once a week.

We got to the shop and Gran told the lady about the pond and me. She took me out to the back of the shop and Oh! how wonderful, there was a pump and the lady said I could have as much as I wanted, and I drank and drank until she got quite frightened and she told Gran that she thought I was going to burst. Anyway, I carried two bottles of water home and Gran gave me only a little each day so as to make it last for the week. Then our Charles came to Gran's for a holiday, and Gran had the same bother about the water with him. She told the farmer that I worked for, that if she had known about our craving for water she would never have had us to stay with her. So he said that if she sent us down to the farm he would give us a bucketful at three pence a time. And so Charles and I would get the water, but Gran would only give us a little each day, because she could not afford it too often.

We have been living in our road for some months but had never spoken to our neighbour, except to ask him the time of day, when one Saturday he could not get his car to start, so Nobby helped him. The two men started talking. Some time later Nobby came in rubbing his hands.

'It just goes to prove Missus, it pays to do a good turn, do you know what that man and his son do for a living? They go rooting for dandelion roots and they have asked me to go along with them for some extra cash. They are lending me a digger, it's a special tool they use. They go to the farms to get permission to dig up the dandelion roots and the farmers are glad for them to do it. There is a chemistry place that buys the roots and give a good price for a sack-full'. 'Whatever do they want the roots for?' I asked. 'Don't know, all I know is I'm glad to get some extra cash'.

'Look what I've brought you Missus, don't say I never think of you' said Nobby. He had bought me a lovely big bunch of cowslips. 'Oh Nobby, what can I say, I feel all choked up for it brings back memories of when I was a small girl'. Oh how lovely my cowslips look on the table, no wonder my mother loved them. She would get me and Ruth to go down to the ground at the end of the street where we could get cowslips and milkmaids, otherwise known as cuckoo flower.

'What do you think of all this talk about war Missus?' Nobby asked. 'I am very frightened at the thought of it', I said, 'but anyway it won't be a long one like the First World War. That's what I've heard'. 'Don't you believe it Missus. Anyway, what I wanted to talk to you about is, if it has to come to it, I want to see if I can get back into the Royal Marines again. I don't want to be called up, I want to volunteer. Do you understand how I feel, Maysie?' 'Oh God, so that's it — now what do I say? 'I understand your feelings, so you can go off and do what you want to do. The children are growing up fast and June and Arthur are a great help now, and perhaps, like I said, it may not be long'.

'You don't know how happy you have made me Missus, and when I'm on the road and think back over the years, all our ups and downs, more downs than ups, I go back over the years and remember the day we were married. Your mother and father, and how they helped us, more than my own mother and father ever did. I can see your mother now, putting her hand on my shoulder, and looking up into my face and saying 'I hope you love her well Nobby, and will look after her. If not, you will answer to me'. And I told her she had nothing to worry about'. 'I wonder why you are telling me all this now, you have never mentioned all this before', I said. 'I don't know Maysie, all I know is I thank God for my Missus'.

'Nanny was a wise old dear'

Lady Susan Seymour
MAIDEN BRADLEY

I shall always retain the mental picture of Nanny dressing herself in the mornings. She would sit on the edge of her bed wearing a long white cotton nightgown, high necked with long sleeves; somehow she managed to get her arms out from the sleeves and then she fiddled under this kind of tent for about ten minutes, eventually pulling it off over her head and emerging fully dressed, corsets laced up and all. This was a performance that never failed to intrigue us. She wore black stockings and, when she took us out, high black boots, the lacing or buttoning up of which also seemed to take a long time.

In the early days Nanny took us out in the pram, with me sitting at the end facing her and my brother Percy* sitting at the opposite end facing me. When we had grown older the pram was given up in favour of things called scooters; these consisted of two wheels joined by a flat piece of wood with something like a broom handle attached to the front wheel hub with handles at the top. You placed one foot on the strip of wood and kicked frantically with the other; when you came to a downward slope the kicking foot joined the other and, if you were lucky, you got a somewhat wobbly free run. Nanny insisted that on alternate days we changed feet, thus wearing out the soles equally and also with the view to not becoming lopsided ourselves. Nanny was a wise old dear.

Poor Nanny, she did not get much free time, only every

*Became 18th Duke of Somerset.

other Sunday afternoon, when Norah took us out, and one evening a week which only started at seven p.m. after she had put us to bed. It was her habit to read to us while we were having supper in bed, but on her evenings off she recited to us instead while she was changing and doing her hair in a more elaborate way for going out. She had lovely long autumn hair and I can see her now standing in front of the mirror rolling strands of hair around her fingers, tying them with pieces of tape and then fixing the rolls on top of her head with hair pins; the result was quite glamorous. She had to be back by ten o'clock and if it was a foggy night, as it often was, I stayed awake until I knew she was safely back.

I missed Percy dreadfully when he first went to boarding school, but while I was feeling lonely and miserable and Daddy was still on leave from the Army we received an invitation from our Cousin Algenon, 15th Duke of Somerset, and Cousin Susan to go and stay for a week with them at Maiden Bradley which, later, was to become my home, although I did not know this then. Some years later, when Duke Algenon died, my Grandfather, who was his heir, became the 16th Duke of Somerset and my parents Lord and Lady Seymour.

I was aged six* when I first went to Maiden Bradley. We were met at Frome Station by a groom with a pony and trap, the pony was called 'Ginger', and our luggage followed in a horse-drawn waggon. We arrived at the house about tea time to be received by the housekeeper, Miss Freeland, an absolute dragon. We were met at the front door by the butler, Seaford, and ushered into the dining room, an enormous and imposing room to me at that age. Soon after our arrival Cousin Susan came in having just returned from her afternoon drive. She was a large formidable looking lady and I was an extremely shy nervous child, preparing to burst into tears if she spoke to me, when she handed me a box of chocolates saying 'I am sorry they are not nicer ones but I could not stay any longer in the shop

*Lady Susan was born in 1913.

because there was a German there'.

It was Mary, the head housemaid, who took Nanny and me under her wing and soon made us feel at home in that big house. Mary was a dear at heart, although a tartar with the under servants. She had the figure of an hourglass, the smallness of her waist being achieved by the tight lacing of her corsets. The staff consisted of Seaford the butler, two footmen called Long John and Little John, a hall boy whose jobs were to wait on the upper servants and to clean and maintain the oil lamps, there being no electricity in the house in those days, cook, kitchen maid and scullery maid, head housemaid, two under housemaids, two laundry maids, and, of course, Cousin Susan had a lady's maid and there were often visiting ladies' maids and valets.

Etiquette in the staff quarters was very strict. At meal times they all sat down together in the servants' hall to eat the first course, the Butler taking the head of the table at one end, the Cook the other end. After the meat course the upper servants left the servants' hall to eat their pudding course in the stewards' room, leaving Mary to reign supreme in the servants' hall. At this point the under servants were permitted to start to talk. Visiting ladies' maids and valets took precedence according to the rank of their masters and mistresses.

Breakfast and supper were brought up to Nanny and me in the nursery. Tea we had with Miss Freeland on a round table in one corner of the dining room, the grown-ups having afternoon tea in the drawing room. This was a very stately ritual; first two footmen carried in the table, followed by Seaford with a silver tray loaded with silver teapot and a silver kettle under which was placed a little special lamp to keep the water hot. The footmen then returned carrying tray-loads of silver dishes of muffins or hot scones and plates of sandwiches, cakes and pastries and very thin bread and butter. Sometimes after tea I was called into the drawing room and invited to sit on Cousin Susan's knee which I hated, but was too polite (or too frightened) to say so. The men retired to the smoking room, the only room in the house where smoking was permitted.

Luncheon was at 1.30 p.m., and I accompanied Mummy to the dining room for this meal, always sitting next to her in case I got into difficulties as I had never before used a knife and fork. I was only accustomed to a spoon and 'pusher', a utensil I have not seen since my childhood. Cousin Susan constantly complimented me on my perfect table manners and always thanked me for wearing a pretty dress; both these references made Nanny swell with pride when they were repeated to her.

It was at Maiden Bradley that I found my first dog friend. Kay-Kay was a charming, most amiable Dachshund. There were also three greyhounds in the house, but they were of uncertain temper and Kay-Kay was the only one I was allowed to touch, so I stroked him, cuddled him, talked to him and took him on a lead for our walks. The dogs all slept, each in his own backet, in the linen room where Mary and the other housemaids sat in the afternoons mending the linen. For years afterwards the linen room smelt of these dogs.

There were also a number of horses in the stables which fascinated me. There was the pair of carriage horses, only allowed out every other day, then there were Cousin Algy's and Cousin Susan's riding horses, her's named Jack used to say 'please' for a lump of sugar with his foot. Also Ginger who pulled the dog cart and was sometimes ridden, later by me, and a most uncomfortable ride she was; also Rebecca, a large roan who pulled the luggage waggon or the dray that took out the shooting parties. On my second visit some two years later after I had learnt to ride, I was allowed to ride a large chestnut mare called Beckie. She pulled quite hard and shied violently at any cars we passed because they were something new which she was not accustomed to seeing. I was escorted out by the head groom called Seal or by his son Jack, they both wore black boots and black gaiters, dark grey habits and wide brimmed black bowler hats. I loved this riding in the beautiful woods on the estate and sometimes we went into Longleat Park, the adjoining estate belonging to the Marquess of Bath.

Something else I enjoyed doing was going round with Long John and Little John while they shut up the house in the evenings. This consisted of putting shutters across the windows, securing them in place with iron bars and then fixing a large bell into a socket above the iron bar. This was done to all the downstairs windows, the idea being that if anyone tried to force their way in the bells would ring, causing the dogs to bark and rouse the household. I doubt if those dogs, closetted in the linen room upstairs, would have heard anything.

In 1920 we moved into the enchanting home my parents had found in North Devon, called Ebberly House. I dearly loved every corner of the garden, every room inside the house and every aspect of it from the outside. My happiest hours were spent by myself riding or on foot with the dogs, roaming the small estate and playing for hours in the stream.

This late Georgian house faced due south and both ends of the front part bowed, a most unusual feature, and this effect was repeated internally with some of the rooms oval and even some of the doors curved to complete the effect. The front door opened on to a large square hall, on the right of which was the large drawing room, with the bowed window at the end. Behind the drawing room was a second smaller hall out of which opened the music room which had the unusual feature of a window exactly over the fireplace, also French windows on the East side. From this second hall rose the very beautiful elliptical staircase. Opposite the front door was the dining room and on the left Daddy's study; beyond this came the kitchen and other domestic quarters, and beyond the kitchen a small stewards' room with the bowed end and window corresponding to the drawing room one. Upstairs there were ten bedrooms and three bathrooms.

On the day of our arrival Percy was sent round to the farm for some milk. He returned empty-handed, saying he could not understand a word they said and they must be speaking French. It took us some time to become familiar with the broad Devonshire dialect, but in a very short time I was speaking it myself, largely due to the fact that I quickly made great friends with Doris Hookway, although she was several years older than me. She was very sweet to me, she taught me to milk the cows and feed the calves, letting them suck my fingers in a bucket of milk. I followed Doris round the farm enthralled from the minute she got back from the village school at tea time.

I also kept ducks, rabbits and guinea pigs. I don't think I had any real affection for the guinea pigs but they did teach me 'the facts of life', something I am sure my mother would never have explained to me. If ever I asked where did babies come from Mummy looked intensely embarrassed and said 'I'll tell you when you are older darling', 'How old?' 'We'll see darling', and changed the subject. But at least I was not put off with fairy stories to make one search under gooseberry bushes and scan the sky for storks as some of my friends did.

These days of rural life were absolutely blissful to me. I used to go to bed at night in happy anticipation of the next day and wake up in the mornings with joy in my heart. I just loved all the animals, the flowers and the beautiful countryside, often standing lost in wonder at the glory of the sunsets and the beauty of my surroundings. I was, at that time, very conscious of the presence of God in that place which filled my heart with such love.

At the age of seventeen, just as I was supposed to 'come out' my Grandfather died so that my London Season and presentation at Court had to be postponed for a year.

I was very fond of Grandad and he of me, he always called me Kiddy and when we went to stay he allowed me to ride his horse. He was also much loved in the village. Six months after my father became the 17th Duke of Somerset, we moved to Maiden Bradley.

We found there had not been very many changes in Bradley House, even since the days when I first knew it. Mary was still there as head housemaid, a little older of course, but still with her 'hourglass' figure. Jack Seal was still in the stable and so was Ginger who lived to the astonishing age of forty-seven.

I shall always feel tremendously grateful to the parents who gave me such a wonderful childhood with such devoted unselfishness and, above all, a home where love reigned supreme.

'Don't play near the railway'

Norman F. Norris M.B.E.
EASTLEIGH and SOUTHAMPTON

This is an account of the early years of my life spent in a town almost entirely dependent upon the railway industry, and covers the years from 1914 until 1932. It will be obvious that the railway, in many ways, had a great interest for me, and I am quite unrepentant that this narrative has a strong railway theme woven into it.

In 1904 my parents left London to live in Eastleigh in southern Hampshire. My father worked at the London and South Western Railway Company's Nine Elms Works as a coach painter and writer until being transferred to that Company's newly built carriage and wagon works at Eastleigh.

The L.S.W.R. had erected their works there in 1889 because their Nine Elms works had become out-dated and inadequate for the construction of the larger rolling stock which began to take its place on the railways of Britain, around the turn of the century.

Eastleigh, lying in the valley of the River Itchen, is situated almost equi-distant between the Port of Southampton and the ancient capital of Wessex, Winchester. Here, upon the extensive flat land of the valley floor east of the railway station the railway company decided to erect their carriage and wagon works, which was followed in 1910 by the construction of the locomotive works.

The re-location of the railway works had a tremendous effect on the area. A glance at the population figures shows that in 1811 46 persons were living there, while a hundred years later the figure had risen to 15,247.

The L.S.W.R., by bringing their works into southern Hampshire created one of the first 'new towns' of this century. The fine purpose built workshops for the construction of railway rolling stock in the good conditions provided, were undoubtedly some of the most advanced in the country at that time.

Into this rapidly growing town I was born in September 1911. My earliest recollection is a of a steam-roller making up the road in which we lived. I was about two and a half years old. The houses where we lived had been built some five years previously. The road was lighted at night by gas lamps, the footpaths were paved with concrete flags, and the road surface was of rolled gravel. In summer the roads were sprayed with water from a horse-drawn water-cart to prevent dust blowing into the houses. In Northlands Road where we lived, there were fifteen houses, seven and a small chapel on one side, and eight on the other. All the adult males, in one way or another, were employed in the railway industry. On one side of the road lived a 'top link' driver, a plumber, a saw-mill foreman, an assistant machine shop foreman, a coach painter, a coach builder and a machine shop labourer. On the opposite side of the road lived a station-master's clerk, an engine fitter, a shunter, a coach finisher, a gas fitter, (most carriages were then lighted by gas) a trimmer, (upholsterer) and a gentleman who was held in some regard by the children, because he went each day to the 'office' wearing a pin-stripe suit and spats. I think he was Mr. Urie's clerk, who was then the Chief Mechanical Engineer. From 1880 until 1909 houses, mostly built in terraces, were erected in their hundreds. To those coming from London the town must have had the atmosphere of a 'gold rush' town. Gradually, however, the streets were drained and surfaced, shops built together with churches, public houses and the inevitable clubs, from the Conservative to the 'working mens'.

As might be expected my friends and I were steeped in railway lore. We knew an engine designed by Mr. Adams from those of his successor Mr. Dugald Drummond. The most elegant of all the locomotives in use on the L.S.W.R., in my opinion, were the T.3's built by Mr. Adams at Nine Elms works in 1893, and which proved to be one of the most powerful express engines of its day. One of these beautiful machines is currently on display at the York railway museum, in its light green livery with the scrolled L.S.W.R. lettering in gold leaf on the driving wheel splashers.

Boys regarded 'top link' drivers as being rather special. The names of some of them spring to mind, there was Mr. Chandler who invariably drove engines on steam trials when they were 'out-shopped' after repair or overhaul, or when emerging from the erecting shop as new. Always identified by the highly polished copper tea-can he carried, was Mr. Alf. Short, long on driving experience, but short on conversation. An outstanding figure was Mr. Snow, a tall bearded, dignified gentleman. We took great care not to kick our ball into his garden. Mr. Stokes, who with his wife and son kept very much to themselves, owned the first motor car in the part of the town in which we lived.

A chum of mine, Wally Notley, lived nearby. His father, an engine driver, often brought a heavy goods train up from the west country which arrived at a distant signal close to a line crossing at about 1 p.m. This crossing, part of a public footpath, had a stile at each side of the tracks, and was known locally as the 'line gates', although gates were non-existent. It was a favourite place for children to watch the trains. The 1 p.m. 'goods' invariably had to wait at the signal until the main London/Bournemouth line was clear. The line from Salisbury, and that from the direction of Brighton, crossed the London line at Eastleigh station and the north/south traffic had priority.

Knowing which turn of duty would find Mr. Notley on the 1 p.m. 'goods' we endeavoured to be there. He would allow us to mount into the cab and after some time had elapsed permitted one of us to pull the lanyard of the whistle so as to acquaint the signal-man in the Eastleigh east box that he was waiting at the signal. When the quadrant dropped, giving him the 'all clear' to proceed, we clambered down from the engine, an H 15 4-6-0 designed and built by Mr. Urie, who had succeeded Dugald Drummond as Chief Mechanical Engineer. The H 15's were usually painted black, had short stove-pipe chimneys and heavy eight wheeled tenders.

These locomotives were the fore-runners of the ubiquitous King Arthur class, which in Southern Railway days were to be seen working on most parts of the system.

On the railway metals at the 'line gates' we children would occasionally place 4" cut nails when we knew that a goods train was due. The engine would flatten the nails changing them into — what we fondly hoped — were knife blades. These we set into hazel sticks to serve as handles. Needless to say our knives were as sharp as tennis balls. As children we failed to see the danger to which we were exposing ourselves. Had our parents known they would have been horrified. I think we became immune to 'now don't play near the railway'.

A stupid and dangerous game we sometimes played, was known as 'under quick'. This entailed crawling below the wagons of a goods train whilst it stood waiting for the signal to come off. We were playing this game and a boy named Stevens had just crawled under between the wagons when the train began to move with a clanging and banging as the engine took the slack out of the coupling chains. Terribly frightened, Stevens nevertheless had the presence of mind to lie flat on his face off the centre of the track, so that the hanging links of the couplings missed hitting him; in this position he remained until the train had passed over him. Most of the goods trains on the Salisbury line consisted of between forty-five and fifty wagons, and I think about eighteen wagons passed over the boy before he emerged safe but shaken.

The days when drivers were allocated an engine which they drove exclusively, unless the engine was 'in shops', ceased many years ago. In the era of 'one engine one driver' a keen competitive spirit existed between engine crews, and this could be seen in the condition of the machines. The polished brass of cab gauges and wheel splasher rims, the gleaming steel of the connecting rods and motion gear and the brilliant shine of the paintwork all provided ample evidence of the interest taken not only by the driver and his fireman, but also by the cleaners and maintenance fitters.

The coaches of the L.S.W.R., prior to the amalgamation of the nation's railway systems in 1921, were quite distinctive in their livery of brown umber panels with a kind of salmon pink above and white roofs. I eagerly looked to see the lovely blue livery of the Somerset and Dorset Railway's engines and coaches at Templecombe, when we travelled to Torquay for our summer holidays.

Up until the late 1920's railway coaches were, in the main, constructed of wood, and prime timber was obtained from all over the world for this purpose. Different woods were required for the framing, the panels, flooring and the inside finishing. My father told me that from the time a coach came from the finishing shop into the paint shop and was ready for the 'road', up to seventeen coats of paint had been applied. Each coat was rubbed down with pumice powder and water, the work completed with two coats of Copal coach varnish.

Those employed in the railway work-shops, the motive power department, the traffic department, signalmen and numerous others, worked a twelve hour day before and during the First World War.

The General Strike of 1926 had a dramatic impact upon the life of the town. Almost at the drop of a hat the great railway works and the motive power department fell silent. It was very strange not to hear the bang and clatter of wagons being shunted throughout the day and night. Noises emanating from the various railway activities to which the towns-people had become accustomed were silenced.

Sentries with fixed bayonets were posted at the railway station, the carriage and wagon works, the locomotive works and at other places considered vulnerable. At Eastleigh the strike passed off, in the short time it lasted, in a good humoured and orderly manner.

As a child there were many things to delight and interest

me, but the railway took pride of place. I think that the zenith of the British railway industry was reached between 1921 and the beginning of the Second World War.

Most Eastleigh boys, on leaving school at fourteen years of age found employment in the railway industry. However, my parents thought it best for me to enter a different industry and arranged for me, when attaining the age of sixteen, to take up an apprenticeship with the firm of John I Thornycroft — now Vosper Thornycroft — at their Southampton ship-building and ship repair yards.

With two years to wait for my sixteenth birthday I took a job as a van-boy for Messrs Brixley and Sons whose bakery and two shops, one in High Street and another in Leigh Road, were well known in and around Eastleigh.

I worked on a country round which covered a wide area, serving outlying villages and hamlets, some of which were without a village shop. The bread vans, manufactured by the Ford Motor Company of Detroit, were well maintained. The van allocated to the country round was a Model T., complete with brass radiator, which I kept resplendent, cleaning it each day with 'Brasso'. I thought it a splendid motor van, and I suppose for its time, it was. The cab doors were barely waist high when we were seated, and a side wind on a wet day ensured that we got wet. There were no screen wipers and no gears as we know them today, and although the side and head-lamps were electric they were dim by today's standards. During the time that I worked with this van I cannot recall a single instance of mechanical failure, which I think remarkable considering the condition of the roads. We had, of course, our share of punctures, the tyres had not reached the high degree of reliability we expect today. In view of the road conditions prevailing then, I think it was the sturdy construction of the vehicle that gave us trouble free motoring.

On Christmas Eve 1927, we left the bakery about 8.30 a.m. loaded to the roof of the van with bread, flour and cakes. It was a cold December day, but free of snow and the heat from the freshly baked bread was quite a comfort to our backs, although the wind-screen frequently steamed over and required wiping with a chamois leather. At 10 p.m. that night we arrived at the homes of our last five customers who lived in the hamlet of Hensting. Here lived a family named Davies who had twenty one children, albeit some had left the parental home. In addition there were two farm houses and a pair of farm cottages. Left in the van were only about five two pound loaves of bread and a few bags of flour. Four days would elapse before we worked the round again. Assuring the customers we would return to Eastleigh in an attempt to bring them bread, and if no bread was available we would return with flour and yeast, we set off. Fortunately the other roundsmen and the shops, had put their unsold bread in the bread store, and so we were able to deliver somewhat belatedly, the bread for the Christmas period. We gathered up a motley collection of bread: white, brown, Hovis, Youma, Bermaline and currant.

All in all, those were happy days, despite coming home, now and again wet through. Journeying into the quiet countryside in all seasons, watching the changing colours of the trees and crops as one season gave way to another, I found most enjoyable.

What a terrific contrast it was to leave behind the peace of the countryside to work in the ship-building industry, where the intolerable din of the riveters and caulkers pneumatic hammers was incessant. At that time Thorny-crofts had on the stocks six destroyers for the Chilean Navy and two for the Canadian Navy. With hulls of 3/8" plate and standing on slip-ways where there was nothing to deaden the sound, the noise had to be experienced to be believed. It is no wonder that many boiler-makers and platers suffer from deafness in later life.

My apprenticeship at Thornycrofts commenced in August 1927, and after a short stay in the ship-yard at Woolston, Southampton, where the new vessels were built, I was transferred to their ship repair works in Southampton Docks.

At that time the docks were a hive of industry, ships of

the major shipping lines constantly entering or leaving the port. The golden age of the trans-Atlantic liner however was drawing to a close by the end of the 1920's. Ships of the Cunard and White Star Lines held pride of place and always docked in the Ocean Dock, the White Star liners at berths 42, 43, and 44, and the Cunarders at berths 46, 47, and 48. The ships of the Union Castle Company in their distinctive colourings could be easily recognised by the vermilion smoke stacks, with their black tops, and hulls painted a pretty lilac. They left weekly for South Africa from the 'dock head' at berth No 36 each Friday at 4 p.m. precisely, despite the seafaring superstition concerning sailing on a Friday.

On one occasion at least, I recollect seeing three 'Star' line ships in the docks at the same time, the White Star's 'Homeric', the Red Star Line's 'Lapland' and the 'Andora Star' of the Blue Star Line.

After the First World War, Germany, as part of her reparations, handed over two of her giant liners to the White Star Line. These were the 'Bismarck' (56,000 tons) and the 'Columbus' (34,000 tons). They were renamed the 'Majestic' and 'Homeric' respectively. The Cunard line acquired the 'Imperator' (52,000 tons) which became the 'Berengaria'.

R.M.S. 'Aquitania' (46,000 tons) was regarded by many as the Grand Old Lady of the Atlantic, and the famous 'Mauretania' after coming safely through the rigours of the 1914-1918 war held the 'Blue Riband' of the North Atlantic for twenty years. The lines of her sleek hull were beautiful, not only were her turbines powerful and practically free of vibration, she also had the graceful slim bows of a yacht. The splendid mahogany panelling lining the corridors and some of the public rooms was ear-marked years ago, and long before she went to the ship-breakers. I understand that the panelling now adorns a rather select club.

The White Star liner R.M.S. 'Olympic' and the Cunarder's R.M.S. 'Aquitania' and 'Mauretania' were all four funnelled ships. I have seen all three plus the 'Majestic' in the Ocean Dock at the same time, and it was indeed a sight to remember.

Occasionally I entered the door situated at the base of the mast of the 'Berengaria' or 'Aquitania' to climb up the iron ladder fixed inside the steel mast, and after a long climb in darkness to emerge into the 'crows nest' from where an astounding panoramic view of the Isle of Wight, the New Forest and Southampton could be enjoyed.

In 1929 the Wall Street financial collapse, which followed the failure of Mr. Hatry's monetary dealings on the New York Stock Exchange had very serious repercussions throughout the United States of America, and almost all the industrialised nations of the world, not the least of these being the United Kingdom. Almost over-night a vast change occurred throughout the British ship-building industry, within a few weeks the only people employed in the work-shop where I worked were the foreman, the charge-hand, a store-keeper and six apprentices.

All the berths at Thornycroft's yacht yard at Northam were occupied by luxury steam yachts, laid up indefinitely as a result of the financial problems which hit all and sundry as the effects of the money crises spread. A sign of the times were the five or six two-berth motor cabin cruisers, built at the Chiswick yard of Thornycrofts, and brought round to Southampton in the hope that they would sell quicker there. These boats were about seven feet in the beam and twenty-four feet from steam to stern. The asking price? A mere £250.

Through the early and mid-thirties the trade depression continued with very little let-up. It was not until Hitler annexed one European country after another in the latter half of the decade that Britain began to realise the strong position Germany had created for herself. Consequently, Britain slowly started to build up its armaments which brought a new impetus, not only into ship-building, but to almost every other facet of industry.

It was into this industrial scene that I started out as a journeyman after serving a five year apprenticeship. I had in my childhood lived through one world war, and was about to experience another, but that is quite another story.

The 'lost' village of Imber on Salisbury Plain

Dorothy Webb
IMBER

My father had been a journeyman baker, but a chance to become his own master occurred when he heard of a bakery attached to a public house at at a village on Salisbury Plain called Imber. I was born in 1907. We moved to Imber when I was only three weeks' old. It became my home for the next ten years.

Looking back now I realise that Imber was a paradise for children. We had few toys or books, no cinemas or television but we were never bored as there were so many exciting things going on outside. This was a purely agricultral village growing acres of corn and tending large flocks of sheep. As the seasons came round there was sheep shearing to watch, then the harvest when every hand was called on to help. We loved to go gleaning the ears of corn left after the rake had been round. What a feast for the hens when we came home, tired out and bitten all over by harvest bugs.

A gate in the wall of our garden led into a field where cows grazed and here we wandered at will birds-nesting or picking cowslips to make tossy-balls.

During the summer we children roamed far and wide over the Plain with no restrictions of any kind and seeing no-one but an occasional shepherd. In due season we went in search of peewit eggs to take home for breakfast, or to fill our baskets with mushrooms. The cry of the peewits and never-ending song of the larks, the beautiful little hare-bells, the rabbit warrens, the sudden start of a hare and above all, the short, springy turf that was so pleasant to walk on, this is what Salisbury Plain, in retrospect, means to me.

We walked hand-in-hand over the Plain, taking half the day as we dawdled along, perfectly happy and absolutely safe in those days.

This idyllic situation ended when the 1914-18 War was declared, and Imber became the centre of military operations that were eventually to sound its death knell. Khaki uniforms were everywhere and the sound of gun-fire shattered the peace of this once slumbering village. We could no longer wander at will in any direction; when the red flag went up, large areas were out-of-bounds. One of my pleasanter memories of this period is of attending a concert given by the military in a large barn opposite our house. Here, for the first time, I saw a performance on a stage. I was intrigued by the make-up on the faces of the performers. For the first time also I heard those haunting songs of the First World War, such as 'If you were the only girl in the world . . .' and 'Keep the home fires burning . . .'

I have never been back to Imber; I could not bear the devastation and destruction.

I often wonder what would have happened to Imber had there been no war. The almost complete isolation could not have continued for ever, and the young people would have wanted to move away to a fuller life. I, for one, shall always consider myself fortunate to have spent my formative years in this unique community on Salisbury Plain. It has given me a lasting love of country life in all its aspects, but, above all, it has given me a feeling of belonging to a tiny part of this country that is no more but that will live on in my memory.

'The warm sweet earth of Wiltshire'

Joan Church
MALBOROUGH

As people always tend to do, we came back to Wiltshire on our retirement, although over the years, we had spent a good deal of time here with relatives who had remained.

My husband was born in Albion House, Devizes, in its grander days. It stands there nowadays looking forlorn and forgotten, but once it was a beautiful house, standing just past the roundabout as you come out of Devizes on the Beckhampton Road. At that time, his father was at Lloyds Bank, Devizes, and their family had been farmers and land owners for over two hundred years, at least, farming in Aldbourne, Froxfield, Pewsey and near Castle Combe. They somehow never made a fortune out of farming, and in those days, of course, there were not the aids to agriculture there are nowadays, so it was easy to begin to slide down the slippery slope and eventually farms were sold and passed out of families' hands forever. This was how my husband's father came to be in Lloyds Bank, and not driving a team of horses over the land.

We bought a house at Shalbourne, in Wiltshire, some years ago, and in the church porch we found the grave of a little boy of our name who died, aged four, in 1876, exactly one hundred years' ago. We did some research and found to our amazement that he was part of the family, and had lived at a farm only a few miles distant. His grandmother is buried in our churchyard. She was a Richens, of which there were many hereabouts.

My father-in-law was in the Wiltshire Regiment in two world wars and fought in France in the First one. His grandfather, John Allan, was the captain of the famous sailing ship, the Thermopylae. He took his wife round the world with him, on board ship in 1870, which was when he had an encounter with pirates in the Indian Ocean. He stood, reputedly, at the rail, and said he would kill the first pirate to step on board. This, he apparently did. He died on that voyage, and his wife returned to England on the ship. When she reached England, she gave birth to a child, which, because they had so much wanted a son, was named Christina Johnny. This child was my husband's grandmother.

The tiny church at Holcombe bears a plaque to the memory of other members of the family. At this little church, there is also a plague grave containing the remains of several hundred people. Behind the church is the grave of Scott of the Antarctic.

My parents-in-law travelled about the country quite a bit after the war, but returned finally to Wiltshire. He longed to buy a farm and to meet the other farmers, but of course, it was much too late for him. He had chosen a different life — in the Army — and although he realised his mistake, early on, life seemed to propel him onwards, far away from the warm, sweet earth of Wiltshire. But it was to the sweet earth of Wiltshire he eventually returned, worn out, and somehow dissatisfied that he had lost his way.

At the end of the nineteen-forties, my husband's parents lived at Stourton, outside Mere. At that time, Stourhead was suffering from post-war depression, as were most large houses and estates. I remember watching Leslie Hoare and his father chopping down trees around the lake. I was offered the 'old convent house' at the far end of the lake for a nominal ('peppercorn') rent of ten shillings a year, but I didn't take it, as there was such a strange air about it.

When I went back there recently, the gardens were glorious, the lake appeared to have been opened up more, and the house the Churches had lived in had been re-named, New Lakeside House, instead of Beech Knoll. The old coach houses opposite the entrance of Stourhead had become a restaurant.

I remember the days when the only flying saucers in that area were the ones coming out of the kitchen of the Ship Inn. Nevertheless, I spent an evening sitting on Cley Hill, hoping to be astounded, but there were no flying saucers about, that evening. All I saw was a mournful young man playing a guitar, his pockets bulging with cans of beer.

Some people I knew, a long time ago, owned a jam factory in Wiltshire (better not say where) and the rumour was that most of it was turnip pulp. Of course, no one really believed it, but I spent a morning there once, and found it was actually true. They must have been good Wiltshire turnips, because it was excellent jam. Only rarely have I tasted better, anywhere.

It seems such a pity that Wiltshire has lost its pigs. When I was young, Wiltshire was famous for them, and nearly every cottager kept one at the bottom of the garden, but new regulations put paid to that, and sadly there aren't all that many Wiltshire pigs about nowadays. I remember all those wonderful pork butchers, with their Bath chaps and brawn and chitterlings, a feast in themselves.

In the autumn, all the lovely Russet apples were stored in the attic, fish was pickled or salted, and there was always a ham hanging somewhere in the house. All this convenience food doesn't taste the same, somehow.

Wiltshire has always seemed to me a measuring rod for the whole country. When you drive over Beckhampton Downs, you can almost see the people whose barrows lie all around. In the dusk, you see the hosts of people who populated the Iron Age settlements. On a foggy night, you see the Roman soldier on guard duty at the top of our road, walking up and down, and whistling his songs of home. Up on the ridge you can hear the tramp of soldiers' feet and the clash of metal. Oh yes, Wiltshire's haunted all right. There's no doubt of that. We are all one with the people who've lived here, and who loved it, as we do.

As Edmund Burke said, 'I would rather sleep in the

southern corner of a little country churchyard, than in the tomb of the Capulets'. As far as I'm concerned, you can make that a Wiltshire churchyard. There's no finer place, anywhere.

The road running above our village (A338) carried pilgrims from Salisbury to Oxford and they would come down one hill into the village, stay as long as necessary, and then make their way back up the other hill, by the mill, and out again on to the main road. There were two inns in the village and it must have been a welcome stopping place, lying as it does, so pleasantly and peacefully in the valley.

The slopes, coming down from the main road, were reputedly used for grape growing by the Romans. Now the harvester careers its precarious way down them to reap the corn.

I remember fields of corn, bright yellow in the sunlight, interspersed with red poppies and cornflowers. Hedge-rows full of cowslips are seldom seen now, but we buy the seed by post and try to re-habilitate them in the lanes. Unfortunately, they *are* so rare, the children are charmed with them and take them home, so it is a losing battle.

To amuse ourselves, we all had hoops to bowl along. And, apart from 'hopscotch' this was all, because we made our own entertainment, jumping over haystacks, riding the ponies, and walking for miles gathering wild flowers, and sometimes blackberries. The only weather guidance and warning the farmer had in those days was to stand long and thoughtfully studying the sky.

There was an old, titled lady living nearby, whose husband liked to keep out the cold with (more than) a drop of 'the hard stuff'. At times, he would chase her down the fields holding a shot-gun, and shouting abuse. No one liked to interfere, since she *was* titled, and I was always mystified by the fact that no one else seemed able to see what I could. They simply turned a blind eye and pretended it wasn't happening. It would have been 'speaking out of turn' to remark on it. I used to wonder what they would do, if he ever actually shot her! (Perhaps leave her where she lay, on the grounds that to notice it would be 'stepping out of place'?)

There was no hankering after large sums of money in those days. One faced life as it was. The natural rhythm of life, the seasons, the decay and rebirth of things, was what governed all. To buy a new dress was an event, to be planned for and thought about for a long time. A mistake was a tragedy. There were very few treats, apart from very simple ones. One didn't travel much in the ordinary way. The countryside and the home were our lives and everything revolved around them. That was the way of life in all the counties.

We had no holidays. We listened with interest to accounts of other peoples', but they were not for us, and we didn't really mind.

People learned to live within their incomes. There was no question of living on credit. People simply didn't do it. They made fantastic stews and vegetable casseroles. The only thought in their minds was how good it was. They didn't think to compare it with anything they were *not* having.

There was very little crime in my youth; at least, we never heard of it! No one would think of locking a car or a door, and we often slept with the back doors unlocked or even open, because no one had bothered to shut them.

People gave each other items of food. One might find a jar of jam on the doorstep and have a good idea who'd left it, perhaps out of real need for bread or meat, so we'd go round with whatever we thought they would want. It was a system of barter, in fact, one that had been in operation for a very long time indeed.

I recall the soup kitchens of those days and the long, long queues at the 'Labour Exchange'. If one went through towns, there were many men standing around on the street corners, with hopelessness written on their faces for all to see. They had a strange look; one I shall never forget; that even as a child, I noted and wondered about; a defensiveness, a shame, that I could not begin to understand. Work had been promised them; but there was no work;

Honour had been promised them, but honour there was none.

Women used to come round to the houses quite often in the nineteen twenties and thirties, asking for any old clothes we could spare. Sometimes they would seize them, there and then, and put them on, with obvious delight, even though they were quite worn, or they would grab a squirming child and force it into a suit of some kind. My mother used to say she felt ashamed that people could be so grateful for what we had discarded. My old pram, with four enormous wheels, was given to a deaf and dumb woman, with four children. I stood, holding on to my mother's skirt, and feeling a strange comradeship and affinity with the children, about my own age, four, because they were taking over something of mine, and their new brother or sister would ride in my pram, and in a peculiar way, be part of me, and I part of them forever.

Since my childhood there has been so much progress in so many ways. Man has been to the moon. Who knows what the next fifty and a hundred years will see?

But Stourton and very many parts of Wiltshire, remain unchanged and as beautiful as they have always been. Long may they remain so.

From pony boy to stud groom to chauffeur

Henry Charles Lansley
EAST WOODHAY

I am now *eighty six years old having been born at East End in Hampshire in 1886 on January 6th. I was one of twelve children — the third son of the family of six sons and six daughters. My father worked as a garden labourer for Lt. Col. Sir F.H.W. Carden Bart at Stargroves Manor House for forty five years until his retirement. Previous to this he had worked in his native districts of Tangley in Hampshire as a dewpond maker and in due course was responsible for making the lake at the west side of Stargroves. My mother was born at Highclere, her maiden name was Allen. Her father was a blacksmith and was related to and worked for the famous family of blacksmiths named Challis of Highclere. One of this family went to Canada and got on so well that he became Mayor of Toronto.

My father at this time was paid twelve shillings a week, so life was pretty hard going. To augment the income he used to team up with five or six others as a gang and go cutting grass with scythes for making hay. They used to go out as soon as it was light and work until it was time to go to their daily jobs, and again in the evening from say six o'clock until it was dark. We children usually had to meet them at some given field with their tea. To give an idea how tough things were, many a time I was sent to one of the big houses to get a pennyworth of dripping to

*This was written in 1972. Mr Lansley died in 1974 and these reminiscences were sent in by his son, Mr. C.H. Lansley. Ed.

spread on our bread.

One annual event was the parade of the East Woodhay Provident Deposit Society. I shall always remember it. It used to take place every Whit Monday beginning with a parade to East Woodhay Church headed by the East Woodhay Brass Band, then back to a feast in East End School followed by a fête in the meadows of East End Farm. The village street was lined with stalls of different things — round-a-bouts in the Sun yard, swing boats in The Meadows. Above the village all kinds of sports and games were held. Fortune tellers were around — one old man, my uncle, Bunny Bastin (nick-named such because he was supposed to be a rabbit poacher) used to run a show of his own. He used to be in a tub with a top hat on and charged a penny a shot at the hat. Two pence back if you knocked it off! The day ending when the pubs turned out at night. Beer in those days was two pence a pint.

I started going to school at East End when I was five years old. The master then was a Mr. Boulter, renowned for the use of the belt. He used to have one on his waist and one on the wall. Sometimes the one on the wall would disappear mysteriously, then the one on the waist came into service.

I went to this school for about two years until the six cottages in the row where I lived were condemned. We then went to live at Woolton Hill and I went to school there. My father continued to work at Stargroves.

About six months after we had moved, the cottages at East End went up in flames and I well remember the fire engines from Newbury galloping past the cottage we lived in at Woolton Hill. The engines were, of course, horse drawn. No motors in those days, and again they came about six months' later when East End Farm was burnt down.

While still at Woolton Hill School during summer holidays the school was added to and we had a much longer holiday than usual, so my mother said I must get some sort of job to supplement the income. I got a job of pig-minding on the stubble at Church Farm which was then run by two brothers named William and Henry Hull. This job was early morning till late at night for three shillings a week. There was an old boar that used to cause me a lot of trouble, every evening when it was time to go to the yard this animal used to wander off to another field where there was a crab-tree, and I had to go off to fetch him back and he didn't always come willingly and I was a bit frightened of him. I think he preferred the crabs to the trough of water that awaited him in the yard.

Part of the time I had to lead the lead-horse in the harvest field while the wagons were being loaded and at times I had to bring the loads down the hill to meet the empty wagons, the mares were very good and knew more about the job than I did.

I left school at ten and a half years old. The local Postmaster Mr. John Dunn, applied for a lad to carry telegrams and I was the one chosen and started work on the following Monday morning. Our first job was to get all the wood ready for the Baker's oven, as this Mr. Dunn ran a Bakery business as well as a shop and Post Office. There were three of us boys and at eight o'clock the post used to arrive by horse and cart from Newbury.

My delivery district was the Hollington one, of course we had to walk everywhere. No bicycles in those days and up to that time there were no telephones. The telegrams used to come over what they used to call the ticker-tape. I could never understand it myself. In those days there were lots of telegrams to be taken out, we used to have to deliver to all and sundry. I think my longest journey used to be to Faccombe Manor, where a Mr. Heath then lived. He had a son who was a boxer and when he was away training, telegrams were often coming. One day I had walked to Faccombe twice and as we were leaving for home at six o'clock, another arrived and I was told to take it. I said 'My feet are too sore' and Mr. Dunn said 'take one of the ponies'. No saddle, of course, only a sack on his back. I thought, 'here's a chance of a ride'. So I jumped up and away but by the time I got to East End Farm I didn't know which was worse, my feet or my seat. Anyway, I left the pony at East End Farm and finished on foot. I was very late home, of course, and my father came to see where I was. I had reported back to the Post Office and started for home but had stopped to rest my feet and went to sleep by Burley Lodge where he found me and carried me home.

After about a year of this my father took me away saying that it cost more for shoe leather than I was earning as I was only getting four shillings a week. My father got me a job as Pony boy at Woolton House Farm. Here I had to look after the pony, lead him for lawn mowing and carry milk from the Farm to the House twice a day. After about three years at this Farm I applied for the job of Pony boy at Malverleys for Mr. Paul Forster. This only lasted about a year when the Boer War broke out and the eldest son of the house was killed in battle in South Africa. This meant the house being closed for a year and I was discharged.

I hardly had my notice when the Stud Groom called and asked me to start work at Stargroves to help them out for a few weeks. I took this one and the few weeks lasted fifty six years. This proved to be very good schooling as they both bred horses and trained them for both driving and riding. In all, there were between twenty and thirty horses here at that time and about six grooms to look after them, groom them and ride and drive them. I learned most of the things that led up to being a Stud Groom and in the end I was in charge of both departments such as the driving in London for the London season, and the hunting and driving in the country during the winter, for the London coachman went deaf and I had to take his place for several seasons, and the Stud Groom had a heart attack and wasn't allowed to drive, so I took his place in the country.

In those early days I was a boy member of the choir, first at East Woodhay then for a time at Woolton Hill, then as a grown-up I sang as a bass, and I still make a bit of a noise. In all I have been singing in choirs for seventy eight years, having started at eight, and I am now eighty six years old.

One of my best memories is of the East Woodhay Mummers who, in my young days used to go round the Parish at Christmas time doing a comic play or plays. I know us youngsters used to follow them round from Public House to Public House. I remember once following them on Boxing Day from North End and found myself at the Crown Pub at Highclere and I got a good whipping from my old Dad when I got home later that night. Another of my early memories is of the lovely Christmas trees, and the treat when as a tiny tot we used to be marched up to Stargroves for the Christmas party in the coach-house when an enormous tree was lit up by hundreds of tiny candles and a lovely useful present for each child was given by the first Sr Frederick and Lady Carden. Afterwards this was carried on by the succeeding Sir F. H.W. Carden and Lady Carden for a great number of years.

From the age of fifteen I lived in a Mess Room at the stables and slept in a room under the clock tower of Stargroves doing my own cooking, washing etc. About this time I first met the sweet lady who afterwards became my beloved wife. I married at the age of twenty six in 1912 and we went to live in one of the cottages in Tile Lane. I lived there for fifteen years when it was decided that it would be better if I lived in the stable yard to be near my work with the horses. It was decided to convert part of the stables into a cottage. My wife bore me one son and we lived and enjoyed being together for fifty-one years.

I carried on being a groom until I was sent to London in 1910 to learn motor driving. The first car I ever saw was about 1896 or 1897. It belonged to the late Lord Carnarvon. Rumour had it that he was travelling to Whatcombe, where his horses were in training. For once rumour was right, for after some wait, along came a car making a lot of *noise*. It was being driven by a Frenchman, who had brought it over from France to instruct a Mr. Trotman, who in due course became Lord Carnarvon's Chauffeur.

The first car I drove was a new 16 h.p. Wolseley. My employer had taken a hunting box in Warwickshire. On my way a terrific snow storm set in and, as there were no windscreen wipers in those days, I couldn't see a thing. So I stopped at Rugby for the night, and went on next day. Luckily the car was a very heavy one (2 ton 5 cwt empty) so it gripped pretty well in the snow. Side and tail paraffin lamps were fitted and the head lamps were lit by acetylene gas, which of course, had to be attended to daily. Also in those days there were no spare wheels. What we had was a *Stepney* which had to be clamped to the punctured wheel. If not on very tight, it would creep and slip and you wouldn't get along at all. Only the rear wheels were braked in those days and as there were no self-starters it was always necessary to swing the handle at the front.

My Wolseley could carry five people inside, and two outside, as well as much luggage on the top. When fully loaded it was sometimes difficult to get up the hills without either the engine boiling, or the clutch slipping, to which those old leather-lined clutches were very prone. I have often had to get out and put pieces of hack-saw blade under the leather, to pack it up. After such treatment it would grip satisfactorily perhaps for some weeks.

In 1913 we acquired another car. This was a French Daracq, which also had a leather-lined clutch, and I often had the same slipping trouble as before. For the first few months of the 1914-18 war I was engaged in driving my employer, who had rejoined his Regiment, to different camps. Then in January, 1915 I joined up with the R.A.S.C.

In due course, things improved and we were able to have two cars. My employers bought two American Willys Knights — and lovely cars they were to drive — so flexible and powerful after English cars. The one drawback was the distributor, which was just behind the radiator, where if we had snow, or a boiling radiator — it would get wet and soon stop the car. But we carried on with these two Willys Knights for about eleven years.

About this time there were electric carriages which used to be called Mother Skipton's Horseless Carriages. They were used mostly for drives in the Parks. Their power came from huge batteries which had to be charged each day.

I have just completed sixty two years of car driving without an accident — for which I am expecting the Veteran Motorist Association's Badge — for sixty two years of safe driving. At the present time I am happy still to be able to drive my own car.

When my employers learnt to drive I was not so much in demand as a driver, so naturally I went back to looking after the riding horses again. I was very lucky for I often got a day's hunting. We had some very good horses in my early days. I used to ride a horse called 'Annanias', who was so good at racing that he won two gold cups in two days at Hawthorn Hill. I am proud to have a painting of him and the dates he won the cups. Another very good show jumper we had was one named 'Brown Boy'. I rode him several times in the show-ring. Another good horse we had was 'Carlow'. He won the Craven Hunt point-to-point members race five years in succession. Quite an achievement. The final one being in 1929. I also trained a horse called 'Venture' which won The Craven Hunt Maiden race one year.

There is one other odd thing I must mention which happened to me in my younger days. When I was about eight years old I had a terrible lot of warts on my hand. They were covered with them and my old uncle (Bunny Bastin) was supposed to be able to charm warts away. My mother enquired of him about this, he said I was to count every one and go to him and tell him the number, which I did, there were forty seven of them. He did not touch me, he simply lit a match, watched it burn to his fingers, then said 'Go home and in two weeks they will all be gone'. True enough all were gone and I have never had one single wart since.

Since my retirement my employer has died and the lovely old place and grounds have been sold and purchased by a member of one of the popular *pop groups. Stargroves is now, I am sorry to say, a home for hippies, which has somewhat lowered the tone of the district.

*Mick Jagger, who subsequently sold Stargroves.

'Bluebells was a very gentle game'

Florence Hannah Warn
BRISTOL

I was born in 1901 at Easton in Bristol. Our street was a cul de sac; there were about 30 houses each side of the road, and as there were lots of families with children, the street was our playground, because back gardens were used for growing vegetables and keeping chickens.

When a tiny child died, the cost of a funeral was beyond the pocket of a poor family, so an arrangement was made to bury the infant at the same time as an adult's funeral. In front of the glass hearse, there was a little glass compartment running the width of the hearse and the little coffin was placed there and so buried in the adult's grave. We had a little brother, Gilbert, who died of pneumonia and this was the form his burial took. None of us attended the funeral, but I remember we had black sashes to wear on our Sunday dresses.

We did not have any pocket money but sometimes we ran an errand for someone and received a halfpenny so we would buy some sweets, and for a farthing there were lots of things one could buy: there was a strip of toffee called Everlasting, (which it was not); a braid of liquorice which broke into strips and were called Shoe Strings; a slab of black toffee called Wiggle Waggle which blackened the tongue and lips; Bulls eyes were marbles of sweet which could be eaten, but when rubbed on a rough wall revealed a flat surface with rings of varying colour, hence bulls eyes; sweet shrimps; white or pink fondant mice (we girls were a trifle squeamish about eating these) — for a farthing, you could get six pretty little boiled sweets called Rosebuds.

Saturday was a busy day and there was plenty of activity in the street. The baker, the oilman and the milkman came and had to be paid.

The oilman called only on a Saturday; he would stand at the bottom of the street and ring a big bell — like a school bell. He had a piece of rope tied on the end of the clapper, and this he shook violently so that everyone would hear and know he was coming. He sold oil for the lamps which lit our rooms (except bedrooms where we used candles), and mats, rugs, buckets, bowls, soap and lots of other oddments. He had a loud voice and everybody knew when he was about.

Sometimes the man selling flycatchers would come. He wore a tall black hat with long strips of sticky paper fastened to it and covered with dead flies, and he would walk up one side and down the other side of the street calling loudly, 'Flies, Flies, Catch 'em alive' and then sell his strips of sticky stuff. Then there were two men wearing long black coats hanging to the ground who trundled a small cart with long handles from which they sold blocks of salt. They called out in very doleful voices, 'Any Salt, Please Lah-di'.

When the baker came, he would gallop his horses to the top of the street and then call at the houses on the way back. At the back of his wagon was a handle at each side and the boys would hang on and have a good run all the way up, until someone would call out 'Wheel, wheel, whip behind' and the baker would slash his whip around and catch the boys' fingers to make them let go.

On very dark, wintry mornings, there was a boy who came around, calling out 'Hot rolls, all hot' but his poor voice sounded so sad and it sounded like 'hot rooolls, all hot', the vowels being dragged out a long way. We were sorry for him as we were snug and warm in bed — we didn't have any rolls of course; money did not run to such luxuries in our house. Often we had a visit from a man with a Hurdy Gurdy which was a portable music machine and a handle turned to give forth jolly music. We children thoroughly enjoyed the merriment and also the little monkey who wore a red pill-box with a tassel on his head would leap around with a collection box for his master. We also had a man selling watercress which was sold in little bunches standing in a bucket of water, and he would say 'Wahder Creese, only ½d a bunch' — whereupon he would lift out a bunch and shower us with water.

Both boys and girls wore dresses until it was time to start school (at five years). My first little friend, who lived a few doors away, used to come to play every day, armed with a little enamel cup and mother would give us a drink of some kind while we were playing. One day, my little friend came as usual but, to me, it was *not* usual, for a little boy stood there, looking very proud of himself. I said accusingly, 'You are a boy!' and absolutely refused to play with him, despite his tears. I thought I had been playing with a little girl. I do not know why at that age it should have mattered to me; I was well used to boys, having four brothers, but evidently it did. When it was time to start school, a little boy was 'breeched' (we called it 'britched') and very proud they were of the first pair of trousers with a pocket in, and neighbours would give a small coin to make a jingle in the pocket.

When we wanted a skipping rope, we went to the green-grocer's and asked for the rope which was bound around orange boxes. It was very rough to handle and we had to join it together, but we didn't mind that, and we would have a lot of good skipping games . . .

Two long ropes were needed for 'German' skipping. Two girls, holding one end in each hand swung them alternately inwards, from left to right, and right to left. The skipper had to stand in the centre of the ropes, and as the ropes were turned alternately, she had to jump over each rope as they came towards her feet, without getting caught or she would be 'out'. 'Snakes' skipping was simple. One long rope and two girls, one at each end. The rope would be shaken vigorously up and down until a long snake would be wriggling across the road, and each skipper had to jump over, without getting tangled up in the rope.

'Bluebells' was a very gentle game. Instead of shaking the rope up and down, it was kept horizontal, flat to the road, and just waved about, so it was a case of a long jump to escape getting caught.

When I was about ten years pf age, I did some housework for a crippled lady, scrubbing cement paths with a long-handled broom bigger than I, then scrubbing a long passage of linoleum and polishing it afterwards, black-leading a huge, old fashioned fireplace, scrubbing floorcloth in the living room and then scrubbing the scullery floor. It must have taken four or five hours. I was paid the princely sum of one shilling but I had to hand it over to Mother and received two pence for myself, but there was no feeling of resentment as it was expected and quite usual.

'A milking pail full of hot gin and cider was provided'

Austin Brooks
GLASTONBURY

Austin Brooks was born in 1836 and died in 1919. This account of life in 19th Century Glastonbury was submitted by one of his descendants (Mrs. Phyllis Ribbons). The first part of the manuscript has never been found.

Austin Brooks was a bespoke shoe maker, who eventually owned his own shop in the High Street of Glastonbury — The Golden Boot. His descriptions, particularly of the travelling theatres, the custom of wassailing and fairs, echo the Wessex novels by Thomas Hardy. Ed.

'. . . offender in the stocks in front of the church when a sympathiser, pitying his condition, brought out a teapot and cup and saucer and offered him some liquid refreshment, but the constable happening to pass at the moment and having his suspicions, took a smell at the contents and chucked the lot into the road, regardless of the waste of good liquor; the pot contained not what it should have done but beer.

There were no policemen in those days, only parish constables, the Police came some time after. They, the Police, wore very light tunics and had leather stocks strapped under the chin to keep their heads upright; they wore top hats with glazed leather tops, and a strip of leather down each side (this was about the period when cricket was played in top hats). The first result of a row was to see the policemen's hats knocked off and trundling down the street. I remember that we boys, when the Police first came, used to congratulate ourselves that, as we thought, the Law would not allow a policeman to run, so that we felt tolerably secure from capture. We, however, found out our mistake later. The present entrance to the Abbey Ruins was, as a good many will remember, The Red Lion Inn, a house much frequented by tradesmen of the town, and I have pleasant recollections of a very delectable brew of mulled stout, grateful and comforting in cold weather, concocted by the daughter of the house 'the Fair Clara' whose charms I have no doubt enhanced the quality of the liquor.

Next door *(now an up-to-date outfitting shop) was occupied by Mr. Geo. Fox as a boot and shoe shop on one side, and on the other by Miss Grange as a china and glass emporium (the best marbles in the town were to be had here). It had old fashioned semi-circular windows with small panes, in fact, there was not a single pane of plate glass in the Town.

There were five public houses all in a group and almost adjoining. On the site where now stands the Abbot's Cafe, there were some old ramshackle brick houses, one of them occupied by the last pawnbroker in business in the Town (Uncle Davey) at any rate the last to show the outward and visible sign of his calling, — the three gilt balls. Next door at the corner of Benedict Street, was a low-ceilinged dilapidated house occupied by a man named Merchant in the trade or profession of watchmaker and jeweller. He was also an expert firework maker and his busiest time was for a few weeks preceding November 5th in preparation for the annual festival, which was kept in those days with much spirit. Monster bonfires were lit near the Market Cross and at the top of High Street, processions of blazing tar barrels were carried on men's heads, squibs and fireworks of every description (a good many of the fireworks' fraternity being in fancy dress) with an effigy of Guy Fawkes for the central figure. In later years it became a more personal affair and anyone who had made themselves unpopular during the year was liable to have their effigy

*Probably circa 1900. Ed.

burnt. This often occasioned much ill-feeling and was one of the principal reasons for the suppression of the Festival.

Messrs. Webb's Garage was then a Plymouth Brethren Meeting House. It was originally a Quakers' place of worship. The markets, and also the fairs which were then held for sheep, pigs, etc., being on the west side of the street clear of the pavement, and the standing for cattle and larger animals on the east side. It was quite an ordeal for a timid person to pass along the street on market days; a good deal of the east side was protected by temporary posts and railings so that pedestrians could get to the houses on that side and to the Town Hall (traces of these barriers are still to be seen). On Fair days the streets were wholly given up to the business on hand and the cattle, etc. used to extend from the Globe Inn through Magdalene Street and High Street to St. John's Church. The favourite spot for showing off the paces of horses was about the centre of High Street, while in every nook and corner were standing for the sale of all kinds of merchandise besides eatables and including oysters.

The name of Mr. Ateyo of Othery stands foremost as the purveyor of those most delectable cakes locally called 'best nuts' and it was considered the correct thing to purchase a quantity of these delicacies for your best girl or other friends.

In addition to the other attractions at Fair time, there was usually a travelling theatre set up near the Cross which stayed for a week or two. (Wildman's Theatre Royal). They managed to rattle off four or five dramas or tragedies in the course of the evening, the whole company coming on the stage in front and performing a dance in the interval between each piece, the same costumes being worn for each play. After the Fair they gave one performance only per night, the favourite one being the Mistletoe Bough, the Company coming on the stage inside and singing a verse of the well-known song between each act, the heroine having to be exhumed from her old oak chest for the purpose looking very frail and ghostlike. I rather think this must have been the theatrical company described by

Dickens in Nicholas Nickleby and that Nicholas and poor Smike must have visited Glastonbury as they were a travelling company and Glastonbury not so very far from Portsmouth. It is fortunate there were no cars tearing through the Town or something tragic would have been inevitable on Fair days. I must not forget to mention that on Fair days anyone who liked to place a branch of a tree at their front door was allowed to sell intoxicating drink; these were called 'bush houses' and judging by the sounds of music and revelry going on they seemed to be well patronized.

Any travelling show was then allowed to set up in the Market Cross at any time, such as wild beast shows, etc., which took up nearly the whole width of the road, leaving only a narrow space for wheeled traffic. During the visit of Woombwell's Menagerie to the Town, the band attached to it was much admired and in fine weather crowds of townspeople would assemble to listen to its dulcet strains, although latish in the evening it was sometimes difficult to distinguish between the beasts and the band.

Singlestick was then still practised at Fair time, the one to draw first blood from his opponent was considered the winner; the most mighty men at this business usually came from Wedmore. Climbing the greasy pole for a leg of mutton was still in vogue, the mutton being fastened at the top of a well greased pole and the first one to reach the top gained the prize. The knowing ones would wait until the grease had been pretty well cleaned off by first comers and would then carry off the prize — the mutton must by that time have been considered well-hung.

Wassail was then observed by up to date cider growers. The mode of procedure as taken part in by the writer was as follows: A milking pail full of hot gin and cider was provided with pieces of toast bread floating in it. The Master of Ceremonies would first take a piece of the toast and place it in the fork of a tree, naming the tree (say a Cadbury) as follows:

Cadbury tree, Cadbury tree,
I wassail thee

> To bear and to blow
> Apples enow
> Hatfulls and capfulls
> And three-cornered sackfulls.

Hulloa boys! Hurrah! Hurrah! Hurrah! There was then a drink all round and the same ritual observed at each of the principal trees in the orchard until the gin and cider was exhausted, which being rather potent, the company dispersed each one assured that their efforts would result in a good crop of apples for the ensuing year and consequently cider would be plentiful.

Street Road — It is difficult to convey an adequate idea of the state of this road many years ago; it was the most unkempt and uncanny place imaginable, especially after dark.

There were no lamps and no path, the side of the road towards the Hill was formerly a deep gully overgrown with thorns and brambles with alder trees and here and there elms and oaks; there was slush and water in the bottom of the gully, traces of which still remain; it was a rare place for bird nesting and snakes. There was no fence or protection at that side of the road but a narrow margin of grass which was cut through at intervals to allow the water to drain off the roads. Steam rollers had not yet come into use so the metalling was out on the roads and the traffic had to wear it in; tyres were then all of iron. The journey between Street and Glastonbury was much dreaded after dark, especially as the rules for carrying lights were not then in existence and very few vehicles troubled to light up.

. . . A very picturesque old house used to stand on the site of Messrs. Classey & Stacey's. It was kept by a Mrs. Ward whose faggots and black puddings were very popular and the perfume far reaching.

The present Post Office is a comparatively new building but about the years 1860-70 the whole of the postal business was transacted in the little squeek of a place about nine feet by four feet between Messrs. Barretts confectionery shop and the gateway leading to the

Assembly Rooms. The hundred and one things which now go through the Post Office were then unknown such as Parcel Post, Telegrams, Telephone, Postal Orders, Pensions, etc; the letters were delivered by old Jenny Haine who carried them in a little basket on her arm. There was a turnpike gate across the road to the gatehouse at the corner of Bere Lane and across the pavement were upright slabs of stone with a turnstile in the centre which would allow only one person at a time to pass. This was to prevent horses and cattle from going round by way of the pavement and so escaping the toll. There was also a turnpike gate at the foot of Coursing Batch.

The gravedigger at St. Johns (Abraham Sellick) used to live in the small cottage No. 28 High Street, opposite the Church and now occupied by a greengrocer. He used to keep his gravedigging tools in his one living room downstairs. It was no uncommon occurrence in digging a grave to cut into an old coffin and sometimes the corpse, grave clothes etc., would appear just as when first laid in the grave but when the air was admitted would in a few minutes fall to dust.

Excursions of any sort were not then frequent but a favourite one and one quite out of the question at the present day was by barge to Ashcott Corner, the party taking their own provisions and getting hot water and other accommodation from some people there who supplied these necessary things. After a pleasant time on the Moor, with dancing and games the return was made to the accompaniment of music and singing; a time was generally chosen when there was a moon for the return journey, the writer being allowed to join the party on one or two occasions and although too young to fully appreciate the romantic feature of the outing, it was quite evident that the elders of the party thoroughly enjoyed themselves.

I do not quite remember what stood on the site of St. Benedict's School, but on the other side, there was then a large barton and rick yard belonging to Mr. Richard Holman who lived at St. Dunstans in the Market Place;

when the time came for threshing (the ricks being mostly of wheat or other grains) there was fine sport killing the rats which were driven out in great numbers when the rick was getting low. All the terriers in the neighbourhood would collect with men and boys armed with sticks and other weapons and give them a most warm welcome. I have seen it stated that foxes and rats enjoy the excitement of the chase — if so, these rats must have had the time of their lives.

It may not be out of place to mention that when the Revd. Parette, Congregational Minister, first came to Glastonbury, he was so struck by the number of unoccupied houses in the town that he made it his business to count them and he found there were over seventy. The old ecclesiastical-looking building now called Tudor Cottage, was a reputed sly house for the sale of intoxicants. These matters were not looked into as they are at present and the old constables would be inclined to turn a blind eye in that direction for obvious reasons.

Mount Avalon was built about the middle of the century, the bricks for which were made on the spot from clay which came from the excavations; the kilns for burning them were much visited by the townfolk, the effect at night being very weird and picturesque. When the house was finished, there was a kind of public rejoicing ending up with the usual feed and congratulatory speeches and a free fight in the evening.

About the middle of the last century it was a great institution amongst the tradesmen and middle classes to meet and drink tea at each others houses. The teas were of a very substantial kind, one indispensable item being a dish of hot buttered toast with the crust cut off, besides muffins and crumpets and other delicacies (people had appetites in those days). The hostess who brewed a good strong cup of tea was very popular (tea was about eight or nine shillings a pound as witness the size of the caddies then in use). These teas were two kinds, those where amusements were provided after and the other called 'tea and turn out' when the guests were supposed to leave soon after tea was over.

One of the amusements of those far off days was playing pranks on the watchmen who patrolled the streets at night proclaiming the time and the kind of weather. One of the jokes I have heard was as the watchman passed along Chillwell Street close under the Abbey wall, the jokers would pour on his head a bucket of filth taken from some cesspool which were pretty plentiful in those days. Very amusing for one of the parties and the language quite up to the standard of the present day golf course.

Another occasional entertainment was when a person was to be hung. People were then hung for sheepstealing and other offences which are now considered trivial; many would walk all the way to Ilchester to witness this tragedy, this being the nearest gaol where executions took place.

Gas had not made much headway and candles were in general use for domestic lighting. Dips and rush lights were the only kinds made locally, the dip had straight cotton wicks which did not consume as the candle burnt, and the snuffers had to be brought into requisition about every quarter of an hour or so; rush lights were simply dips with pith of the common rush for wicks; they burned slowly and gave a poor light but were comparatively cheap. Mould candles, which did not require snuffing, were considered quite a luxury and were not made locally. The stringy parts of the fat, the residue from the candle making, were sold in the hucksters' shops as articles of food and were called scollops.

In my young days there were lots of people living who could remember the housing of French prisoners of war in the churches during the Napoleonic Wars and trinkets were to be had which were carved by them in bone and wood and sold. They seem to have had a pretty good time enjoying much freedom and mixing quite freely with the inhabitants; for these entertainments they would execute dances and ingratiate themselves in other ways. En passant, the Writer can almost claim a link with the Battle of Waterloo as he can remember the funeral of the great Duke of Wellington.

The dislike of people to new fangled ways may be illustrated by old Tommy . . . who was laboriously trying to light, with the flint and steel which was then in general use, but the tinder being damp it would not ignite. His son who was standing near seeing his difficulty and being an up-to-date young man, had some newly invented Lucifer matches in his pocket and said; 'Wait a moment, and I'll give you a light', at the same time striking one of the Lucifers (no safety matches then) and offering it to his father who, turning in great wrath exclaimed 'Get out wi yer paltry pride and ambition, I'll have none o it here' and went on in the old time honoured fashion trying to woo Lucifer from the damp tinder.

The medical profession was represented by Dr. Ling.

He was a gentleman with a wooden leg — not one of the modern clockwork and steam description but a real old timber toes, straight from the hip downwards; the sound of his good old stump approaching must have brought joy to many a sick room.

What strikes one in these strenuous days is the great amount of leisure enjoyed by doctors at that time. They never seemed to be particularly busy and one of them was generally to be found in the Reading Room of the Literary Institute. I suppose people in those days were content to just die natural deaths.

There was a newspaper published in Glastonbury before the advent of the C.S. Gazette; it came out at uncertain intervals but very few knew where or by whom it was printed; it was of a rather scurrilous nature and consisted mostly of take offs, or skits, on persons and current events of the day. One can distinctly remember . . . a rather prominent young lady of the Town, the pretty Polly . . . who was quite a leader of the fashions of the day, and so caused much envy among others of her sex. At the time umbrellas and parasols were first coming into use, this lady was the first to have one and some doggerel appeared in which this occurred:-

And she can hardly walk at all
Unless she's got a parasol.

The Abbey ruins years ago, I am sorry to say, were not well looked after, in fact they were *wrangle-common to anyone who liked to go there. Of course, when boys have free access the result is usually the same — destruction; picnics and dances were frequently held there and dancing and games played on what is now considered sacred ground, — the nave and choir. Fortunately, they have lately been in better hands and are now held in proper reverence, but with all the restoring that has been going on, the making of a new bridge, levelling off and making paths in every direction, it looks almost as if new ruins were being re-built.

A very notable feature of years ago in Glastonbury was the chiming of St. John's Church clock at three, six, nine, and twelve to the tune of 'We love the place of God'. The first line at three, two lines at six, three lines at nine and the whole tune at twelve. Its discontinuance is much to be regretted. Bruges had not got it all its own way in those days.

One of the most striking alterations is the removal of the old conduit which stood in the roadway in front of Mr. Crocker's boot shop. It was surrounded by cobble stones sloping to a sink and at the four corners were upright stones worn smooth by constant practice of leap-frog by boys and from being supported by loaders which in those days more than at present were to be found hovering about the neighbourhood. Close at hand was the public weighbridge which has only recently been removed. The conduit was one of three which used to supply the town. It was usual at any hour of the day to see a group of people waiting to fill their buckets, especially in the Market Place, and as the only source of supply was from the Edmund Hill conduit it took a long time in dry weather to get the buckets filled. The method usually adopted for conveying the water was by two buckets and a hoop, the person carrying standing inside the hoop and

*Wrangle — used in the sense of free access combined with free speech. i.e. a noisy, rough place. Ed.

the buckets hanging over the edge, one on each side, this prevented the buckets from dangling against the legs.

The origin of the old local saying 'Middling Mary', is as follows. Poor old John lay dying. His wife, who had been a great termagent, was weeping copiously and trying to convince John and others within hearing and also perhaps to soothe her own conscience by constantly exclaiming: 'I've been a good wife to you John, I have, I've been a good wife to you!' John smiled and faintly replied; 'Middling Mary! Middling'.

The Glastonbury waters were at one time noted for their curative properties, but unscrupulous persons took to hawking it about the country and often taking river or other water instead of the real thing, so that in time it got into disrepute. The following is a version of Matthew Chancellor's dream, which first brought the waters into notice.

'This is to certify to all whom it may concern, that I, Matthew Chancellor, of the parish of North Wooton in the county of Somerset, yeoman, had been very much afflicted with an asthma almost thirty years till some time about the middle of October, 1750, when I had a violent fit in the night and afterwards fell asleep and dreamed that I was at Glastonbury, some way about Chain Gate, and that I was in the horse trace and there saw some of the clearest water I ever saw in my life. I kneeled on my knees and drank of it and I could plainly perceive the splashing of the horse on both sides. As soon as I stood up there seemed to be a person by me who pointing his finger said unto me: 'If you will go to that freestone shoot and take a clean glass and drink a glassful (fasting) seven Sunday mornings following and let no person see you, you will find a perfect cure of your disorder and then make it public to the world'. I asked him why seven Sunday mornings? He said: 'The world was made in six days and on the seventh God Almighty rested from His labour and blessed it above other days'. He said likewise: 'This water comes from out of holy ground where a great many saints and martyrs have been buried'. He told me something

concerning our Saviour having been baptized in the River
Jordan but I could not remember it when I awaked. The
Sunday morning following, I went to Glastonbury, which
is about three miles from the place were I live, and found
it according to my dream but as it was a very dry time, I
could scarce see the water run in the shoot so I dipped the
glass three times into the hole under where the shoot
dropped and took up the value of a glassful and drank it,
giving God thanks and so I continued to do so seven
Sundays and by the blessing of God, it recovered me of my
disorder'.

All I know personally of the affair is that I have heard
old people say they could remember a row of crutches
fastened to the wall at Chain Gate left there by people
who had been cured by the waters as a testimony to their
having been healed.

'My mother said Do you realise you will have to answer the door yourself?'

Lady Lister-Kaye
DORCHESTER

I was born in 1915 while my father was serving with the Dorset Regiment in India. My mother joined him when I was eight months' old and I was left in the care of elderly grandparents in Dorchester.

My first recollection of life was sitting with a nanny (of course on a rug) watching the German prisoners making the Borough Gardens in Dorchester. I was bathed in a tub, and every morning and evening my grandfather tooted the horn on the big Avel Johnston car under my nursery window when he was taken and fetched by a chauffeur to and from his office.

When I was four years' old my parents returned from India, bringing with them a small brother whom I had never seen and we set up house at Martinstown where my father owned an estate of 1200 acres.

In 1920 and 1921 another brother and sister arrived, so we had to enlarge the house and import a Norland nanny at the princely sum of two guineas per week, also a governess for myself and my elder brother. Of course, all meals were eaten in the nursery, brought up by the kitchen maid, while the houseparlour maid attended to the adults in the dining room. Only when we were in our middle teens were we allowed down to dinner at night and then I had to wear a dress with long sleeves and my brothers, suits (never sports jacket and trousers).

The highlight of the year was the annual shooting party on Boxing Day when my father and grandfather asked their special friends to come. Lunch was always provided for the guns and a big roaring fire was lit in a hut on the estate with straw bales and a trestle table. This was done by the oldest farm worker who brought the meal up in a horse and cart and took back whatever game was shot.

The Vicar of Martinstown was forced into the profession by his mother. His main interests were carpentry and making model engines, so in the spring, when everyone's gardens were bare, the vicarage garden was ablaze with *wooden* daffodils and tulips.

When I was 18, I 'came out' at the Portman Hunt Ball held at Bryanston School. In those days we were chaperoned by our parents and had small programmes with a pencil attached. If my father did not approve of a gentleman whose name was on my card he would tell him 'I am very sorry — I am having that dance with my daughter'. Besides hunting with the Cattistock hounds, I rode round our estate on Sunday mornings with my father. Those were the days when it was not considered correct to have a job.

In the years 1934-1935 when Col. 'Freddie' Digby was the Colonel of the old Dorset Yeomanry, my father was the Col. of the Dorchester Battery and my brother was a 2nd Lieut. I was invited to a military week-end house party at Sherborne Castle. The week-end started on Friday evening. General Allenby of Palestine was the principal guest. There were at least 30 other guests of all ranks.

I was given a lady's maid who spread out the dress and accessories which *she* thought I should wear that evening. Dinner was served in the Main Dining room and we ate off silver plates and footmen in livery served the meal. It was a beautiful summer evening and I remember seeing the Hunt horses very close to the windows of the castle, but of course they were really divided by a 'ha-ha'.

After dinner the older members of the family and their guests played bridge, while we younger people were allowed to play around in the crypt of the castle until about midnight.

Saturday breakfast was more informal. There were two

long side tables in the room — one with large cold joints, ham, tongue, cold beef etc., the other with all the hot foods one could imagine — fish, hot rolls, eggs done in every way, scrambled, poached or fried with bacon and sausages.

After breakfast a footman came in and emptied all the remaining food from the *hot* table into a huge cauldron on the balcony outside and stirred it up with a big pole and then this was fed to Mrs. Digby's Keeshonds, *there were more than twenty, as this was her main hobby.

During the morning we could play tennis, our racquets being brought down to the courts by a footman.

We were never taken abroad for holidays but we had a cottage on a farm near 'White Nothe'. We went for six to eight weeks between July — August. The journey of about thirteen miles took most of the day — my mother drove the family car with myself and my sister, the nanny and the governess, while the two boys in the family were allowed, as a great treat, to travel in the back of the lorry taking the bedding and enough coal for about two months. The maids sat up in front with the driver, one holding the whisky decanter and the other the kitchen clock. Lastly, a farm boy of about sixteen called Albert, drove the family cow the whole distance of about thirteen miles and while on holiday his job was to milk it, fetch up water from the well for the cook and for our weekly baths, empty the two earth closets and bring down the tea to the beach each day, also a deck chair for my mother. The local fishermen provided lobsters at seven and six pence each for the Sunday evening meal and also large quantities of prawns.

Christmas Day was always spent at home with our own family and no guests. After a huge mid-day lunch of turkey and plum pudding, my father always used to go out and saw up a log — just to show us that he could do manual work and also to help digest the meal.

When I announced to the family that I was going to

*Keeshond — a breed of dog originating in Holland

marry a Dorset farmer, hands went up in horror — my mother said 'Do you realise you will have to answer the front door yourself?'.

I had a very happy thirty eight years with my farmer husband — we rented a small house (as his mother was still alive) at £1 a week and I brought up three children with the help of a local girl who stayed with us for twenty one years.

My dear husband died on our 38th wedding anniversary after a long painful illness. For seventeen years he was Chairman of The South Dorset Hunt and was a well known judge of Dorset Down Sheep — not only at local shows but at Smithfield, The Royal Show and The Royal Highland Show.

The next year my only son died aged thirty four, leaving a wife and young family — his wife still gallantly carries on the farm, although we have not such a large acreage. Until the death of my second husband, Sir John Lister-Kaye, I still lived in The Old Rectory, but have now had to move to a small cottage.

Glow-worms in the hedges and sand-castles on the beach

Hazel Austin
WATCHET

My father came from Somerset, and my mother from Devon, but when he was a young man my father went to work in the pits of South Wales. I was born there on January 23rd, 1917 and for the first ten years of my life Wales was my home.

However, each summer we went back to Wessex for two weeks' holiday with my grandparents at Watchet in Somerset. This was something my brother and I looked forward to the whole year through. Our grandparents' house was at the top of Cleeve Hill. There was a magnificent panoramic view from the front of the house, which extended from the Quantock Hills to the Brendons.

There was a pump in the backyard, but the water (when it was there) was suitable only for household jobs, such as washing clothes. Rainwater was collected in three ship's water tanks, for drinking, one at the front of the house, and two at the back. Water was extremely valuable, especially in summer, and not a drop was wasted.

My uncle Jim kept a few hives of bees in the small orchard at the side of the house. Honey was stored for winter use, and the beeswax was used for rubbing the inside of ticking pillow-cases before the feathers were put in. This would help to make the ticking feather-proof. The wax was used too, for making furniture polish. A block was used for rubbing the flat-iron, so that the iron would glide smoothly over the clothes. Grandmother made mead from the honeycomb.

There were no refrigerators in those days, and when the weather was hot, the cream was kept in a covered milk-pail which stood in the stream that flowed through the farmyard. Stones packed around the pail kept it steady in mid-stream. A couple of stepping stones enabled the farmer's daughter to reach the pail when someone came to buy cream. There was a thick crust on top.

We spent many happy hours on the beach and to get to it we went out of the back garden gate into a cornfield. There was a good view from the steep field. To the left was Blue Anchor Bay and North Hill, Minehead.

On the beach we built sand-castles and forts with moats. We carried endless buckets of water to fill the moats, but the water just soaked away. We caught crabs in the rock-pools or sailed our yachts and Indian canoes.* The donkeys worked hard, carrying limestone from the beach in panniers on their back, to the lime-kiln not far away. Here it was burnt to make lime.

For many years, as well known character lived in a dis-used part of the lime-kiln. He was known as 'Windmill Jack', for when Father was a boy, he used to make and sell windmills to the children. Once a child was almost knocked down when running across the road to him. He was so upset that he ceased making the windmills. He was a kindly old fellow and an ex-soldier. It was rumoured that he belonged to a well-to-do family, but he had chosen to live the simple life. He did odd jobs on local farms. In his cave-like dwelling, he had a table and chair and there was a mat on the floor. His shining knife, fork and spoon were usually laid on the table, together with his crockery. His bed was a hole in the wall, where at one time, the fire was kindled to burn the lime-stone overhead. The bed was hidden from view by a blanket curtain, which hung across the opening. Mother always said he was 'as clean as a new pin'. He grew marigolds, pinks and ever-lasting sweet peas in the little garden. If he was at home when we went to the beach, we always called to see him. He gave Mother seeds from the everlasting sweetpeas, but they never flourished in our garden as they did in his cliff-top one.

When it was time to harvest the corn in the field outside

*Indian canoes — home-made paper boats.

the back gate, we children would stand and watch the reaper, as it moved around the field, the centre patch getting smaller and smaller. Men with guns stood ready to shoot the rabbits as they bolted out of the last patch of standing corn. Then there was rabbit pie for dinner the next day. The one thing we didn't like about the corn-cutting was the harvest bumps which used to appear on our arms and legs, and sometimes on our tummies. Grandmother would put a saucer of vinegar on the kitchen table, then when the bumps were particularly irritating we could dab them with the vinegar, which made them smart, but it stopped the itching.

At night, I used to look for glow-worms in the hedges. I thought there was something magic about them to make their little lights shine in the dark. Sometimes I managed to find two or three to put in my jam jar. Excitedly, I would take them indoors, and grandmother let me put them in one of the potted plants in the front room window.

The local name for a conger eel is a 'glat'. Glatting, then, is hunting congers which have been left stranded by the out-going tide. Some congers can be as much as ten feet long, with large mouths and vicious teeth. A few men from the West Street area were very keen on hunting for conger eels. They took strong wooden sticks to prise up the stones on the flat mud banks, then the dogs would attack the eels, yelping and barking, while the men wielded their sticks. Often, both men and dogs returned home splattered with mud.

Lifeboat Day was usually held on August Bank Holiday Saturday which, in those days, was at the beginning of August. Grandfather began the proceedings by firing a maroon from the harbour slipway. A party of men would pull the Lifeboat on its carriage across the Esplanade to the slipway, where it would be launched. There was no shortage of men to pull the boat. After the launching there would be demonstrations of the self-righting Lifeboat, life saving, and other Lifeboat procedures. Then the fun began with the Miller and the Sweep. Two men, each in a rowing boat, would bombard each other with flour and soot, until one or the other fell into the water. The greasy pole was good fun too. A long pole would be fixed on to the end of a cargo vessel and covered in thick grease. One by one the swimmers would attempt to walk the pole, but would fall off, with a great splash into the sea. The winner was the person who walked the pole and grabbed the flag at the end. Then there was a wild Duck Hunt. Swimmers would chase a duck as it sped over the water.

The bedroom we always occupied in Grandmother's house, while we were there on holiday was one in the back. In a recess near the window stood a pretty dressing table which looked like a table with one drawer. The top was covered in pink material, and the same material, fully gathered, hung around the sides. Over this was draped a dainty patterned lace. The swing-mirror on the top was free-standing. A piece of lace, similar to the one which covered the dressing-table was draped over the mirror, and tied back each side with a bow of pink ribbon. There was a china tray and two matching candlesticks, but the latter were never used. We carried a candlestick from downstairs when we went to bed.

A crochet-edged cloth covered the top of the mahogany bow fronted chest of drawers. A beautiful shell-box stood in the middle, which I greatly admired. Mother wouldn't allow me to touch it, but occasionally Grandmother would put it on the bed for me to take a closer look. Each year, as soon as we arrived for our holiday, I would go to the bedroom to check that the shell-box was still there.

On the wash-stand, was a matching set of toilet ware. A large china water jug with bowl, soap dish with a lid, and a jar for holding tooth brushes. Two chamber pots stood on the shelf underneath. The decoration on the ware was a wide band of pink, with narrow gold lines each side, on a white background. The towels were spread on a mahogany towel-horse, and a china slop pail, with lid, stood beside it. The feather bed was so comfortable — all the feathers having come from Grandmother's poultry. We didn't have feather beds at home — this was a luxury! Snowy white valances draped the sides of the bed, and on top was a white honeycomb quilt with a fringe.

Best of all, I liked the rugs that Grandmother made from rabbit skins. Whenever Grandfather caught rabbits, the skins were saved. Grandmother would cure them, then when they were ready, she would stitch a number together to make a rectangle. This was then stitched to a base of thick felt (from the Paper Mill) which had been vandyked around the edges. The felt was larger than the furry section, so that a border extended beyond the rabbit skins. When you walked, bare footed on the rugs, the fur tickled your toes: I thought they were the most wonderful rugs I had ever seen.

All the tramps called at the house, and there were quite a few! At breakfast time, there was always an extra kettle of boiling water on the range ready to make tea for the tramps. At about half-past eight there would be a knock on the front door. When it was opened, a voice could be heard saying 'Morning, me dear, 'ave ee got a pinch o' tea for me can, an' a drop o' boiling water?' A moment or so after 'An' I do like a bit o' sugar and a drop o' milk'. When he was given the tea, he would probably ask for a 'crust o' bread'. This usually resulted in two thick slices of bread spread with farmhouse butter. Some mornings, the appetizing smell of bacon or steak frying would encourage a tramp to ask for fried bread. He would be sent on his way with instructions not to tell his mates, but almost always, ten minutes later, a second tramp would call. Then there was more tea and more fried bread to be given away.

The tramps walked from the Workhouse at Dulverton to the one at Williton. It was a very long way, so the tramps rested for the night at New Barn. This was a very old building, which originally belonged to the monks of Cleeve Abbey. New Barn was only about two miles from Grandmother's house and hers was the first house on the second stage of the journey to Williton. Unbeknown to my Grandparents, their house was 'honoured' with the tramps secret marking — a chalk cross on the wall of the house.

'Those evenings held a kind of magic for us'

Gertrude McCracken
SUTTON VENY

As most people know, the older one grows the clearer to one's memory does the dim and distant past become. I was born in 1907 in Sutton Veny. My family name was Humphreys and we lived in Dymock's Lane, now Home Farm.

There was, of course, no electricity in the cottages in those days, but we obtained our light from the 'Lamp' and candles. Mam's lamp really was a thing of beauty. It had a heavy pierced stand with a glass reservoir for the oil and a chased glass globe on the chimney glass. After the tea things were cleared away a chenile cloth was placed on the table and the lamp was lighted. Dad always sat with his back to the lamp to read the paper, or sleep. Mam always sat in the circle of light with her mending and either talked to us or sang. She had a rather nice voice and was also known for whistling. I think those evenings held a kind of magic for us with the fire glowing and blinds drawn. It gave us I think a feeling of security. Being a large family, Mam always seemed to have a needle in her hands. There was no money to spare, so jumble sales were a great help. Home would come the jumble to be washed, unpicked and remade into garments. She had no patterns and after the garments were tacked together, the recipient had to stand still whilst Mam pinned her in for what she called 'Sherri-ping', in other words shearing bits off with the scissors. How I hated those fittings. To stand still for about twenty minutes was to me an utter waste of precious time. I remember Dad having to do it once. Mam had bought a dark blanket and door curtains for threepence and made him a pair of working trousers. He came though the ordeal very well and thought it was a great joke. Those threepenny pants lasted Dad nearly two years.

In the summer at that time we were allowed out to play within call but not in the winter. In the summer the mending was taken outside to be done whilst Dad did the gardening. Mam was allowed a small patch for her beloved flowers, the rest all had to be put down to spuds and cabbage. Summer and winter were alike with our children's routines which were always the same, the elder ones helping the smaller ones, boots off and cleaned ready for the next morning school. In those days, we all wore black boots which stretched well up the calves of our legs, generally laced up (buttoned ones were considered very posh). We all wore long black stockings held up above our knees with garters (or sometimes string). The boys wore shorts, Norfolk type jackets and celluloid collars which were sponged off. The girls had dark frocks and white pinafores which, in my case, always needed washing every night.

In the summer, supper was usually bread and butter or marg and home made lemonade. In the Winter we sometimes made toast in front of the fire on which we spread home made lard or dripping. Otherwise we had 'Kettle broth', stale bread seasoned with fat of some sort, dripping was the favourite, and soaked in boiling water. There was no money for luxuries. My mother had eight children and her housekeeping money was at that time fourteen shillings a week, which had to include the rent. In those days the rent was, I think eighteen pence a week.

Most cottages in those days kept their own back yard pig, feeding it on household scraps and vegetable peelings boiled up in the washed copper and mixed with meal. The day the pig had to die was all bustle. The copper filled and lit, a bonfire was made ready to burn the hairs off the carcass. A little man called Mr. Payne cycled from Warminster and, if we were within earshot it was ghastly, the pig squealing like billy-oh and then utter silence.

Nothing was wasted from the pig, the offal and the flec (tummy lining) made faggots, brawn from the head and trotters, black pudding from the warm blood. The sides were cured and hung up in the back kitchen. The fat was rendered down for the lard and we children ate the scraps that were left after the lard was melted.

Writing of the lard reminds me of the queerest use I have ever heard of a cure from home made lard. A Mrs. Sewel, who was a large fourteen stone woman, used to walk from the Paulk Cottages at Tytherington to my aunt's twice a week to do the washing and ironing. Her wage was a midday dinner and five pence. But Mrs. Sewel was very pleased as she always had tea and bread and butter before starting work, a good midday meal and a snack before leaving about 3.30. This particular day, Mrs. Sewel's very young baby had a dirty piece of rag around its little finger. On being asked what was wrong, she replied (and these were the words more or less I heard) 'Oh the "babby" was lying on the floor kicking and I stepped on her little finger. I squashed the top of her finger off, so I popped it in a basin of home made lard and stuck it on'. I think this was true because when auntie re-bandaged the baby's hand with cleaner linen, the little finger had a bluey red ridge around the top joint and she, auntie could move the finger top.

Apart from the usual home made cures of those days — Elder flower steeped in boiling water for ladies' complexions, goose grease and camphorated oil for the chests of wheezy people, water in which cow parsley roots had been boiled to soak the feet to harden them and prevent corns, etc., — I think that the most appalling remedy I ever heard was this. At that time whooping cough was rife at school with three weeks' isolation for the victim. The popular remedy was to take the child into a flock of sheep in an enclosed space. This certainly seemed to help but this child's mother went one better. After fourteen days she returned to school so we children promptly told her that it could not have been whooping cough. 'Oh yes 'twas' says she. 'My mum caught a mouse and baked it and gave it to me in bread and butter'.

It was about this time that one of the villagers came to my mother and asked her 'would she like a basin of dripping'. 'Thank you madam' said my mother, and got the reply 'I would like to see curtsying returned. Would your children start this and the other children would perhaps copy'. 'Madam' returned my mother, 'my children bend their knees to two people, God and the King', so my mother never received her dripping.

Each Sunday at that time stalls were set up in Weymouth Street in Warminster, and about nine o'clock both the fishmonger and the butcher would start to auction off some of their goods so father used to cycle to Warminster and that way we always had fish tea on Saturday, more often than not bloater or herrings. He also got a cheap Sunday joint and a pound of boiled sweets. They were unwrapped, at sixpence a pound, old money. Of course, being unwrapped, our sweets soon became sticky, but who cares about stickiness when one is young. No-one wasted money on packaging.

There was, of course, no National Health Service in those days and most families paid a few pence 'surgery money'. By doing this, they had the services of a Doctor and free medicine. At one time any village housewife could deliver a baby without sending for a Doctor or a Midwife, unless complications set in. But in the early part of the century a law was passed stating that only a qualified person was allowed to separate the mother and child. We were lucky enough to have a Midwife living in the village. Nurse Jane, as she was known, was on call twenty four hours of the day. The Doctor was usually summond with a note carried by a school child. The Doctor made up his own prescriptions and again it was usually a child sent to fetch the medicine. The school master would keep the register open until 9.30 a.m. in case a child was on such an errand.

Later on, as the old age pension was instituted by Lloyd George, the 'surgery money' was dropped, but then we paid into a Hospital fund to ensure free Hospital treatment.

In place of Social Security was the Parish Relief, but this was not always a lot of help. Before 1914, it usually amounted to half-a-crown a week and a four pound loaf. Recipients were usually looked down on and considered feckless by other villagers.

In those days there were two pubs in the village, the Woolpack and the Bell. These opened from 10 a.m. until about 11 or 12 midnight, and always seemed to be full up. As one woman expressed it to Mam 'to pass by the pub be like going past the Tower of Babel'.

There was no daily delivery of milk at that time and children used to go to Greenhill Farm before going to school. We generally fetched neighbours' milk as well as the family milk and carried it in cans with wire handles. This was painful especially in cold weather, with, perhaps, three or four cans in each hand, so we all made sure to wrap the palms with rag or a hanky.

To begin with the War did not at first make a lot of difference. Pig keeping was dropped as the meal for young piglets became too dear, but most families went gleaning to keep a few hens. When the camp building for the Army started it was like an invasion, all sorts and sizes of men appeared, even men with one arm or leg, most of them sleeping rough or taking over the huts as they went up.

The first lot of troops entered Sutton Veny on the 27th April, 1915. I was farmed out to a neighbour's back bedroom that night while Mam gave birth to a son. I spent most of the night listening to the bugles and watching the lights under the trees. Not all the camps were finished. A lot of troops went under canvas.

I think that the Scots made a great impression in my childish mind. I remember so vividly when in full dress, they marched through the village. It was a warm sunny day and it seemed as if their spats and kilts moved as one. They moved up the hill road with their pipes and I stood there speechless as the sound of the pipes gradually moved away. I gave a great sigh and said, 'Coo, if I grow ever so old, quite fifty, I shall always remember this day' and what is more I can still see them with my minds eye. Age is something one can't grasp when one is young. On my sixtieth birthday, my two young grandchildren said, 'Gran, do you mind if we only put one candle on your cake. We haven't got enough money to buy you a hundred'.

Incidentally, the Highlanders were good fighters even in their leisure time. The pickets came down the village in the evenings about eight o'clock carrying a stretcher followed by a van. This was to carry away a few of the lads when the beer started to talk and they went to fight. They brewed a good beer in those days.

At one time during the war, sewage overflow pipes were opened and the fields alongside flooded. Probably as a result of this the wells in the village, or a lot of them, became polluted and pronounced unfit for drinking. Water was brought from Shearwater, and later on standpipes were fixed at the side of the main street. There were six. Just imagine what a lot of water was needed and how far some cottagers had to carry it. Think of the weekly washing for eight or nine people, and they had no sinks or indoor drains either, so it all had to be carried outside the house again. We had open gutters down the streets, both sides, and it was accepted as the usual thing to see the housewives come out with their enamel pails in the early morning and throw the slops from under the beds down them.

Lots of shops sprang up with the filling up of the Army camps. Several lock-ups appeared and a large drapers between the Woolpack and Jasmine Cottage. There was a butchers, a large canteen, and a shoe shop. The cobbler repaired children's boots, soled and heeled for about one and sixpence; but lots of mothers repaired their own children's shoes. I know our boots were done at home. Mother's last was a very posh affair. Three legged with a flap for heels, one for children's shoes and one for adults.

The postman used to cycle from Warminster round the village and retire for breakfast to a small hut where the village notice board now stands. He made two journeys a day in a seven day week, and would take letters and stamp them himself, or parcels for the villagers. Our roads were swept by an elderly man named Vincent whose descendants still live in the village. Mr. V. took an immense pride in his work. All hedges and banks were always kept trimmed and the gutters both sides of the street were brushed every day.

Picture houses, as they were then called, were also built in the village; there was one at the bottom of Dymock's Lane. The Manager of this cinema had a daughter my age and used to put two chairs inside for us to see such films as Harold Lloyd and Charlie Chaplin and then send us home. At that time some of the ladies of the village started a Girls Friendly Society. The older schoolgirls sat knitting socks, the lady on duty turning the heels etc., or gloves. Mam said she though the poor tommies had enough to put up with without trying to use these articles, and they should make the P.O.W.'s use them. The lady on duty always read to us. One evening one of them interrupted her knitting to say 'I hope that none of you children have been to that den of iniquity the picture house'. A lot of us had so we were warned if we went again we would have to leave the G.F.S. Two or three weeks' later the same lady and the same question, only two of us were brave or foolish enough to admit we had, so pointing to the door she said in a dramatic voice, 'Leave this room immediately, before you pollute the minds of these innocent children'. Ah well, that's life.

The winter of 1916-17 was a particularly hard one, so everybody wore coats and mittens in school. Most of the fingers looked like sausages, they were so swollen with chilblains. We had a married couple as teachers — a Mr. and Mrs. Thomas with two young children. When these children had measles, I was sent to babysit, a job which I thoroughly enjoyed. Mam soon knocked the conceit out of me by sending a note to school. In it, she said that as I was as daft as a brush, she wanted me to have all the education I could, but if they thought I was unteachable, she could do with help with her own smaller children.

There were no school dinners in those days, so the schoolmaster would make cocoa for those who had to come some distance and bring sandwiches. One playtime,

I saw the schoolmaster going up the road and did something I had always wanted to do. I jumped the fence between the two play-grounds and played football with the boys. The teacher returned, I was caught and sent to sit in the infants room for two weeks with my arms folded. This was for daring to show my legs in such a fashion, black stockings and all.

The schools closed down for a week to allow the children to go potato picking and help with late harvests. We always had a special treat each summer. We were conveyed to Shearwater for the afternoon by coal cart. These had been hosed down and cleaned, and with a mug tied round our waists we sat in the carts and sang all the way. If it was a fine day, we had tea in the open, a boat ride round the lake and games. Each child was given an orange and a quarter of sweets before leaving. We sang, or rather yelled all the way home.

In those days, the police used their sticks, or the toe of a boot and it was taken for granted if you were caught you were cuffed. It was the same at school. We didn't go home crying if we had been caned. As long as the cane had only been used on the palms of the hands, Mam would only say 'Serve thee right'. I only remember once when my Mother complained to the school. The headmaster had rapped me across the fingers with the side of the ruler. My fingers were badly swollen with chilblains and split easily. She marched me up to school and into the Head. She told him. 'You have a very difficult job and I always uphold you when you use the cane properly. But if you do this to any child of mine again, I will sweep the floor with you. I am keeping her home until these fingers are healed, so don't bother with the Attendance Officer'.

Most of the big houses had their laundry done by someone in the village. Mrs. Crouch told me years later that she started work straight from school. She started at five a.m. in the summer and eight a.m. in the winter, finishing at five p.m. The wages were nine (old) pence a week and she was given breakfast and dinner. Breakfast was usually bread, butter and tea and dinner — 'Monday was good meat and fried vegetables and always a cup of tea. Tuesday was scraps of cheese, the rest of the week was a stomach full of something'. Mrs. Crouch stayed at this job for years until she married. I don't know what age she was, but she had saved five pounds which paid for her bed linen.

Some of the village women, including Mrs. Crouch, took in washing at home as well, which was no mean feat. Usually the copper was in the back kitchen, the water had to be fetched from a well or pump. As there were no drains, the water often had to be carried out again afterwards. If the weather was wet, everything had to be dried indoors. A good fire was needed on ironing days to heat the heavy irons which were spat on to test the heat. A round bottom iron was used for bed linen, shirts and stiff collars, and a goffering iron, rather like a pair of curling tongs, was used on all the frills and laces of the ladies' clothes. As War progressed, many cottages took in soldiers' washing to augment their housekeeping. The prices were:- Socks one penny, Two handkerchiefs one penny, Shirts two pence, White shirts three pence (old money) and the women also had to replace missing buttons and mend the garments for these prices.

After 1919, the village started to deteriorate. Unemployment was high — many men returning from the forces had worked for a time in the camp and helped to dismantle it, but after that there was nothing. Some villagers, my father among them, used to cycle to Netheravon on Sundays and return the following Saturday to dismantle the temporary army camps on the plain. Many girls went away to work in service in the bigger towns and villages. I left the village when I was nineteen and only returned for holidays until the Second World War broke out.

The first pack of Girl Guides was started in the village by Miss Joan Singer who lived at the Knapp. Major Hoare, owner of Sutton Veny House, allowed us to use their laundry as headquarters. My patrol was the Pimpernel, not solely because of the flower but also because of the books by Baroness Orczy. In my patrol were Major Hoare's youngest daughter Pamela, and the sister of the Marquess of Bath. I was told how lucky I was, but didn't always think so as some of their escapades worried me to death, they seemed to know every trick in the book.

We are all now used to the wonders of radio and television, but when 'Wireless' first became popular, many of the villagers looked askance at it. My grandfather called it 'the toy of the devil and no good will come on it'. The lads started making their own receiving sets called, for some obscure reason, 'Cats whisker wireless'. My brother made one with two headphones in the living room and he could also switch it through to his bedroom to listen from his bed. When Dad first listened it was unfortunate that he received only atmospheric disturbance through the headphones and said, 'T'aint nothing but a lot of cats squawking' and refused to try it again for a long time. However, hearing that an international boxing contest was to be broadcast, changed his mind and from then on, was a devoted fan. He could sleep with the headphones going full blast, but woke as soon as the referee would call 'seconds out'. We were not allowed to make a sound during any sport broadcast and he would glare over his spectacles at any offender.

One evening, Mum had an old friend call in for a chat. This lady had never heard radio and sat enthralled for some time. Then she started chattering and saying all that she wanted to tell Mum, still wearing the headphones. My brother, in desperation, switched the set through to his bedroom and crept away. For some peculiar reason, all he could receive was the chatter from the two ladies, mostly from the visitor. After some time, he lost patience and shouted downstairs, 'you silly old coot, shut up and go home'. There was an appalled silence then Mrs. C. . . said 'Did you hear that? If that's what wireless does to them, my boys aren't having any'.

Later, when loudspeakers were fitted to the sets, I visited a very elderly lady. Her set as usual had the volume control turned full on as she was somewhat deaf, and an opera was blaring out of the speaker. 'Oh dear', she said to me. 'I do wish she would hurry up and finish'. When I suggested she could switch off, she replied 'Oh no, I can't hurt her feelings like that. After all, she ain't done I no harm'.

When the Second World War broke out on September 3rd, 1939, I was living in married quarters at Borden, Hampshire. Food rationing started again, this time very restricted: twelve ounces of sugar a month, eight ounces of butter, twelve ounces of tea, and I think twelve ounces of fat per month. We queued for hours at the butchers with whom we were registered, for the chance of getting some offal but were not always successful. The two things I disliked most were the dried egg and dried fish. The egg always seemed to taste and smell musty. The fish, elegantly named 'toerag' by the local people could be disguised with herbs.

When Coventry was attacked in a seemingly unending series of daylight raids the planes passed over the village. I was peeling potatoes somewhere around midday when I heard the roar of the planes. Outside I could see the planes, German bombers, flying so low, it was possible to read the markings. For a moment I was too astonished to be frightened, then a single Spitfire appeared out of the clouds. It attacked and shot down one of the German planes and then flew away. I remember with amazement that the other German planes seemed to take no notice and flew onwards until they were out of sight.

Summer time was introduced during the War, but met with scant approval from the country people. They said that 'playing with the clocks' would upset the weather. One elderly lady remarked to me 'Ah, we got those old jerries now — they don't know we've altered the clocks, and they do think its later than it is — that'll show 'em'.

After the War ended, changes, although slow to happen, took place in the village. The first council housing estate was built. The school had been enlarged and extended, with dinners now being cooked on the premises. The children are now allowed a lot more freedom and I envy them when I look back at my own school days. I see the children today dressed in shorts and T-shirts doing P.E., or at Sports Day. I remember being made to sit with my arms folded, doing nothing for days as a punishment for daring to kick a ball with boys and that was while wearing thick black stockings, boots and a long skirt.

*'The hedgerows were a blaze of wild violets,
horse daisies, cowslips and daffodils'*

R. C. Forcey
GODMANSTONE

I shall try to portray a picture of Bushes Bottom valley as seen though the eyes of a lad of five years of age until I was ten and a half.

We came to this valley in the summer of 1909 from Martinstown where I had started school at the age of three. At Bushes Bottom, there was no road, only a cart track and bridle path from Grimstone in one direction, and the same to Godmanstone in the other.

The valley at this time was open country as far as the eye could see, dotted with trees, gorse bushes and wild flowers. The grass was grazed short by cattle. I learned later that about a hundred red Devon steers, one or two Shire colts and sheep were left to roam these hills and feed on the grass. This made a lovely picture, but it was the valley itself which was so beautiful, the trees, the bushes, gorse and wild flowers beggar description. And the wild life, well, I had never seen so many rabbits, and even in broad daylight we saw several foxes, stoats and weasels. It was wild and primitive but to a child of my age it was awe-inspiring.

When we reached the farmstead, which nestled in a break in the main valley, our house was the first of a pair of cottages adjacent to the farmyard. All this land was farmed by a very well-known farmer and landowner, a Mr. Henry Duke. At this time, I believe Mr. Duke controlled some seventeen thousand acres. He was a considerate employer.

The cattle were rounded up in the autumn. This was

done by Mr. Smith the farm manager, who lived at Godmanstone. He would come with two of his stockmen all mounted on horses, and the cattle would be driven down from the surrounding hills into the yard. They would then be divided up, those ready for market would be penned in the cowshed, the others would be freed.

In the spring the hedgerows were a blaze of colour with primroses, wild violets, horse daisies, cowslips and daffodils. I could never understand how great clumps of daffodils came to be growing wild, they must have been planted at some time. The hedgerows themselves were red and white may, dog roses and honeysuckle and when they were in bloom it was a magnificent sight. Later in the season the foxgloves grew everywhere.

Winter in the valley was pretty grim as I remember. That long walk to school in the bitter cold and the rain and sometimes snow. There were days in the winter when we just couldn't get to school. But even then a certain wild beauty remained. One of my most vivid memories is of walking to school in the early morning when there had been a hard frost and the gorse bushes and trees were festooned with cobwebs which glistened with the frost and looked like fairy land. Another was the bird chorus in the spring. There was a wide variety of birds — to name but a few, there were blackbirds, thrushes, jays, bullfinches, and I have never seen a place where so many goldfinches lived, in the spring mornings they sang so much that you could hardly hear yourself speak.

There were also a lot of owls, they mostly lived in the barn but after dark they would fly around the trees and surrounding bushes and there was a constant hooting. This, with the distant yapping of foxes, was a nightly chorus we became accustomed to.

Just as it was getting dark in the summer evenings, the bats that lived in the barn would come out and fly around and we used to throw our caps at them in the hope of bringing one down, but without every having any success.

Foxes were numerous. My father kept chickens and I

remember he seemed to have a constant battle trying to protect them. The pen and chicken house had to be very strong and foolproof. My young sister had a pet rabbit and in spite of all our efforts to protect it the foxes had it one night.

I feel that this only emphasises the way the valley was then, totally unspoilt by man. But would anyone live there today under the conditions we lived? I doubt it.

At that time, which was prior to the First World War, the total number of people in the farmstead was nineteen. They came from three families and there always seemed to be a spirit of friendliness among them. So much had to be shared, such as the milk, pig killing, shopping, gathering fuel etc., that I suppose co-operation was inevitable for survival.

The standard of living at Bushes Bottom was, in some ways, better than most farm workers enjoyed in those days. The average weekly wage for a farm labourer then was sixteen shillings per week, a stockman or carter's wage was eighteen shillings. At Bushes, the workers received two shillings per week more than this to encourage them to live in such an out-of-the-way place. In addition, a cow was provided to supply milk for the three families, which was shared between them. Also the cottages were rent free. Provisions were made for pig keeping, each family kept one and these were killed at the relevant times, but I remember clearly, that would only be when there was an 'R' in the month. We were allowed to catch as many rabbits as we liked and this provided a valuable source of meat. If you add these emoluments together with the wages, it compared very favourably with the normal standard of living, and whilst the living conditions in the valley were primitive and removed from civilisation, it was a good job.

In each cottage there was an oven which would be filled with wood and gorse faggots and lit and fired until it became white hot. It was then what was known as 'scuffed out' with a wet sack on the end of a pole to clear the bottom of the ashes. My mother baked beautiful bread in this oven, and it lasted well too. Each Wednesday she made enough bread for the week. The rest of the cooking had to be done over the large open fire. Built into the chimney was a large iron hook, and on this hook we hung a large black cast-iron boiler. All vegetables were cooked in nets especially designed for the job, all in the same pot. Some had very fine mesh for peas and the like, others were larger for cabbage etc. The tops were tied up with a string and when they were dropped into the boiler these strings were left hanging over the side and made fast by placing the lid on tight which helped to make it easier to get them out.

It must be remembered that no tradesman of any sort ever came to Bushes Bottom. Those who lived there were completely isolated, therefore the families became dependant on each other.

All letters had to be collected from Godmanstone Post Office and so did the weekly newspaper, which was the Western Gazette. Of course, there was no radio, no telephone, and news of any importance always reached us days late. But what did that matter? Life was slow and easy in those days.

Our nearest Doctor was at Cerne Abbas and provision had been made that in the case of an emergency a little white cob roamed free in the valley with the other cattle. He could be caught and ridden for help, but he was not very co-operative and was very difficult to catch, so a small weight on a chain was strapped to one foreleg. This prevented him galloping off and made him easy to catch.

Another of the advantages of life was that we kept plenty of chickens. We always had eggs and a fine cockerel at Christmas. On Magiston hill, mushrooms grew in profusion. These made a fine addition to our diet. Then, of course, there was the fruit and the garden produce.

Each house had a large garden with blackcurrant, gooseberry bushes, rhubarb etc., and at the bottom of the garden was a large wagon shed which was the length of the gardens. This housed all the wagons, carts and farm implements, these used to be taken great care of and on wet days, when the men were unable to work on the land they would spend their time cleaning and greasing them.

The stables housed four horses, they were Shires, very large, fine animals with great white fetlocks and were my father's responsibility. He always took a great pride in his horses. I remember mother jokingly saying on more than one occasion that he thought more of his horses than of her. However, he would never sit down to a meal until his horses had been cared for. They were well fed and they always looked fine. I have always thought of them since as gentle giants.

I think in those days we lived well. There was no shortage of food, but money was another matter. There wasn't much of that, but living in a place like that valley in the years before the First World War, this was no disadvantage to us children. In any case all the other children at school were in the same position.

Great care had to be taken because of the snakes. Slow-worms and grass snakes were dangerous but adders were very prolific and in the winter they would often conceal themselves in the barn or stable loft.

I remember too, a family of wild cats, very large ginger cats. They were extremely wild and vicious. I imagine they must have descended from some tame cats belonging to an earlier resident, and been left to fend for themselves, thus becoming wild.

Grandma had been left a widow in 1881, grandfather was a shepherd and he died of exposure in a blizzard caring for his sheep. My mother was eleven years old at that time; there were two sisters and a brother as well, so my grandmother had to provide for them on her own. She did this by knitting fishing nets for the fishermen of Bridport, and one of the things I used to do as a boy when we went to see her was to wind the twine and fill the wooden needles for her. She must have worked very hard.

During the Easter holiday, the great potato planting took place. Mr. Duke used to set aside a field for this and all the employees in the district were given a day off to plant a line of potatoes right across a field. This was usually some distance from our farmstead, over the hill towards Sydling, but all the families took part.

The furrow was opened by a kind of double furrowed plough throwing the soil each side and leaving a nice trench for planting. Our job was to place the potatoes in this furrow properly spaced, then this 'Bock' as it was called, drawn by one horse, was driven up between the rows. This had the effect of not only covering the potatoes but hoeing them up at the same time; consequently they needed no further attention until they were harvested. This came in the autumn, always on a Saturday, when the children were home from school. The same instrument was used to plough the potatoes out and our job was to pick them up and fill the sacks. When this was completed a fire was made with all the dead *haulm and hedge trimmings, and large potatoes were pushed into the embers to bake. After the carts were loaded we wended our way homeward eating hot, baked potatoes.

During the holidays, we children were allocated certain duties. One of these was to gather pine and fir cones for kindling from the wood down the valley. These were put into sacks and collected by horse and cart. Sometimes trees would be blown down, when we found them our parents were told and the men usually came with a large crosscut saw and cut them up. Then we could carry the logs to the edge of the wood where they would be picked up by horse and cart and taken home, shared and stored for the winter. A great deal of gorse was cut as well in the summer, bundled and left to dry for winter fuel.

One day when we were out rabbiting, I noticed what appeared to be two tiny silver balls. I pulled them out of the soil and found a tiny purse. I opened it and behold there were five golden sovereigns! I can remember it vividly to this day. I couldn't believe my eyes. We ran home. My mother was astonished but she decided that the purse and money should be put aside until Mr. Smith, the farm manager, came on Sunday. When he came, father took the purse and its contents out to him and explained

*Haulms — potato stalks.

how we had come by it. It was Mr. Smith's opinion that it had been lost by one of the lady huntswomen who rode with the hounds last winter and I remember his comment to my father. 'I think you can do more good with it, George, than the person who lost it', so we had new boots and clothes to go back to school in after the holiday.

During the Easter holidays, we used to walk miles bird nesting. In those days it was usual to collect birds' eggs and blow them and put them in a case of cotton wool. One had to be careful not to take more than one egg from any nest. These were labelled and it was surprising what a collection could be built up. Of course, it has been illegal now for a long time and very necessarily so, otherwise there would be few birds left.

One interesting job that used to take place in the winter evenings was making rabbit snares. This my brother and father did and I never tired of watching them. They would have three strands of thin copper wire which they would double, leaving a loop at one end. Through this loop was passed a rod; on to the other end of this wire was tied a flat iron. This was spun round many times until the wire had been twisted into a strong six stranded wire. The flat iron was then removed. The end of the wire was passed through a loop making a wire noose. A cord was then made fast to the wire at one end, the other end of the cord was fastened to a peg about a foot long and when the trap was set for the rabbit, this peg would be driven firmly into the ground. The noose would be set up on a split stick in a regular rabbit run and when the rabbit ran, its head went through the noose and that was the end.

The men in the valley also used a long net for catching rabbits. This was about one hundred yards long and was taken out by the men on a moonlight evening and set up along a hedge by the side of a field or round a rabbit warren. Then the men would spread out and walk round converging on the area where the net was. My part in this was to stand at one end of the net and my friend, George, at the other and hold the string that closed the net. When the net began to vibrate considerably we knew that it contained one or more rabbits. We would then give a shout and the men would close in and untangle the rabbits and we would move on to another site. We were allowed to catch as many rabbits as we liked but being situated in such a remote and out of the way place, it was not easy to sell them, so no great effort was made to catch more than was needed from day to day.

When I revisited the farmstead sixty nine years later, I found the little farmhouse in a wonderful state of preservation. It had obviously been well cared for. I saw a young man mixing cement and he was doing some work around the back of the house. I enquired from him if the bridle path to Bushes Bottom still existed. With a curious look he assured me it did and then his curiosity got the better of him and he asked me why I was interested. When I told him I used to live there he became quite enthusiastic.

The only thing missing that I could see on that little farmhouse was the honeysuckle over the front porch, otherwise it is exactly the same, but I have a feeling that it is no longer a small-holding, everything looked so clean and there was no sign of any animals or chickens.

We then set out to walk to Bushes and reached the edge of the wood, but it had all changed. There were no fir trees and the wood seemed to be very thin. In the days I remembered it, it was very dark inside and at least twice the size it is today. However, we could not get through as there was corn growing in the field where once the path ran, so we went up the hill a little way opposite the wood until we could just see the large tree at Bushes Bottom. And when my grandsons, who were with me, saw where I wanted to go, they backed out. There was no way that I was going to persuade them to walk up that valley. But I noticed that the lovely hedge that had extended right up the valley at the time I lived there had gone and had been replaced by a wire fence. All the gorse, bushes and trees were gone and as far as the eye could see was golden corn.

One could go on and on writing about the beauties of that valley. I have tried to paint a word picture of it, but only those who lived there, or others who saw it, could ever appreciate what it was really like.

Imagine walking home from Grimstone Station after dark, the sounds of the night, rabbits scuttling away as one approached, perhaps a hedgehog or a fox, the squeal of a rabbit caught by a stoat, and then all along the bank under the hedgerow, the glow-worms in their dozens, and yet, in this lonely valley walking home after dark aroused no fears such as are experienced today if you walk our streets after dark.

I have thought so often of our last summer at Bushes Bottom, nineteen fourteen had come. My brother left school and although life seemed to go on the same, there were distant rumblings in the air. I heard the adults talking about war, but it all seemed too far away to affect us children. My brother used to keep pigeons and he had four carriers. That summer the police came and took them away saying they would be returned if all went well. They never came back. It was that summer I saw my first aeroplane.

August came, and with it the school holidays. We spent our time as usual in the harvest field and went happily on our way. Then one day father came home with a newspaper. War had been declared on Germany. I can still vividly remember my father reading aloud Sir Edward Grey's words. 'The lights of Europe are going out. We shall not see them relit in our time'. Those words have made a very deep impression on me and I have never forgotten them. As children, at school, we were never allowed to forget that we were subjects of an Empire upon which the sun never sets.

One thing is certain in my mind, never again will families struggle to survive in such primitive conditions as we did all those years ago.

AT THEIR DEPARTING
A Childhood Memoir
Nancy Thompson

Armistice Day 1918. Grey, bleak Middlesbrough, haunted by
unemployment, poverty and the grim war years, put on its
Sunday best and danced and sang — a revelation to one
three-and-a-half year old observer for whom life was just
beginning. Nancy Thompson's vivid memoir recalls the
pleasures and dramas of childhood: the excitement of learning
to read; the wonder of music; a magical visit to cousin Liz at
Huck-a-Back far away on the moors; the traumatic trip to the
seaside when sister Bessie almost drowned. Each treasured
episode conveys a fresh awareness of life and death and the
fearful, inevitable growing-up.

Through a child's acute vision there emerges a picture of life
in the North East that is deeply moving and quite
unforgettable.

'A really wonderful account of a working class childhood,
rich in detail, vivid in presentation, and absorbing from
beginning to end. A real pleasure'
ALAN SILLITOE

'Fascinating . . . a valuable collection of memories of northern
life after the First World War'
TIMES EDUCATIONAL SUPPLEMENT

'The past is astonishingly alive to this accomplished author'
YORKSHIRE LIFE

FUTURA PUBLICATIONS
NON-FICTION/AUTOBIOGRAPHY
0 7088 3251 2

All Futura Books are available at your bookshop or
newsagent, or can be ordered from the following address:
Futura Books, Cash Sales Department,
P.O. Box 11, Falmouth, Cornwall, TR10 9EN.

Please send cheque or postal order (no currency), and
allow 60p for postage and packing for the first book plus
25p for the second book and 15p for each additional book
ordered up to a maximum charge of £1.90 in U.K.

B.F.P.O. customers please allow 60p for the first book,
25p for the second book plus 15p per copy for the next
7 books, thereafter 9p per book.

Overseas customers, including Eire, please allow £1.25
for postage and packing for the first book, 75p for the second
book and 28p for each subsequent title ordered.